THE PROBLEM OF
RELIGIOUS LANGUAGE

CONTEMPORARY PROBLEMS IN PHILOSOPHY

George F. McLean, O.M.I., *Editor*

THE PROBLEM OF
RELIGIOUS LANGUAGE

M. J. Charlesworth
UNIVERSITY OF MELBOURNE

PRENTICE-HALL, INC.
Englewood Cliffs, New Jersey

0-13-720011-0

Library of Congress Catalog Card Number 73-17264

PRINTED IN THE UNITED STATES OF AMERICA

10 9 8 7 6 5 4 3 2 1

PRENTICE-HALL INTERNATIONAL, INC., London
PRENTICE-HALL OF AUSTRALIA, PTY. LTD., Sydney
PRENTICE-HALL OF CANADA, LTD., Toronto
PRENTICE-HALL OF INDIA PRIVATE LIMITED, New Delhi
PRENTICE-HALL OF JAPAN, INC., Tokyo

Contents

Foreword

The purpose of volumes in "Contemporary Problems in Philosophy" is to introduce the reader to a philosophical analysis of basic issues in contemporary life. By describing the nature of the problem and presenting related materials by recent philosophers, the works lay the bases for initiating philosophical reflection on crucial themes.

To do this, each volume has an extensive introduction which presents the history of the development of the problem in order to clarify the nature of its components. In addition, the relation between these components is analyzed, and the precise nature of the problem at the present time is determined. Finally, the introduction points out the most promising routes toward progress in further reflection. The main body of the volume consists of selections from major statements on the problem. A few are representative of the historical background; most illustrate the major contributions to the contemporary dialogue; some are by the pioneers of new and stimulating directions in thought.

In such a series the problem of language concerning God, upon which the present volume is centered, holds a special place. The general problem of language has been a central concern, especially in Anglo-Saxon philosophy. Its focus is not the broad issue of communication but on the more precise question of external, social statements of what man can know. Hence, the problem of the language about a certain reality is in reality a question of what man can know and share about its meaning. By application, it becomes a question of the role that can be played by that truth in building our social life.

The problem of language concerning God has become particularly central for an age in which calls for honesty in the use of religious language have been paralleled by a restriction of all meaning to the secular. More radically, some would draw from this the condemnation of man to a freedom without meaning and a life without hope. For this reason, the question of language concerning God promises to become even more central as work progresses on rediscovering the meaning of man and rebuilding the foundations of meaning itself. *The Problem of Religious Language* by Maxwell Charlesworth is focused upon this issue.

The introductory essay, written with great care and insight, clarifies the precise nature of the problem and provides an appreciation of its historical background. In this light the series of readings becomes especially significant. One by one they exemplify the gradual search by the Anglo-American mind on this question. All major positions are reflected, from a negation of all descriptive meaning by A. J. Ayer, through the "poetic" meaning of George Santayana and the "sui generis" meaning of Ludwig Wittgenstein, to quasi-metaphysical and metaphysical meanings.

By coordinating these efforts to clarify the kind(s) of meaning of religious language, this work renders great assistance to those who search for a sound appreciation of the nature of man's awareness of his relation to God. As cultures traditionally have based all else upon this relation, this volume by Professor Charlesworth opens an important route to discovering the meaning not only of religious language but of all else as well.

G. F. McL.

Part 1
INTRODUCTION

Religious language is that used by the religious believer in three distinctively religious contexts. On the first level, there is the language used when he is engaged in such distinctively religious activities as expressing belief in God and living his life in the light of his belief in God, praying, worshipping, performing rituals, or witnessing. Here the believer is, so to speak, performing or engaging in his religion rather than just talking about it. The concepts, forms of expression, presuppositions, modes of reasoning, and justification that he employs as part of this whole religious way of life constitute a special "language," just as the concepts and expressions that we use when we are engaged in moral activity constitute a "language."

At a second level, however, there is the language that the religious believer uses in his theorizing about his religious activities. For example, the Christian believer may say that he believes that Christ is really present in the Eucharist, and then, as a distinct act, invoke the theory of "transubstantiation" or the theory of "transignification," either to "explain" how Christ can be really present in the bread and wine on the altar, or at least to show that he is not talking stark nonsense. This is the level of theology and theological language.

Again, at a third level, there is the language that is used to speak about the presuppositions made by the religious believer (the "preambles of faith," as Aquinas called them). The Christian believer, for example, presupposes that the concepts of God and of a supernatural order of things are intelligible and not self-contradictory or incoherent. In fact, he presupposes (at least *prima facie*)[1] that that first-level religious language expressing beliefs in God, praying,

---

[1] *Prima facie*, because, as we shall see, this assumption that religious locutions describe or refer is itself questioned by certain thinkers.

worshipping, etc., describes or refers to certain objects or states of affairs. In so doing he cannot avoid making certain philosophical assumptions: for example, that a radically materialist view of reality is false. The critical scrutiny of these presuppositions of religious faith has traditionally been called natural theology or philosophical theology, and just as there is a language of religious belief and a language of theology, so also there is a language of natural theology. Thus, in a sense, one might say that the statement "God loves the world" has a different meaning for the religious believer when he is practising his religion, when he is theologizing about it, or when he is "apologizing" philosophically for it.

Though these three levels of religious language are logically distinct, they interpenetrate each other in practice. The believer cannot simply believe as an act of religious faith that God loves the world without at the same time either implicitly or explicitly invoking some kind of theological interpretation of what God's love of the world means, or without implicitly or explicitly making some kind of philosophical presupposition about the possibility of the term "loves" being used of God in a nonanthropomorphic way. In reality, the famous "simple believer," who naively believes in God without theological interpretation or philosophical assumption, is a fiction and an impossibility. Despite what Barth and the Barthians say, we cannot believe save within a particular "frame of reference" or philosophico–theological schema or context.

I.
THE PROBLEM OF RELIGIOUS LANGUAGE

Ordinary Language : Extraordinary Object

Given this as the general meaning of "religious language," what now is the problem about it?[2] As a first rough approximation we may put

---

[2] Recent general discussions on the problem of religious language include: *New*

it in the following way: when the religious believer expresses his beliefs he is apparently speaking about very peculiar objects, states of affairs, events, and processes that are nonmaterial, nonspatiotemporal, not empirically observable, and not subject to limitation or imperfection. In other words, it would seem that the believer is speaking of objects that are not wholly within the world of our experience, but over and above this world, and that, in some sense, make the world of our experience possible. *Prima facie*, at any rate, this appears to be what the religious believer is doing when, for example, as a specifically religious act he recites the Nicene Creed: "I believe in one God, the Father Almighty, creator of heaven and earth...."

Yet the only way the believer can speak of these religious objects is in a language that has been devised to deal with the material, spatiotemporal, observable, and limited objects of our ordinary mundane experience. For example, when the believer says, "I believe in God, the Father Almighty, creator of heaven and earth...", he is using either quite ordinary words ("Father," "mighty," "earth") or technical words ("God," "creator") that can be analyzed out into ordinary words. If I explain what I mean by the technical term "God," I have to say something like, "a supreme personal being on whom the world depends for its existence and value," and all the terms in this translation are ordinary and familiar words whose proper use we learn in mundane contexts. Similarly, if I define the technical term "creator," I say, for example, that a creator is one who makes things or brings things into existence "out of nothing,"

Essays in Philosophical Theology, ed. A. Flew and A. MacIntyre (London: S.C.M. Press; New York: Macmillan, 1955); *Faith and the Philosophers*, ed. J. Hick (New York: Macmillan, 1964); *Faith and Logic*, ed. B. Mitchell (London: Allen and Unwin, 1957); *Religion and Understanding*, ed. D. Z. Phillips (Oxford: Blackwell, 1967); C. B. Martin, *Religious Belief* (Ithaca: Cornell Univ. Press, 1959); F. Ferré, *Language, Logic and God* (New York: Harper, 1961); H. Meynell, *Sense, Nonsense and Christianity* (London: Sheed and Ward, 1964); N. Smart, *Philosophers and Religious Truth* (London: S.C.M. Press, 1964); A. Plantinga, *God and Other Minds* (Ithaca: Cornell Univ. Press, 1967); I. T. Ramsey, *Religious Language* (London: Macmillan, 1957); J. Macquarrie, *God-Talk* (New York: Harper, 1967); D. M. Evans, *The Logic of Self-Involvement* (London: S.C.M. Press, 1963); W. Blackstone, *The Problem of Religious Language* (Englewood Cliffs, N.J.: Prentice Hall, 1963).

that is, without presupposing any preexisting material out of which the things are made or brought into existence. Once again, all the words in this explanation are perfectly ordinary words used to describe the objects of our experience.

The difficulty is that these ordinary mundane words, when used of the extraordinary supramundane objects of religious belief, appear to be so outrageously stretched and strained and subject to so many qualifications that they lose all intelligible meaning. Thus, for example, the believer says that God makes things out of nothing, and he relies upon the term "make" having its ordinary sense. As we all know what "make" means, we are given the illusory sense that we understand what is meant by "God makes things out of nothing." But the qualification "out of nothing" renders the ordinary concept of "making" unintelligible, for in ordinary discourse we cannot be said to "make" anything unless it is possible to ask, "out of what was it made?" If when a person said "I have just made X," we asked him "Out of what did you make X?" and he thereupon replied, "Out of nothing," we would say that he did not understand how to use the term "make" properly. At first sight, to say that God makes things out of nothing seems to mean that there is a special kind of making that only God can do: ordinary mortals make things out of other things, but God can make things out of nothing. But we now see that this whole way of speaking is meaningless, for we have so qualified "make" that it no longer possesses the meaning that we started out with and upon which we relied. We seem to be saying something intelligible, but we have used ordinary language in such a way that it ceases to have any real content. It might be said that exactly the same trick of "taking back with one hand what you give with the other" is practiced with every other term of ordinary language used in religious contexts. When we say that God is a person, that He is good, that He is loving, or that He is powerful, we are here using terms with which we are familiar in our ordinary experience; but as used of God they have to be so qualified that in the end they lose their original meaning.

This then, in its first formulation, is the problem of religious language: how can we use ordinary language to speak of the extraordinary objects that religious language signifies? We cannot escape using ordinary language; yet, when we use it of religious objects it has to be so qualified that it ceases to have any meaning. It is in this form that the problem presents itself to Edouard Le Roy, for instance, in his essay *What is a Dogma*? Thus Le Roy claims that when the believer says that God is a person, he means by this first of all that God is a person in much the same sense as human beings are. But then the believer qualifies this by saying that God is a person in a completely different way from human persons; in fact He is a person in a way which is quite unique and indefinable. Thus, the believer ends up by admitting that the term "person" cannot really be applied to God.[3]

From quite a different point of view, Carnap objects that the believer does not really give any content to his propositions because he cannot specify what evidence would make them true or false. Hence, despite their grammatical appearance, religious propositions do not really "propose" anything; they are vacuous or "meaningless."[4] Ramsey also admits that religious assertions are "unavoidably paradoxical" in that they attempt to speak of "something more than observables" in language invented to deal with observables. However, Ramsey also wants to argue that certain of these religious paradoxes can be meaningful in that they evoke "disclosures" about religious realities.[5]

Religious Language : Descriptive or Not ?

The assumption on which this whole view of religious language rests and which, so to speak, causes the problem about religious language is that the only, or at least the primary, way in which language in general can be meaningful is for it to describe states of affairs or facts. In other words, it is assumed that the main function of language is descriptive.[6] From this, it follows that if religious language is to be

---

[3] See below, pp. 181–2.

[4] See below, pp. 129–30.

[5] See below, pp. 157–9.

[6] I use the more neutral terms "descriptive" and "nondescriptive" instead of "cognitive" and "noncognitive," for this latter usage begs the question as to whether nondescriptive locutions may have some cognitive function. In other words, it begs the question as to whether there can be "practical knowledge."

meaningful, it must also be descriptive in some way—not, of course, descriptive of ordinary natural or empirical facts or states of affairs, but of "supernatural" facts.

It might be argued that this assumption has only to be brought out into the light for it to be seen as untenable. It is evident that we use language meaningfully for purposes other than that of describing "what is the case" about things. When, for example, we say "X is good," we are not describing X but rather evincing our approval of X. Again, when I say "I agree to X," I am neither describing nor approving X but using language to effect a performance (for example, ratifying a contract or promise).[7]

Although contemporary analytic philosophers in particular have been concerned to expose what they call the "descriptivist fallacy" (namely, that language is meaningful only insofar as it is descriptive in function), and to show what a wide range of non-descriptive functions language has (prescriptive, emotive, performative etc.), this "pluralistic" view of language is in fact a very ancient one. Protagoras, for instance, and Plato and Aristotle after him, recognized that, apart from propositions making true or false statements about "what is the case," there are commands, requests, and questions that are meaningful in a way different from that of propositions. For example, "The door is open" (proposition) is meaningful in that it is a true or false description of what is the case; but "Shut the door!" (command) is not true or false, and neither is "Would you open the door?" (request), or "Is the door open?" (question). There is no state of affairs to which these latter locutions correspond, or of which they are true; yet they are (or can be) used quite meaningfully. The contemporary Analysts have attempted to show how this view of language helps solve many of the difficulties connected with moral language. If we assume that terms such as "good" must be descriptive in some queer way in order to be meaningful, we will be led to suppose with G. E. Moore, for

---

[7] Cf. J. L. Austin, *Philosophical Papers* (London: Oxford Univ. Press, 1961) p. 272: "When I say, 'I name this ship the Queen Elizabeth,' I do not describe the christening ceremony, I actually perform the christening: and when I say 'I do' (sc. take this woman to be my lawful wedded wife), I am not reporting on a marriage, I am indulging in it."

example, that "good" describes some "nonnatural quality" in the things of which it is predicated. In this view, to say "X is good" is to say in effect that along with all its other "natural" qualities, X has attaching to it a nonnatural quality. But, so it is argued, when we see that the function of "good" is not to describe qualities but rather to express performatively an attitude of approval towards the object or state of affairs of which it is predicated, then all the problems attendant upon the postulation of "nonnatural qualities" vanish.[8]

The price that one pays, however, for this solution is that moral locutions can no longer be construed as true or false, for the properties of truth and falsity apply only to descriptive locutions.[9] All that we can say is that nondescriptive locutions are appropriately or inappropriately (or, with J. L. Austin, felicitously or infelicitously) used. Thus the command, "Do X" where X is impossible, is not false but inappropriate or infelicitous. Similarly, the question, "Is the door open?" is not false but inappropriate if, say, the questioner is in a forest. It is obvious that we are faced here with a formidable difficulty for (unless we wish to embrace subjectivism) we must specify the conditions that make a locution appropriate or inappropriate and presumably must do so without recourse to facts or states of affairs describable by true or false propositions. Thus, for example, if I construe "X is good" as a nondescriptive locution whose function is to express approval of X, then, on the nondescriptivist view, I cannot ask whether this locution is true or false, but merely whether it is appropriate or not. But how am I to specify whether "X is good" is being used appropriately or not? If I say that "X is good" is used appropriately only in those contexts where, for instance, "X is pleasurable" or "X is a means to self-realization" is true, then nondescriptive locutions such as "X is good" will be meaningful only if certain descriptive locutions are meaningful. In more general terms, the nondescriptive functions of language will then be dependent

---

[8] Cf. P. Nowell Smith, *Ethics* (London: Penguin Books, 1954); M. Warnock, *Ethics Since 1900* (London: Oxford Univ. Press, 1960).

[9] And, as a corollary of this, such locutions will not have certain logical properties that true or false propositions have. For example, they will not admit contradictories as genuine propositions. This will make it difficult to see how there can be real disagreement in morals.

upon its descriptive function and hence will no longer be distinct and autonomous. We will return to this problem later.

This distinction between the descriptive and nondescriptive functions of language enables us to pose the problem of religious language in a more radical way by asking: what kind of meaning does religious language have? If religious locutions are descriptive in function, they will enjoy the logical advantage of being true or false, along with the other properties that follow therefrom. But the price of this is that they will then be subject to the difficulties we exposed before, namely, how we are to specify the extraordinary or supramundane facts or state of affairs they purport to describe. On the other hand, if we take religious locutions to be nondescriptive in function, seeing them, say, as emotive expressions or as quasi-moral expressions of attitude, then we escape these latter difficulties, for if it is not the function of religious locutions to describe certain peculiar facts, we cannot meaningfully ask for any proof or demonstration of these facts. Once again, however, as the price we pay for this logical advantage is that religious locutions are no longer true or false, we then must face the difficulty of how we are to justify them as appropriate or inappropriate without having recourse to true or false propositions about facts.

We also face the consequent difficulty of explaining the difference between theism and atheism. If both theist and atheist are not speaking descriptively when they say respectively, "There is a God," and "There is no God," then they are not contradicting each other but merely, it would seem, taking up differing attitudes or expressing differing emotions. One might put the problem thus: on the nondescriptivist hypothesis, how is disagreement over religion possible?[10]

There are, then, logical advantages and disadvantages on both sides, and the proponents on both sides argue for their respective positions by emphasizing their own advantages and pointing to the disadvantages of their opponents' position. The religious descriptivist

[10] That is, disagreement between the theist, who holds that religious discourse is meaningful, and the atheist, who holds that it is absurd. See on this R. D. Broiles, "Logic and Religious Language," *Sophia—A Journal for Discussion in Philosophical Theology*, V (July, 1966), pp. 10–14.

highlights the fact that, on his view, religious locutions can be justified as true or false so that atheism is, as it appears to be *prima facie*, a contradiction of theism. On the other hand, the nondescriptivist points to the difficulty of verifying religious locutions in terms of supramundane facts and emphasizes how his view enables one to evade this difficulty. As so often happens in philosophy, both sides maintain their own positions by scoring off each other. They are, so to speak, parasitic upon each other.

In the selections in this volume we can see this dialectic at work very clearly. G. D. Marshall, for instance, points to the untoward logical consequences of interpreting religious assertions as expressions of attitudes; he argues that if religious belief is to preserve its distinctive character, then assertions of religious belief cannot be so interpreted. On the other hand, nondescriptivists such as Santayana, Le Roy, and Arnold labor the difficulty of verifying religious assertions in terms of any facts or states of affairs, and put forward their own solutions as the only way out.

II.
HISTORY OF THE PROBLEM

The problem of religious language, as just formulated, has been a perennial one in the history of Western philosophy. No doubt, the problem has been framed in a particularly acute way by the contemporary philosophers of Analysis who have been preoccupied with questions of meaning and language and with the differences in "logic" of the various forms of discourse. But we did not need to wait for the Wittgensteinian era to become aware of the paradoxical nature of religious language and of the difficulties that spring from the ambivalence between its descriptive and nondescriptive characters. As R. M. Hare notes,[11] Plato was very much aware of the problem in his account of the Form of the Good—that being which for

---

[11] See below, p. 238.

Plato cannot properly be called *a being* since it is the ground of all other things, that in virtue of which there are beings (just as, to use a limping analogy, the standard metre in Paris is not itself a metre in length since it is that by which any length is deemed to be a "metre"). Similarly, the Neo-Platonists (Plotinus, Proclus, and Dionysius) in their own way were aware of the problem of using ordinary language to describe an extraordinary object like God. Their theory of the "negative way" (that we can speak of God only in negatives, that is to say, by denying of God predicates that are properly affirmed of His creatures) is supposed to solve this problem. For Aquinas also, and the medieval philosophers in general, the problem of the "Divine Names" was central. As we shall see, Aquinas's theory of analogical predication—worked up from Aristotelian and Neo-Platonic elements—is a very bold attempt to show that it is possible to use some at least of the terms of ordinary language to apply to God, without falling into anthropomorphism on the one hand or unintelligibility on the other. Again, the problem came up in Kant's attack on the "cosmological" proofs of the existence of God, for Kant alleged that all such proofs involve an illicit use of categories, such as the category of causality. These function meaningfully *within* the world of our ordinary experience but become meaningless when used of things outside and beyond that world. It was Kant also who foreshadowed the nondescriptivist approach to religious discourse by arguing that God is a postulate of the "practical reason," that is to say, the notion of God becomes intelligible only when it is seen as that which makes human morality possible. For Kant, the point of religious language is not primarily to describe the structure of reality (as for example, it was for Aquinas); it is rather "practical" or moral in intent.[12]

This same view of religious language was taken up in different ways in the nineteenth century when the advent of science seemed to make any descriptivist view of religious language impossible. Thus, both Arnold and Le Roy assumed that science had rendered untenable the traditional view that religious assertions were true descriptions of supramundane facts. Therefore, they construed these asser-

---

[12] Cf. Kant, *Critique of Practical Reason*, 138 (236), where Kant argues that the concept of God is meaningful only within the context of morality.

tions in the "practical" mode, so that (despite their grammatical appearance) they are to be seen as expressions of moral and other practical attitudes. Like Kant, these thinkers suppose that the practical sphere is quite autonomous, that is to say, it is not dependent upon any 'facts' about what is or is not the case.

Within the contemporary movement of phenomenological existentialism one can also discern the same kind of quasi-Kantian approach to religious discourse. Thus, for Jean-Paul Sartre, God must have the being that is proper to "être-pour-soi" (the being had by conscious and free subjects and which, in a sense, can never be described since it is essentially an openness to an unlimited future). Further, Sartre argues, if this be so then God cannot be immutably perfect or possess the property of "aseity."[13] For Gabriel Marcel, also, God is not a describable object or entity, but rather a "presence" that evokes an attitude on my part.[14] In the whole Kierkegaardian tradition, religious assertions only make sense within the realm of human "subjectivity," which is taken to be quite distinct from the realm of facts that are described by science.

Although at first sight the contemporary movement of Analysis seems to be radically different from the mainstream of traditional philosophy, there runs through it the same Kantian distinction between the realms of fact and value, religious discourse being situated within the latter. For what might be called the Logical Positivist wing of the movement (for example, Carnap and the Vienna Circle philosophers, together with A. J. Ayer and Anthony Flew in England) religious discourse is meaningless, since it does not satisfy

---

[13] But then, Sartre argues, if this is so God cannot be immutable and perfect or possess "aseity," since this would mean that God's being was the being of "être-en-soi," that is, the kind of being that describable objects have. The traditional idea of God, Sartre concludes, is therefore contradictory since it attempts to define God in terms both of "être-pour-soi" and "être-en-soi." See *Being and Nothingness*, trans. H. Barnes (London: Methuen, 1943), p. 662.

[14] Gabriel Marcel, *The Mystery of Being*, Vol. 1 (London: Harvill Press, 1950), p. 205: "We could say that the man sitting beside us was in the same room as ourselves, but that he was not really *present* there, that his *presence* did not make itself felt. . . . When somebody's presence does really make itself felt . . . it reveals me to myself, it makes me more fully myself than if I should be if I were not exposed to its impact."

the conditions of meaningful descriptive language.[15] For the Wittgensteinian wing of the movement of Analysis,[16] however, although
religious language might be meaningless if taken as descriptive in
function, it can nevertheless be meaningful if taken as having a
nondescriptive function. Thus, on the one hand, for Braithwaite and
Hare religious locutions express attitudes—quasi-moral attitudes in
the case of Braithwaite and quasi-metaphysical attitudes in the case
of Hare. On the other hand, for Wittgenstein himself (as interpreted
by Hudson, Malcolm, and others) religious locutions have their own
peculiar and irreducible function. The religious "language game,"
as Wittgenstein calls it, has its own peculiar rules or "logic."

The Selections

Within this general historical context let us now look in detail at the
selections published in this volume. These particular texts have been
chosen to illustrate the perennial and pervasive[17] character of the
problem of religious language, as well as to bring out in a systematic
way the main aspects of the problem and the various attempts that
have been made to solve it. The solutions represented here are certainly not exhaustive, but they are the basic ones that have emerged
in the history of this problem, other solutions being, I believe, variations on these primary ploys. As for the choice of texts, along with the
intention to illustrate the respective positions clearly and aptly, an

[15] A. J. Ayer, *Language, Truth and Logic*, 2nd edition (London: Gollancz, 1946);
A. Flew "Theology and Falsification," *New Essays in Philosophical Theology*, pp. 96–
99; *God and Philosophy* (London: Hutchinson, 1966).

[16] J. Wisdom, "Gods," *Philosophy and Psychoanalysis* (Oxford: Blackwell, 1953),
pp. 149–168; R. M. Hare, "Theology and Falsification," *New Essays*. pp. 99–103;
"Religion and Morals," see below, pp. 223–38; P. Winch, "Understanding a Primi-
tive Society," *American Philosophical Quarterly*, I (October, 1964), pp. 307–325; D. Z.
Phillips, "Faith, Scepticism and Religious Understanding," *Religion and Understanding*
pp. 000. N. Malcolm, "Anselm's Ontological Arguments," *Philosophical Review*,
LXIX (January, 1960), pp. 41–62; W. D. Hudson, "An Attempt to Defend
Theism," *Philosophy*, XXXIX (January, 1964), pp. 18–28. Cf. *L. Wittgenstein:
Lectures and Conversations on Aesthetics, Psychology and Religious Belief*, ed. C. Barrett
(Oxford: Blackwell, 1966).

[17] Pervasive, in the sense that this problem comes up in quite different philosophical traditions and contexts.

effort has been made to get away from the usual run of texts that appear and reappear in anthologies on this subject of religious language. Thus, for example, instead of using the much cited chapter on religious language from A. J. Ayer's *Language, Truth and Logic*, I have chosen Rudolf Carnap's powerful and lucid essay, "The Elimination of Metaphysics." Again, in place of Braithwaite's equally overexposed *An Empiricist's View of the Nature of Religious Belief*, I have included the remarkable essay, "What is a Dogma?" by the French philosopher Edouard le Roy. Though written as long ago as 1905, Le Roy's essay anticipates most of Braithwaite's main points and, to my mind, makes them more subtly and plausibly. It seems to me also that R. M. Hare's essay "Faith and Morals" republished here is a much more substantial piece than the same author's earlier essay in which the notion of "bliks" first appeared, and which has received more notice.[18]

III.
THE DESCRIPTIVIST RESPONSE

The first set of texts presented here argue that religious locutions are descriptive, though in different ways. *Prima facie* at least, the central religious locutions do seem to be making statements about certain supramundane objects, states of affairs, or dimensions of experience. Traditionally, at any rate, these statements have been held to be true. Thus, a believer was "orthodox," or defined as a Christian, insofar as he held the statements of the Creeds to be true, and a person was defined as a heretic insofar as he denied or impugned the truth of the Creeds. In this view then religious belief or faith is a matter of assenting to certain truths. Of course, certain practical consequences may follow from these beliefs. For example, if a man assents to the truth of the proposition, "God became man in the person of Jesus Christ in order to save men," then we may expect that his attitude towards his own life and towards other persons will be influenced by this belief. But, although these practical consequences

[18] R. M. Hare, "Theology and Falsification."

follow from the belief-assents, they do not constitute the act of faith. Put in another way, in religious faith *belief that* certain things are so is primary; *belief in* God, as expressed in certain attitudes of trust, hope, confidence, optimism, is secondary.

This "intellectualistic" view of religious belief, as Le Roy calls it, was certainly the dominant one in the Western Church until the time of the Reformation.[19] No doubt, as a matter of history, this view of religious belief and of religious language was influenced by the part that Greek philosophy played in the early development of Christian theology. But, historical circumstances apart, and whatever one may think of the role of Greek thought in Christianity, there are powerful logical considerations that make this position a very plausible one. Thus G. D. Marshall argues, in the first text in this anthology, that if we wish to hold that religious beliefs are (i) "performances in the rational mode" and not just expressions of irrational feeling; (ii) justifiably true and not just expressions of subjective whim or taste; (iii) responsible and intentional acts and not just dispositions over which we have only indirect control— then we must interpret religious beliefs as assents to propositions. Putting this into the formal or linguistic mode, we must construe religious locutions as being descriptive in function.

The descriptivist challenges the nondescriptivist then to show how the latter's position can escape the difficulties just mentioned, for if religious locutions do not describe any facts how can they be justified? As we saw before, even if we say that they are neither true nor false but are rather appropriate or inappropriate, we may still ask, what makes them appropriate? What, for instance, makes "God talk" in general appropriate and atheist talk inappropriate? The descriptivist has a clear answer to this question: religious language is appropriate or meaningful in that it describes certain religious facts, and it is those same facts that justify it. But it is not at all clear, at least at first sight, how the nondescriptivist can answer this question.

---

[19] However, there was also a long and respectable anti-intellectualistic tradition in the Church, which emphasized that religious faith was primarily a matter of the "heart." Pascal is in this current of thought when he says (*Pensées*, IV.277), "The heart has its reasons that reason knows nothing of."

Religious Experience

If we agree on the formal or "logical" point that religious language must be descriptive in some way, we still have to discover in what particular way it is descriptive, for it is obvious enough that religious locutions are not descriptive in the same way as are scientific or empirical propositions. One classical attempt to answer this question is in terms of religious experience.[20] In this view, religious locutions are meaningful in that they refer to or describe certain quite distinctive experiences that the believer has undergone. For example, in Rudolf Otto's famous essay *The Idea of the Holy*, part of which is reproduced in this volume, the meaning of religious utterances is based ultimately upon our experience of what is called "the Numinous." At first sight, the appeal to religious experience appears very simple and attractive, for there are obvious analogies with other forms of experience. Thus, if we are asked what "green" means, the answer is given in terms of visual experience: green is what you see—the visual experience that you have—when you look at a given visual object. Similarly, if we are asked what "toothache" means, we can only answer by referring to certain pain experiences. Again, what we mean by saying that a work of art is "beautiful" can only be explained in terms of certain aesthetic experiences. Finally, to the question "What does it mean to say that you are *in love*?" we can only reply that being in love means suffering certain experiences of attraction, joy, exaltation in the presence of another.

In all these cases the meaning of the terms in question is given by referring to certain experiences which involve (i) knowledge by direct acquaintance, as opposed to abstract knowledge about things

[20] On the notion of religious experience see: R. M. Hepburn, *Christianity and Paradox* (London: Watts, 1958; New York: Humanities Press, 1958); C. B. Martin, "A Religious Way of Knowing," *New Essays*, pp. 76–95; A. MacIntyre, "Visions," *New Essays*, pp. 254–60; J. Baillie, *Our Knowledge of God* (London: Oxford Univ. Press, 1939); H. D. Lewis, *Our Experience of God* (London: Allen and Unwin, 1959); W. D. Glasgow, "Knowledge of God," *Philosophy*, XXXII (July, 1957), pp. 229–40; William James, *The Varieties of Religious Experience* (1902; London: Collins, 1963); R. C. Zaehner, *Mysticism, Sacred and Profane* (London: Oxford Univ. Press, 1957).

and also to knowledge obtained by inference; and (ii) "subjective" or private knowledge, as opposed to "objective" or publicly testable knowledge. Reference to experience implies that you must "see for yourself" or undergo the experience for yourself. I cannot describe what "green" means to a blind man; I cannot describe what "beauty" in music means to a tone-deaf person; I cannot describe what "love" is to someone with no affection or feeling. So also, religious experience implies that the experiencer has had a direct contact or acquaintance with God or religious objects and that this experience is private or subjective and not publicly testable, in the sense that it cannot be adequately described to one who has not had the experience for himself.

The general notion of "experience," however, and the notion of "religious experience" in particular, are not as clear as would appear at first. Thus, "experience" may mean first of all that the subject of the experience is experiencing certain psychological and neuro-physiological states that he can introspect and describe. A person may say, for instance, that he feels edgy and tense. From this kind of experience, which we may loosely call *psychological* experience, nothing follows with regard to its "objects" or causes. As it has been put: "An experience cannot of itself yield us any information about anything other than the experience."[21] And again: "The only thing that I can establish beyond correction on the basis of knowing certain feelings and sensations is that I have those feelings and sensations."[22]

But "experience" may also mean that the subject of the experience is engaged in some intentional act. Thus visual experience is experience *of* some coloured object. Visual experience does not consist in having certain color-sensations (from which we infer the existence of colored objects), but rather in awareness *of* color. Again, an emotional experience is an experience *of* or *at* some object. Thus the emotion of anger does not consist simply in certain feeling-states of the subject, for to give an account of the emotion we have to specify at what or with whom we are angry.[23]

In this sense we may say that visual experience and emotional

[21] C. B. Martin, "A Religious Way of Knowing," p. 79.

[22] A. MacIntyre, "Visions," p. 256.

[23] Cf. A. Kenny, *Action, Emotion and the Will* (London: Routledge and Kegan Paul, 1963).

experience is intentional, that is, that *ipso facto* it has an object, as opposed to psychological experience, which does not necessarily have any object. There is, however, a price to be paid for this "objective" character of intentional experience, for, unlike psychological experience, it is open to the possibility of error. If I rest content with reporting my psychological experiences ("I feel pain" etc.) there is, as Descartes saw, a sense in which I can never be mistaken about them, so that this kind of experience is infallible or incorrigible. But if I have an intentional experience *of* some object then the possibility of error is immediately introduced. Thus, with visual experience it is always possible to say, "I seemed to see X, but I was mistaken," and the same possibility attaches to all forms of intentional experience. In summary, then, we have a choice between experience that is infallible, at the cost of being purely psychological or subjective, and experience that is objective, at the cost of being fallible. We cannot have experience that is both infallible and objective.

This ambiguity of "experience" is reflected in "religious experience," for sometimes "religious experience" seems to mean the suffering or undergoing of certain psychological states, and sometimes it seems to mean an intentional awareness of some specifically religious object. Thus, "I have had a religious experience" may mean "I have had certain peculiar feelings and sensations quite unlike ordinary feelings and sensations," and here I am describing certain psychological states that obtain within me. On the other hand, "I have had a religious experience" may mean "I have had an awareness *of* God or some religious object," and here I am not just talking about my subjective states but about an intentional act. I am claiming to be aware of God just as I am aware of the color green.

Otto does not always distinguish clearly between these two senses of religious experience. Thus, at times he suggests that the experience of the *numinous* is describable in terms of such psychological states as feelings of awe, dependency, etc.; from these we infer that there must be some object or reality answering to those feelings, as though God, the Holy, or the Numinous had to be postulated as the only possible explanation of those feelings or states.[24] At other times, however—and this appears to be his main position—Otto

[24] Cf. *The Idea of the Holy*, below, p. 78.

claims that religious experience gives us direct awareness of and acquaintance with religious objects.[25] Horsburgh also speaks of religious experience in this way as against those critics who reject appeal to it on the ground that we can never certainly infer from subjective states to objective reality. This argument avails, Horsburgh admits, against those who espouse the psychological form of religious experience, but it does not touch, so he argues, those who rely upon the intentional form.[26]

What, then, are we to say of the claim that it is possible to have a direct intentional experience or awareness of God or other religious objects in the sense just described? First, as we have already pointed out, if an experience is intentional there is *ipso facto* a possibility of error with regard to it. In other words, on some occasions it will be possible to say that I thought I experienced God but actually did not experience Him. This implies that we must have some means for distinguishing between veridical and erroneous religious experiences. However, this is not a fatal objection, as some religious sceptics have alleged. The following objection has been raised: "How are we to decide whether at least some religious mystics truly experience God or whether all such mystics have very unusual illusory experiences? We cannot check the claims of mystics in the way we often check possible cases of illusory experiences, such as mirages, because we cannot observe whether or not there is an object experienced. We can, for example, go to the location in the desert where a man claims to have seen an oasis and carefully investigate the whole area, but we cannot in any comparable manner go to the region in which the mystic claims to have been aware of God."[27] This objection is in fact a very weak one, for it assumes that it is only empirical checking of experiences that is acceptable. Certainly, we may reply, if we wish to hold that we can have intentional experiences of God, then there must be some tests for distinguishing between veridical and mistaken experiences; but those tests need not be empirical tests.

We might compare here religious experiences with aesthetic

[25] *Ibid.* p. 80.

[26] See below, p. 89.

[27] J. Cornman and K. Lehrer, *Philosophical Problems and Arguments* (New York: Macmillan, 1968), p. 290.

experiences. Thus, I may experience a work of art as beautiful and yet be deceived about this. The test that I use here to see that I was wrong and to correct my experience is simply that of looking again at the work of art, attending more closely to it, purging my mind of possible prejudices, and so on. Surely we can do the same, *mutatis mutandis*, with religious experiences. No sceptical conclusions follow therefore from the fact that there is a possibility of error in religious experiences, any more than they follow from the fact that error is possible in sense perception or in aesthetic experience. If it is possible to be mistaken, it is also possible to correct one's mistakes; if it is possible to go wrong, it is also possible to be right. However, the fallibility of religious experience does remove one of the usually claimed attractions of the appeal to it, namely that it is infallible and "self-authenticating" in a special way. It may be remarked in parentheses that religious experience is taken here to be distinct from supernatural faith. The Christian holds that God may by His grace enable or empower men to believe in His infallibility. But the religious experience that we have been discussing is presupposed to any such extraordinary or supernatural faith "experience."

Criticism of Religious Experience

If one is nonetheless prepared to admit the fallibility of religious experience, then there seem to be no *a priori* arguments against its possibility, unless some kind of prior empiricist assumption (namely, that only *sense* experiences are possible) is made. All the same, there are powerful circumstantial arguments against religious experience being the normal basis of religious belief. First, this position seems to imply that there is in us a quite distinct religious sense or faculty over and above our ordinary sense powers and faculties. In Horsburgh's ingenious example, the man who possesses this power of religious experience is like the one man, from a group of congenitally blind men, who possess the power of sight or visual experience.[28] In one sense this is a kind of factual claim about the structure of the human psyche and not unlike claims made about extrasensory powers of

---

[28] See below, p. 91.

perception. Of course, the only way of seeing whether or not this claim is true is precisely by seeing whether or not we have the experience. This, however, needs to be qualified, for there are conceptual limits as to what we can claim to experience. Thus, if a proponent of extrasensory perception were to claim that tests had shown that some people were able to perceive future contingent events, including acts of free will, then on the ground that it is conceptually impossible directly to perceive future states of affairs, we would be strongly inclined to say that these claims were false or at least misinterpretations. In other words, the possibility of the object of experience is not proved by the actual having of the experience, for if the purported experience is of something that is conceptually impossible, we say that the experience has been "misinterpreted." It is this, of course, that is primarily at issue in the matter of religious experience, namely, whether what the experience is alleged to be *of* is conceptually possible or not. The believer who appeals to religious experience implicitly assumes that it is possible, or at least not impossible; the atheist will deny that it is possible and will insist that the experience to which the believer appeals will have to be reinterpreted (for example, as by Freud). It is not being argued here that we must first of all prove that the objects of religious experience are possible, in a positive sense, before we can claim to have had experience of them. But at least religious experience assumes that its objects are not impossible and this, as we have seen, sets a limit to its claims.

There is a second circumstantial argument against religious experience being the normal basis of religious belief. The claim to religious experience implies that we are normally capable of direct contact with God or "the Holy"; what, in Judaeo-Christianity at least, is thought to be an extraordinary and privileged relationship with God (as in the Beatific Vision or in exceptional mystical states) is here made into a kind of normal state. Thus, Otto certainly speaks at times as though everyone is capable of religious experience just as everyone is capable of aesthetic experience and as though this is a fairly normal state of affairs. Within this context it is very difficult to maintain any distinction between our natural knowledge of God and what we know by revelation, for if our normal access to God is by direct contact, what place is left for revelation and the whole supernatural order? If direct awareness of God is, in a sense, our right, what place is there for God's grace? Of course the matter is different if it is claimed that religious experiences are produced by God quasi-miraculously by a suspension of our natural powers and psychological processes, and on rare occasions as manifestations of His grace. But then, of course, religious experiences will not be the normal basis of belief.

Thus, the appeal to religious experience, despite its immediate attractiveness as a solution to the problem of religious language, turns out on examination to be fraught with formidable difficulties. This is not to deny that some people do have extraordinary religious experiences; what is being said here is that the meaning of religious language cannot typically be given by reference to religious experience in the same way that the meaning of words like "green" is typically given by reference to certain visual experiences.[29]

Analogy

The theory of analogy is the other main classical attempt to give a descriptivist account of religious language.[30] As developed by Aquinas and his followers, it is a theory of considerable philosophical sophistication and subtlety and cannot be dismissed as easily as certain nondescriptivists pretend. It is curious, for example, that Le Roy does not even advert to the theory in his attack on what he calls the "intellectualistic" tradition. If we take "God is a person" as a true proposition, Le Roy argues, we fall inevitably into either anthropomorphism—God is a person just like a human person—or into unintelligibility—God is a person in a quite distinctive (*sui generis*) sense. Le Roy does not consider the possibility that "person," as predicated of God, might be used analogically.

[29] A good deal more careful phenomenological description of the various modes and varieties of religious experience, both within and without the Christian tradition, still needs to be done.

[30] For recent discussions on analogy see: E. L. Mascall, *Existence and Analogy* (London: Darton, Longman, and Todd, 1966), ch. V; A. Farrer, *Finite and Infinite* (London: Dacre Press, 1943); R. McInerny, *The Logic of Analogy* (The Hague: Nijhoff, 1961); P. T. Geach, *Three Philosophers* (Oxford: Blackwell, 1961), pp. 117–125.

Again, from one point of view, Ramsey's theory is an attempt to do the same job as the theory of analogy, by showing that certain terms may, if "infinitized," disclose or evoke something about God. But Ramsey gives no account of why this process works with some terms rather than others: why, for example, talk of "infinite love" or "infinite mercy" is meaningful and discloses something about God, whereas "infinite solidity" or "infinite redness" is meaningless and discloses nothing. It is precisely this latter question that the theory of analogy is concerned to answer.

The theory of analogy is not, as has sometimes been claimed, solely concerned with the attributes or properties of God—it being assumed that God's existence has already been established in some way or other.[31] We cannot in fact show that God exists unless we can give some description of the attributes of God, and in this sense we must know what God is (albeit inadequately) in order to know that He is. Aquinas's dictum that we cannot know *what* God is (*quid est*), but only *that* He is (*quia est*), is not to be taken as meaning that we cannot characterize God at all. In fact, Aquinas himself goes on to give such a characterization in some detail. Rather it means that no characterization of God can define the "essence" of God.[32]

If we consider the God that emerges from Aquinas's natural theology, we have a being of the following general description: *a necessarily existing being that is the total cause of the existence and activity of all the contingent beings in the world of our experience.* This is what might be called the minimum description of God. Now it is obvious that the problem that we discussed before comes up *a propos* this description, for it involves using ordinary words such as "necessary," "existing," "cause," in an extraordinary way; we have to show how such words can still retain intelligible content even though they are being used in this qualified way. Thus, it might be said, since "necessary" is a logical term ordinarily used only of certain propositions (such as

[31] Mascall, *op. cit.*, p. 95: "The question of analogy does not arise at all in the mere proof of the existence of God; it arises only when, having satisfied ourselves that the existence of finite being declares its dependence upon self-existent being, we then apprehend that no predicate can be attributed to finite and to self-existent being univocally."

[32] P. T. Geach, *op. cit.*, p. 177.

propositions that cannot be denied without contradiction), it is clearly being used in an odd way when it is said that God is a "necessary existent." Again "existent" and "cause" are ordinarily used of the spatiotemporal things within our experience, whereas applied to God they are obviously being used in a radically different context. Therefore, we have to show how these terms can be used of God without being deprived of intelligible content and without being mere metaphors. If all our talk about God were metaphorical, so that when we said "God exists," "God is the cause of the world," etc., we meant, "God *as it were* exists," "God is, *as it were*, the cause of the world," then the notion of God would lose all meaning.

Once we have established the logical legitimacy of the minimum description of God mentioned above, that is, once we have shown that it is neither metaphorical not unintelligible, we will have an additional basis for ascribing predicates to God, for if God is the total cause of all the contingent things within our experience, then, since a cause precontains what is in its effects, He will "precontain" in some way all that is contained in His creation.[33] Thus, we will be able to ascribe to God any predicates that are ordinarily ascribed to contingent things within our experience, so long as those predicates are not logically restricted to a specific class of things. Thus, on the principle that whatever is predicable of God's creation is predicable of the total cause of that creation, we will not be able to say "God is colored," for as a predicate "colored" is logically restricted to material and extended things; it would be nonsense to say "X is colored but not a material extended thing." On the contrary, we will be able to say "God thinks," "God wills," "God is a person." God's creation contains thinking and willing beings or persons and, although the only thinking, willing, and personal beings we are directly acquainted with are *human* beings, analysis of thinking, willing, and the concept of person will show that it is not nonsense to suppose that disembodied thinking and willing, and disembodied persons are possible, or at least not self-contradictory, concepts.

This way of putting things neutrally expresses the gist of the contentious Neo-Platonic theory of "perfections" that Joyce refers

---

[33] See Joyce, below, p. 106. This principle, that the cause precontains what is in its effects, obviously needs further analysis.

to in his account of Aquinas's theory of analogy.[34] Aquinas' theory mixes together two distinct subtheories: first, a theory about the "logic" of certain predicates, which he derives from Aristotle; and second, a metaphysical theory of Neo-Platonic inspiration to the effect that (i) there is a distinction between those properties of things that represent "perfections" and those that do not; (ii) these "perfections" may exist in a mode quite different from the limited mode in which they exist in material things; (iii) these perfections may be ascribed to God on the ground that He is the most perfect being. It is, however, difficult to make sense of the metaphysical theory of perfections,[35] and it seems to me that the essence of Aquinas' theory of analogy can be expressed in purely logical form without bringing in Neo-Platonic metaphysics.

Whatever might be said about the possibility of ascribing predicates to God on the basis of the cause-effect relationship obtaining between God and His creation, it is obvious that this will not work with regard to the predicates that constitute what we have called the minimum description of God. One of those latter predicates is the predicate "cause" ("God is the cause of the world"), and we cannot show that this predicate is legitimately applied to God on the ground that He is the total cause of creation. It is here that Aquinas invokes an Aristotelian idea about the "logic" of certain predicates.[36] These predicates are not "univocal" or class-predicates ("X is *red*," for example, can be translated as "X is a member of the class of red things"), but are rather what might be called "class-transcending" predicates, in the sense that without equivocation they can be applied within various classes. "Exists" and "good" are two such class-transcending terms. "X exists" cannot be translated as "X is a member of the class of existent things," since there is no such determinate class, ("being is not a generic term," as Aristotle says).[37] Similarly, "X is good" cannot be translated as "X is a member of the class of good things," for there is no such determinate class. To use

---

[34] See below p. 105.

[35] See my discussion of the theory of "perfections" in *St. Anselm's 'Proslogion'* (Oxford: Clarendon Press, 1965), pp. 60–61.

[36] Aristotle, *Metaphysics*, IV, 2, 1002 a 35; IX, 6, 1048 b 5.

[37] *Ibid.*, III, 3, 998 b 20.

an example suggested by P. T. Geach,[38] these terms function a little the way "the square root of" functions in "the square root of 4," "the square root of 9," "the square root of 25." In one sense, "the square root of" means the same in these instances of it; but in another sense, of course, what it means varies according to the particular instantiation of it. Thus "the square root of 4" is 2, the "square root of 9" is 3, and so on. So also when we say, "The Taj Mahal exists," "The number 2 exists," "Minds exist," and so on, "exists" in one sense means the same in all its instantiations,[39] but in another sense its meaning varies according to the particular instantiation. Similarly with "good": if we say, "This knife is a good one," "Socrates is a good man," "This climate is good," "good" is not being used here equivocally, yet neither is it being used univocally. These particular predicates, which are neither equivocal nor univocal nor metaphorical, may be called *analogous* predicates. (It should be noted that the term is rather misleading in that this notion of analogy has very little to do with analogy in the ordinary sense, as when, for example, Plato says that there is an analogy between the structure of the soul and the structure of the state). In addition to "exists" and "good," predicates such as "possible," "necessary," "cause," "acts," also seem to function in the same "class transcending" or analogous way.

Criticism of the Theory of Analogy

The significance of this doctrine of analogy for religious language is obvious enough, for if these analogous predicates are not logically restricted in their application to a determinate class of things, they can possibly be applied to God without equivocation or metaphor. The difficulty, however, is that we do not, so it would seem, know what these terms mean as applied to God. We know that we can legitimately say, "God exists," "God is the cause of the world," "God is good," and so on, but we do not know what these predicates signify here, except that they do not signify what they signify in their

[38] "Good and Evil," *Analysis*, XVII (December, 1956), p. 38.
[39] Assuming that "exists" functions in some way as a predicate.

other applications to mundane subjects. We know, for example, that "exists" does not signify the same with regard to God as it signifies with regard to the Taj Mahal, for when we say "The Taj Mahal exists," we mean that the Taj Mahal is a material, spatiotemporal object. But when we say, "God exists," what exactly do we mean by "exists" here: what positive meaning does it have?

One traditional way of meeting this objection is to have recourse to a mathematical analogy. Thus, it has been said that God is to His existence and goodness as, say, this cabbage is to its existence and goodness. The analogy here is with a sum of proportions: X is to A, as B is to C; we are given the values of A, B, and C and are required to find the value of X. But obviously the analogy limps, for though we know what "exists" and "good" mean in the case of a created entity such as a cabbage, we do not know what they mean in the case of a supramundane entity such as God. In this case the two sides of the proportion, so to speak, belong to quite different orders, whereas with a proportional sum the values that may legitimately be substituted for the variables A, B, C, X, must be of the same order.

Perhaps the way out of this difficulty is to remember that for Aquinas "exists," "good," "cause" etc., are only predicated of God within the context of an explanation of certain fundamental cosmological facts, for example, that the world is mutable or contingent. In order to explain adequately how a contingent world actually exists we find ourselves logically compelled, so Aquinas claims, to postulate the existence of a necessary existent that is the total cause of the contingent world. In other words, we find ourselves logically compelled to use the predicates "exists," "cause," "necessary," and so on, in a way quite different from the way they are used of mundane subjects within our experience. We know, for example, what "necessary existence" or "total cause of contingent existents" mean *within the context of the explanation*, but we do not know what they mean *in themselves*. An illustration may help here: in order to explain certain phenomena a scientist may be compelled to postulate that there exists a fundamental particle with certain peculiar properties, though this particle may be as yet unobservable. In this sense, it might be said that the scientist knows *that* certain predicates must be applied to the unknown X, even though he does not know what the unknown X is like in itself. The illustration, however, has limitations for at least the predicates applied to the postulated unobserved particle are of the same order as the predicates applied to observed particles, and this is not the case with the predications made of God, or involved in speaking of God.

There are, then, difficulties with the theory of analogy, and it clearly needs a good deal more detailed working out if it is to provide a satisfactory answer to the problem of religious language. As it appears in Aquinas, it is little more than a sketch of a possible theory —a theory that is, moreover, confused by Aquinas' mixing of logical (Aristotelian) points and metaphysical (Neo-Platonic) ones. I have suggested that the theory in its primary form ought to be seen as a logical one (albeit with metaphysical implications) about the use of certain predicates, and that we ought to make a sharp distinction between those predicates that constitute the minimum description of God, and those that may subsequently be ascribed to God on the basis of the cause–effect relationship between God and His creation. These latter predicates are analogous only in a secondary sense. For example, we can only apply "thinks," "wills," "loves" to God if we first show that thinking, willing, loving are not purely physical operations, as the materialist or brain-physicalist would claim, so that they are not necessarily restricted to material bodies. Thus, the notion of a disembodied mind capable of acts of thinking, willing, and loving is shown not to be self-contradictory, as would be, for example, the notion of an act of disembodied anger. With regard to analogous terms of the primary kind ("exists," "good," "cause") all that we have to do is to inspect the way in which they function by pure logical analysis without involving any prior metaphysical assumptions. With regard to analogous terms of the secondary kind, however, we have first to make certain assumptions. For example, as we have seen, we have first to show that the brain physicalist or materialist is wrong and that the notion of a disembodied mind capable of mental acts is not self-contradictory. Again, even supposing that the theory of analogy explains how we can meaningfully use terms such as "good," "exists," and "cause," of God without equivocation, these predications are merely on the level of natural theology. In other words, the God they describe is the God of natural theology rather than of religious revelation, for example, the God described in the Old and New Testaments. To some extent the pre-dicates applied to God by revelation overlap with the predicates ap-plied to God by natural theology, for example, "God is good," "God is all-powerful," and "God is all-knowing" etc. But there are also revelation predicates that go beyond those of natural theology, for example, "God is one in nature but triune in personality," "Christ is really present in the Eucharist." If these statements are taken to be descriptive and to have some intelligible content, then the terms "person" and "really present" are being used analogously. But it is obvious that they are not being used in their "ordinary" analogical sense, as when we say, for example, at the level of natural theology, "God is a person," or "God is present in His creation." In summary, we may say that the theory of analogy clearly has some-thing to it; indeed, if one wishes to maintain some kind of descripti-vist view of religious language then some such theory is absolutely necessary. As presented by Neo-Thomist thinkers, however, it faces formidable objections. In order to meet them we need to get away from the stereotyped thinking about analogy within the Thomist tradition and attempt to think the theory out afresh.

Verificationism and Religious Language

To the nondescriptivist, however, the objections to the doctrine of analogy are fatal. Either the predicates we apply to God are anthropomorphic and metaphorical, or they are used in some radically qualified sense that makes them unintelligible. This is the nub of Carnap's criticism of religious language, namely that we cannot specify any "criteria of application" for the word "God" or, what comes to the same thing, we cannot *verify* whether or not the word "God" is being used correctly. For Carnap and the logical positivists in general, the "verification principle" was supposed to be a purely formal criterion of the meaningfulness of any locutions.[40]

---

[40] On the Verification Principle, see C. Hempel, "Problems and Changes in the Empiricist Criterion of Meaning," *Semantics and The Philosophy of Language*, ed. L. Linsky (Urbana: University of Illinois Press, 1952), pp. 163–185; A. Plantinga, "Verificationism and Other Atheologica," *God and Other Minds*, ch. VII.

In other words, they held that—quite independently of whether it was true or false—there were certain formal or logical conditions that any proposition must satisfy if it were to be an instrument of meaning. The main condition was that of verifiability, in the sense just explained. In this purely logical form the verification principle is innocent enough; so long as the believer is willing to specify what kind of evidence is relevant to determining the truth of his religious assertions, the principle does not exclude them as meaningless. But, it is obvious that Carnap and the logical positivists assume that the only kind of propositions that satisfy the vertification principle are the empirical propositions of the natural sciences; for them "veri-fiable" means in effect "empirically verifiable." This assumption is of course highly contestable; it is also meta-logical in the sense that no logical analysis of the conditions of meaningfulness can show us that empirical propositions alone satisfy these conditions. That one particular type of proposition alone satisfies the verification prin-ciple involves a "factual" or meta-logical judgment that does not follow immediately from the principle itself, for whether any prin-ciple does or does not apply to a particular instance cannot be deduced from the principle itself.

Given this identification of "verifiability" with "empirical verifiability" in the sense of observation and experiment, as in the natural sciences, the verification principle reads: only those proposi-tions that are empirically verifiable are meaningful. In this case, of course, religious language (at least if it is taken to be propositional or descriptive in form) is *ipso facto* meaningless. As we have said, how-ever, this form of the principle involves meta-logical assumptions that are open to question. In addition, it is much too stringent a criterion of meaningfulness for it excludes as meaningless not only moral propositions (since, for example, we cannot empirically verify propositions such as "Deliberately killing innocent people is wrong"), but also the theoretical statements of science which cannot be directly verified.[41]

[41] Certain consequences may be deduced from a theory, and these may be empi-rically verifiable. However, it does not follow that the theory itself is therefore verified. If p implies q, then if p is true it follows that q is true. But if q is true it does not follow that p is true. In other words, the verification of q does not entail that p is verified.

Nevertheless, even if the verification principle is very questionable and Carnap's attack on religious language, as it stands, is not conclusive, it does at least put the onus on one who wants to hold that religious language is descriptively true to specify how religious propositions may be verified. As a recent writer has put it: "To believe is to believe *something*, and if there is anything that one believes, we ought to be able to say in some way—if not in the very narrow terms of sense-experience—what the difference is between what one believes being true and what one believes not being true."[42] With a certain kind of contemporary religious talk it is very difficult to say what kind of evidence would be relevant to showing it to be true or not true; its assertions seem to be compatible with any and every state of affairs so that, in effect, they say nothing determinate at all. Whatever might be said about the logical status of the verification principle, it is a good practical rule, particularly in the realm of religious language, always to try to conceive what would verify or falsify one's statements. A lot of high-sounding theological nonsense would be shown up for what it is if this simple rule of method were rigorously applied.

Carnap and the logical positivists had assumed that if a proposition was not descriptively meaningful it was therefore meaningless. It is true that Carnap is not altogether consistent in this, since he seems to think that mythological and poetic locutions have some point even though they are not verifiable; again, A. J. Ayer in his celebrated book *Language, Truth and Logic*, was constrained to admit that moral locutions had "emotive" meaning even though they were not verifiable. However, neither Carnap nor Ayer exploit the idea that there might be other forms of meaning besides descriptive or propositional meaning. This is brought out in Wittgenstein's later work, *Philosophical Investigations*,[43] where he proposes a "pluralistic" theory of meaning and rejects what we called before the descriptivist fallacy. It is also implicit in the position of older thinkers represented in our selections, such as Arnold, Le Roy and Santayana; as we shall see, Randall, who is certainly not a Wittgensteinian, also adopts this view.

[42] B. Williams, "Has 'God' a Meaning?" *Question*, I (February 1968), p. 51.
[43] (Oxford: Blackwell, 1953.)

IV.
THE NONDESCRIPTIVIST RESPONSE

We may now turn to the nondescriptivist solution of the problem of religious language. In part, as we have seen, the nondescriptivist view derives a good deal of its plausibility from the fact that it enables us to escape the difficulties of the descriptivist view. If religious locutions are not to be construed as descriptive, then, at one stroke, we escape all the problems about the verification of those locutions. There is another powerful reason, however, upon which the nondescriptivist also relies, namely, that religious locutions do have a quasi-practical character that the descriptivist or intellectualistic theory has difficulty accommodating. We said before that, for the descriptivist, religious belief or faith consisted essentially in assent to the truth of certain propositions. Although certain practical conclusions as to how the believer ought to live his life and what attitudes he ought to adopt might follow from these acts of assent, these practical effects of belief did not constitute religious faith. For the descriptivist, what defines one as a believer is that one assents to certain propositions as true; if one does not adopt any practical policies or attitudes as a consequence of these assents, one may be classed as a hypocritical or inconsistent believer, but he will still be a believer. It is precisely this possibility that the nondescriptivist rejects. For him religious belief cannot be merely speculative, a matter of assent to the truth of propositions; of its very essence it is practical, a commitment to certain attitudes. On the descriptivist view it is at least theoretically possible to say, "I believe in God, but this makes no difference to the way I live my life." For the nondescriptivist, however, this is impossible, for to say, "I believe in God," is precisely to commit oneself to lead one's life in a certain way. There is a logical gap for the descriptivist between religious belief and action: belief in God or other religious objects does not in their regard logically entail action. For the nondescriptivist, on the other hand, belief tends to be identified with action or at least is translatable into terms of action. This practical character of religious language is a constant refrain in the nondescriptivists represented in our anthology. Randall, for example, emphasizes what he calls the "impressive" character of religious language, meaning by this that it evokes emotional responses in us and so aids certain kinds of action. In addition, a little like poetic language, it causes us to see the world and ourselves in a new light. For Ramsey, also, religious language's main function is to provoke insight through paradox. Again, for Le Roy, Arnold, and Santayana the function of religious language is a directly practical one, that is to say, religious locutions are really practical recommendations to act in a certain way or to adopt certain attitudes. Le Roy interprets practice in a general sense, but Arnold and Santayana see it mainly in terms of moral practice, albeit with an emotive or poetic overtone. For Hare, on the other hand, and to some extent Wittgenstein, the function of religious language is to express and evoke not moral attitudes, but rather quasi-metaphysical "attitudes"—certain fundamental ways of seeing the world and ourselves.

We may remark that even if the effect of religious language is to bring about "insight" or other cognitive attitudes, this does not mean that their own function is a cognitive or descriptive one. The evoking of cognitive states is itself not a cognitive but a practical act. In other words, on this view we do not ask whether religious locutions are true or false, but whether or not they are practically effective in evoking insight.

Reductionism

There is, however, a fundamental distinction among the nondescriptivists. Some identify religious belief with the taking up of practical attitudes—so that religious language becomes a species of moral or metaphysical discourse. Others wish to hold that the essential point of religious language is expressible in practical terms, without, however, identifying the two. The positions of Le Roy and Ramsey are examples of the latter, for both these authors assume that God and an order of religious realities exist independently of the practical attitudes that may be adopted towards them, though what right they have to make this assumption in terms of their own theories is another question. Arnold and Santayana, however, appear to identify religious and moral languages without remainder. In rather a different context, Hare and Wittgenstein seem to suggest that it makes no sense to speak of God independently of our attitudes to the world and to life, so that for them religious language is apparently identified with a kind of metaphysical language. These latter views might be termed "reductionist" views of religious language, for they imply that religious language can be reduced to practical language of one kind or another without remainder.[44] Arnold, for example, sees religious language as simply one species of moral language, distinguished from other kinds by the accidental fact that it also has emotive force. In the same way, R. B. Braithwaite's position in *An Empiricist's View of the Nature of Religious Belief* implies that the function of religious language is identical with that of moral language, the only difference being that religious language has an imaginative or mythological component. So, for Braithwaite, the only difference between the atheist and the religious believer seems to be that the latter feels the need to tell himself mythical "stories" to give himself psychological support in carrying out his humanistic moral intentions.[45]

[44] On reductionism in theology see J. C. Thornton, "Religious Belief and Reductionism," *Sophia*, V (October, 1966), pp. 3–16; E. L. Mascall, "Theological Reductionism," *Sophia*, VI (June, 1967), pp. 3–5; H. Meynell, *Sense, Nonsense and Christianity*. Cf. G. C. Colombo, "The Analysis of Belief," *The Downside Review* (Winter, 1958–59), p. 23, on theological reductionism in the late nineteenth-century modernists: "If asked what is the meaning of the words they pronounce during the divine service, the modernists would give a consistent interpretation throughout. 'God exists' is just the objectivisation to transcend ourselves, and to aim at an ideal. 'Creation' is the satisfaction of our need to feel ourselves dependent and limited. The resurrection of Christ is another way of saying that the faith of the disciples recovered after a moment of crisis, and so on." Colombo cites a letter written by George Tyrrell to von Hugel in 1904: "It is not, as they (the traditional theologians) suppose, about this or that article of the creed that we differ; we accept it all; but it is the word 'credo', the sense of 'true' as applied to 'dogma', the whole course of revelation that is at stake."

[45] P. 27. "It is an empirical psychological fact that many people find it easier to resolve upon and carry through a course of action which is contrary to their natural inclinations if this policy is associated in their minds with certain stories. And in many people the psychological link is not appreciably weakened by the fact that the story associated with this behaviour is not believed."

For the reductionist, then, the problem of religious language is solved by showing that there is no such thing as religious language, at least as a distinctive and autonomous realm of discourse. This is hardly a solution to the problem; it is rather a denial that there is a genuine problem. It would be more honest as well as being an aid to clarity if the reductionist admitted this quite openly instead of pretending to tell us what the "real meaning" of religious language is. What, after all, is the difference between an atheist humanist who denies that there is a God while taking up certain humanitarian policies and attitudes and a religious reductionist who says that he believes that there is a God but that the "real meaning" of this belief is to be interpreted without remainder in terms of practical commitment to precisely the same humanitarian policies and attitudes? There is, of course, the same ambivalence in a good deal of contemporary "secular" theology, which interprets the meaning of the Gospel in "secular" humanitarian terms and yet at the same time resists being called a form of atheistic humanism. Paul van Buren, for example, appears to be saying that the meaning of Christianity can be wholly expressed in terms of practical commitment of a more or less secular kind. Thus van Buren translates "Christ rose from the dead" as "The Apostles, after Christ died, had an Easter experience."[46] If we were to take this kind of translation at its face value we would have to say that God and the religious order did not exist independently of men and their practical attitudes.[47] But the secular theologians still apparently think that there is some distinctive point in religious belief and religious language. If this is so, then they must be presuming that there is after all an order of religious realities

---

[46] P. Van Buren, *The Secular Meaning of the Gospel* (London: S.C.M. Press; New York, Macmillan, 1965), p. 116.

[47] Cf. P. Tillich, *The Shaking of the Foundations* (London: Peguin; New York: Scribner, 1960), p. 63: "The Name of this infinite and inexhaustible depth and ground of all being is *God*. That depth is what the word *God* means. And if that word has not much meaning for you, translate it and speak of the depths of your life, of the source of your being, of your ultimate concern, of what you take seriously without any reservation." Tillich is, however, apparently speaking here in a phenomenological way since he insists elsewhere that statements about God are not reducible to statements about men and their attitudes.

existing independently of our attitudes. God, so to speak, would still be there even if there were no men engaged in practical action in the world, indeed, even if there were no world at all. (This, surely, is the view of God that emerges from the Old Testament.) Just as, in a sense, the religious reductionist wants to have his cake and eat it, so also do many contemporary theologians of the kind just described.[48]

The Justification of Religious Language

Let us however leave these matters and return to the fundamental objection made, as we saw before, by the descriptivist against all forms of nondescriptivism. If we are forbidden to say that religious locutions are true or false, and if it is held instead that they express attitudes, how exactly are we to justify the adoption of any set of attitudes? Why adopt the Christian "agapeistic" attitude to life, as Braithwaite calls it, instead of, say, that of Nietzsche? However, the issue of the justification of religious language is a more complex matter than it appears at first sight, and on this issue it will be worth-while to look in some detail at Wittgenstein's approach.

The notion of justification or verification, Wittgenstein suggests, varies according to the particular "language game" in question; we must not expect all justification to be of the same kind. The justification of moral or aesthetic judgments, for example, will be quite different from the kind of justification appropriate to mathematics or science. Again, while we can justify particular judgments within morals, or aesthetics, or science, or mathematics, it is a different

---

[48] See for example, Bishop J. Robinson, "Has 'God' a Meaning?" *Question*, I pp. 56-61. Cf. p. 60: "Someone has said that the question of God is the question of whether man is alone in the universe or not. This is misleading, I think, if it implies that everything turns on whether there is some other invisible Person, like man, somewhere around. But it is right if by that is meant that the question of God is the question whether persons and personal relationships are simply on their own, up against it, in a fundamentally alien universe. For to believe in God is to affirm that at the heart of things, as the most real thing in the world, is a love and a purpose to which persons and personal relationships are, so far, the highest *response*. This is the way the grain of the universe runs."

matter to justify morals or aesthetics, or even mathematics and science, as a whole.

What, for example, can we say to someone who questions the value of the objective, empirical knowledge that science provides, or to one who questions the process of scientific induction? What can we say to one who claims to see no point in morality, or no value in art? We can justify our use of language within a language-game, but the justification of the language-game itself is a different matter altogether. Wittgenstein seems to suggest that all we can do is to remark that such and such language-games happen to be played— such and such "forms of life" just are, as a matter of fact, lived by men. The justification of language-games, in other words, consists in the fact that they are played.[49]

It is easy to see how these ideas may be applied to the religious "language-game." We can justify locutions within the religious language-game, but the justification for playing the religious game at all is simply that "this game is played."[50] If this seems an arbitrary and unsatisfactory answer, we have only to recall that it is the same kind of answer that we must give in justification of science, morals, aesthetics, and so on.

Perhaps we can go further than this for, as Hudson suggests in the extract included here, a man who sees no point in morality or no meaning in moral language is no longer a man in the full sense.[51] We

[49] *Philosophical Investigations*, 654. Cf. J. Hick, *Faith and the Philosophers*, pp. 238–239.

[50] See N. Malcolm, "Anselm's Ontological Arguments," pp. 55–56. Referring to Psalm 90, Malcolm says: "Here is expressed the idea of the necessary existence and eternity of God, an idea that is essential to the Jewish and Christian religions. In those complex systems of thought, those 'language-games', God has the status of a necessary being. Who can doubt that? Here we must say with Wittgenstein, 'This language-game is played'! I believe we may rightly take the existence of those religious systems of thought in which God figures as a necessary being to be a disproof of the dogma, affirmed by Hume and others, that no existential proposition can be necessary." Cf. S. Toulmin, "Ludwig Wittgenstein," *Encounter*, XXXII (January, 1969), p. 70: "In this second phase, Wittgenstein apparently implied that ethics and religion have 'forms of life' of their own, within which ethical and religious 'language-games' become—in their own ways—as verbalisable, as meaningful, and even as true or false as any others."

[51] W. D. Hudson, see below, p. 253.

would tend to say that such a man was in a pathological or sub-human state. Similarly, a man who saw no point in art or no meaning in aesthetic language would in some sense be an impover-ished man, though perhaps we would not say that he was sub-human. Hudson suggests that this is true of religion and the reli-gious language-game also: a man for whom religious language was really meaningless would be in an impoverished or diminished state.

However, while perhaps most people would agree that anyone who really did not see the point of moral or aesthetic language was humanly impoverished, this is not at all obvious in the case of reli-gious language. After all, the atheistic or antireligious "language-game" is also played; for those who play it religious language is nonsense, and the fact that some people see sense in such language is a sign of infantilism on their part.[52] One might, perhaps, take a different tack and argue that, just as the attempt not to play the moral language-game involves paradox, so the attempt not to play the religious language-game also involves paradox. William James suggests, for instance, that an essential presupposition that one must make if one is to play the religious language-game is that life is "serious." For one with an attitude of what James calls Voltairean "*je m'en fichisme*" (an "I-couldn't-care-less" attitude to life) religion will have no point at all.[53] On this basis, religion might be defined as taking up a serious view of life, which implies in turn that one sees some values as absolute or ultimate. From this point of view, one might argue that just as one who says, "I choose to be amoral," involves himself in paradox in that this is a moral choice, so also one who says, "I choose not to take anything seriously, or absolutely, or ultimately, but rather to live a completely unserious, flippant, dilettante, superficial life," equally involves himself in paradox. Just as the choice of an amoral life is a moral choice, so also the choice of an unserious life and the denial of any absolute values itself in-

[52] See K. Nielsen's attack on what he calls "Wittgensteinian Fideism," *Philo-sopy*, XLII (July, 1967), pp. 191–207. Cf. Hudson's reply: "On Two Points Against Wittgensteinian Fideism," *Philosophy*, XLIII (July, 1968), pp. 269–73.

[53] *The Varieties of Religious Experience*, pp. 53–54.

volves making a serious choice of this and giving it an absolute value. Just as for Descartes we cannot doubt that we are thinking or are conscious, without thereby presupposing that we are conscious, so also we cannot deliberately reject absolute values without thereby presupposing them.

There is, no doubt, something to this argument, but the definition of religion in terms of "seriousness" or the adoption of absolutes (or of Tillich's "ultimate concern") is too broad, general, and accommodating, for according to this definition even an atheist or agnostic would be "religious." The really areligious man would be, on this view, like the amoral man—a pathological or subhuman specimen. We do, of course, speak of certain forms of atheism (Marxism, for instance) as "religions," and this is something more than mere metaphor, for they share with religion a serious view of life and a world-view organized around certain absolute values that exact "ultimate concern." It may be argued that this is the essence of religion and that the content of the world-view or what specific values are deemed to be absolute does not matter; though the Christian will identify differently from the Marxist the content of his world-view and the values that he takes as absolute, this is of secondary consequence. If Buddhism, which denies the existence of a God or of any other supramundane religious objects, is accounted as a religion, why should not Marxism or any other serious and absolutizing world-view be deemed to be a religion? Why should religion be defined as the option for a world-view *organised around certain supramundane objects and values* and not just the option of a world-view *tout court*? Religion may traditionally have been defined in this way, but this does not mean that it is necessarily the right, correct, or solely permissible definition.

The only answer that can be given to this objection is that, if there is a God and a realm of supramundane objects and values actually existing over and above the world of our experience, then we will need some term to mark the difference between world-views organized around such objects and values and world-views (such as Marxism) organised around "secular" values. Traditionally, the term "religion" has been used to mark this supposed difference. However, if we deny the existence of a supramundane world of objects and values, or if we translate talk about this world wholly into "practical" talk, then the term "religion" will be applicable to any world-view at all.

This discussion about the justification of religious language shows how complex and difficult a matter it is. When we reflect how hard it is to justify the moral language-game or the aesthetic language-game, the descriptivist's objections a propos the justification of religious language lose a good deal of their sting. At the same time, there are special difficulties about religious language, so that the analogies drawn between it and moral and aesthetic language, while illuminating in many respects, do not finally settle the problem of religious language. Many of the nondescriptivists seem to think that it is possible to dispose of the problem of religious language by pointing out that moral language shares the same problematic. But regardless of how we account for the evident meaningfulness of moral language, there are, as we have seen, difficulties quite peculiar to religious language. In a sense, it is not really possible to deny that moral language is meaningful; here, the only difficulty is that of giving a correct analysis of the kind of meaning had by moral locutions. But, at least *prima facie*, it is quite possible to deny that religious language is meaningful; here, we are faced not just with the problem of giving an analysis of what in some sense we already know to be meaningful, but with the more fundamental problem of showing that it is meaningful at all.

V.
THE IMPASSE OVER RELIGIOUS LANGUAGE

We have now seen the respective advantages and disadvantages of both the descriptivist and the nondescriptivist approach to the problem of religious language. As far as the Judaeo-Christian religious scheme is concerned, both approaches can claim scriptural warrant; one cannot really say that either one or the other is more in line with the religious view that emerges from the Old and New

Testaments. Thus, on the one hand, the Old Testament, by insisting that God is independent of His creation and of our attitudes to Him[54], supports the descriptivist view. On the other hand, the Biblical view of God is such that, as Malcolm says, we could not believe that He exists and "not be touched at all by awe or dismay or fear."[55]

The strength of the descriptivist view, as we have seen, is that it provides a clear-cut answer to the problem about the meaning of religious locutions: they are meaningful in that they describe supramundane objects. But the difficulties of this position lie in showing how religious locutions can be said to describe these objects and in accounting for the "practical" character of religious locutions. Its danger, as Le Roy shows very acutely, is that it will end as a form of intellectualism where religious belief is seen wholly in terms of pure speculative assent to propositions. This, in turn, would lead to a kind of religious esotericism where only those few who are capable of this speculative assent will be capable of religious belief or faith in the full sense.[56]

These weaknesses of the descriptivist position are precisely the strengths of the nondescriptivist position, for the latter evades the difficulty of verifying the truth of religious locutions by denying that they are verifiably true at all. By adequately accounting for the "practical" character of religious language, it also escapes the danger of esotericism. But its difficulty lies in avoiding reductionism (religious language being reduced to a species of moral, poetic, or quasi-metaphysical language) and in preserving the distinctive and autonomous character of religious language. Further, the nondescriptivist faces the formidable difficulty of justifying religious locutions (if they are to be taken as the expressions of practical attitudes of various kinds) and indeed of justifying the religious language-game as a whole.

We have here a typical philosophical problem, inasmuch as the

[54] Cf. *Genesis* I:1; 2 *Machabees* 7:28; *Isaiah* 41:4; *Psalm* 39.

[55] N. Malcolm, "Is It a Religious Belief That God Exists," *Faith and the Philosophers*, p. 107.

[56] See below, pp. 169–195.

alternative solutions each have advantages and disadvantages and maintain themselves by focusing attention on the weaknesses of the other's position and on the strengths of their own position. (The body–mind problem, where the materialist on the one hand and the dualist on the other keep each other in business, is very similar in this respect to the problem of religious language.) In such an impasse, it is a sign of wisdom to examine whether or not the problem itself has been posed correctly. To my mind, this is something that urgently needs to be done a propos the problem of religious language. In fact, very little thinking has been done in this area, and here I can only indicate very sketchily the kind of assumptions that need to be reexamined.

Reexamining the Problem of Religious Language:

Basic to the whole problem we have been discussing is the assumption that it is possible to make a clear-cut distinction between assents and attitudes, between the speculative and the practical orders, between the true and the appropriate or felicitous, between fact and value, between propositions and performative utterances, and between descriptive and the nondescriptive discourse.

Recent discussion, however, has shown that this distinction is not nearly as clear-cut as it looks at first sight, for there are many locutions that have both descriptive and practical dimensions at the same time.[57] Hare argues, in the essay included in this anthology,

---

[57] Cf. J. L. Austin, *How to Do Things with Words* (Cambridge: Harvard Univ. Press, 1962), p. 141: "Can we be sure that stating truly is a different class of assessment from arguing soundly, advising well, judging fairly, and blaming justifiably? Do these not have something to do in complicated ways with facts?" On the application of Austin's ideas to religious language, see "J. L. Austin and the Religious Use of Language," by Jerry H. Gill, *Sophia*, (July, 1969), pp. 29–37. See also in this connection M. Merleau-Ponty, *The Phenomenology of Perception*, English trans. (London: Routledge and Kegan Paul, 1962), pp. 174–99. For Merleau-Ponty language is a species of bodily expression, and it is to be classified along with emotional and artistic expression.

that the distinction we make between facts and our attitudes to the facts itself depends upon a kind of primordial metaphysical attitude.[58] One might equally say that this is a primordial metaphysical "fact" about the world—this is how the world describably is. It is interesting in this respect to note that Plato's account of the Form of the Good, to which Hare refers, is the source of both reality and value; in other words, Plato's Form of the Good is both "factual" or describable and, at the same time, that which evokes a practical response in us. Similarly, when we describe God and the religious order in general we are describing not merely an order of objects in addition to the mundane objects within the world of our experience, but objects without which there would be no mundane objects at all. These are the objects that represent, in Kant's terms, the "conditions of possibility" of the objects of our experience. What we are describing in fact are the conditions that make ordinary description possible and the primordial "option" we must make if we are to speak or use language at all. It seems then that the kind of description that is typical of religious language is a very odd, but nevertheless very real, kind of description, and one that also possesses a "practical" dimension.[59]

Perhaps it is this same point that Malcolm is getting at in the passage mentioned before:[60]

> If one conceived of God as the almighty creator of the world and judge of mankind how could one believe that He exists, but not be touched at all by awe or dismay or fear? I am discussing logic, not psychology. Would a belief that He exists, if it were completely non-affective, really be a belief that He exists?...

[58] See below, p. 236.

[59] The description of paradigms is also the setting up of an evaluative standard. For example, to describe the standard metre is to set up an evaluative criterion— that in reference to which a length is judged to be a "metre."

[60] N. Malcolm, *op. cit.* This affects the Kantian argument against the possibility of a theistic ethics. See on this, Basil Mitchell, "Ethics and the Will of God," *Sophia*, I (July, 1962), pp. 1–7.

So many philosophers who discuss these matters assume that the first and great question is to decide whether God exists: there will be time enough later to determine how one should regard Him. I think, on the contrary, that a belief that God exists, if it was logically independent of any and all ways of regarding Him, would be of no interest, not even to God.

Seeing religious language in this light does not of course solve the problem about it, but at least it helps us to see more clearly the peculiar meaning possessed by religious locutions and to remove misunderstandings and confusions about their appropriate mode of verification and justification. If it is the beginning of wisdom to have the right expectations with regard to any subject, then to have the appropriate expectations about religious language is to have at least the beginning of the solution to the problem of religious language.

VI.
CONCLUSIONS

This discussion of religious language points to a number of issues that need further analysis and clarification if we are to overcome the descriptivist–nondescriptivist impasse and reach a solution that will do justice to the valid insights on both sides.

First, we badly need a genuine and detailed phenomenological description of religious "phenomena." It is, of course, supremely difficult to let religious phenomena speak for themselves, as Husserl would say, without soliciting them or interpreting them in the light of preconceived ideas and misleading models. But it is of first importance to recognize and respect the variety, complexity, and idiosyncratic character of all those phenomena that we classify under the term "religion," before we can begin to theorize about religion in any really profitable way. What we need in fact is a complement to *The Varieties of Religious Experience*. James's brilliant work is already over sixty years old and it has had no real successor, despite the fact that there has since been a vast amount of data provided by research in comparative religion, psychology of religion, and sociology of religion.

Second, if religious language is to preserve its own distinctive and autonomous character, it must in some way be descriptive, and if it is descriptive then it must be analogical. Thus, there is an urgent need for further philosophical investigation into the logic of analogical predication. Certainly, the elements of a theory of analogical predication are present—though in a confused state—in Aquinas, but the theory must be divorced from its neo-Platonic trappings and worked out with much more logical rigor and in much more detail.

Third, further work needs to be done on the mode of verification or justification that is proper to religious language. When we are dealing with religious phenomena we are, as it were, on the outer edges of our experience; religious language, like metaphysical language, is close to what the Wittgenstein of the *Tractatus* called "the limits of language." It goes without saying then that the verification proper to religious language will be very different from the mode of verification proper to scientific language. Here, no doubt, comparison with the kinds of verification proper to moral and aesthetic language will be useful and enlightening. At the same time, we must be able to specify in some way what the difference is between believing in some religious object and not believing in it. That may seem to be a very simple requirement, but in fact it is one that is flouted by a good deal of contemporary theological talk. What, for example, would constitute nonbelief or atheism for Tillich and Robinson?

Fourth, while religious language must be descriptive (and so analogical, and so verifiable) in some sense, any adequate account must also give due weight to its "practical" aspect. It is here, as we have seen, that we need to look once again at the assumptions that underlie the descriptive–nondescriptive dichotomy. The relationships between thought and action are very difficult to spell out clearly and precisely, and the distinction between "pure" or "speculative" reason (which simply pictures or mirrors the facts or what-is-the-case, without making any value-judgments about them), and "practical" reason (which guides and directs action by judging certain ends or goals as valuable), is not as simple or clearcut as it looks. If we could become clearer about this whole general problem of thought and action then we would be able, perhaps, to see how the descriptive and the "practical" aspects of religious language could be reconciled.

Part II

READINGS

Section A
RELIGIOUS LANGUAGE AS DESCRIPTIVE

1

Religious language must be descriptive

G. D. Marshall

In the following essay, G.D. Marshall attempts to show by a purely formal analysis of the notions of *assent, attitude, belief,* and *faith,* that religious beliefs cannot be understood as declarations of attitudes. They must rather be seen as acts of assent (beliefs *that*) to propositions of a special kind, although attitudes (beliefs *in*) will typically follow on these assents.

Marshall does not concern himself with the content of religious beliefs, nor even with the question whether religious beliefs are, in fact, genuine species of rational belief. Rather, he simply delineates what one might call the logical properties of acts of assent and attitude respectively and concludes that if religious belief or faith is to have certain logical properties that have traditionally been accorded to it—properties, indeed, that it *must* have if it is to retain its distinctive nature—then it must primarily be a matter of assent and not a matter of practical attitude. Thus, Marshall argues, if religious beliefs were expressive of attitudes: (i) they would be neither true nor false, but rather mere evincings of feelings; (ii) they would not be intentional acts subject to rational control and appraisal and able to be changed by reflection and argument; (iii) they would not be able to be justified or defended, nor would the believer be responsible—and so praiseworthy or blameworthy—for espousing them.

Marshall supposes, on the contrary, that religious beliefs must in some sense be true or false, subject to rational control and change, capable of being justified, and such that we are responsible for holding them. Religious beliefs must therefore be acts of assent to propositions describing special objects or states of affairs. Or, put in another way, religious locutions must be primarily descriptive in function.

Dr. G.D. Marshall is a philosopher at the University of Melbourne, Australia, and this essay, "Faith and Assent," first appeared in *Sophia—A Journal for Discussion in Philosophical Theology.*

There appear to be at least two views of what faith is: what I shall call the *attitudinal* view and the *propositional* view. No doubt few hold either view these days to the complete exclusion of the other, but many at least incline strongly to the one or the other, even if they prefer the *via media*. This solution is very tempting, of course, but it is not clear to me that it is right or even possible. Whether or not it is, is the main question I shall try to answer here.

The attitudinal view may be characterised, I hope without being too unsubtle, as the view that faith is a spiritual condition which is *displayed* in the beliefs one holds and the actions one is disposed to perform; a spiritual condition which is a function of the whole person and not merely of his thought, and which is more like confidence than conviction. What one says and does *expresses* one's faith and rests upon it in a causal rather than logical way. According to the propositional view, however, the opposite is true. One's faith *is* the belief that certain propositions are true, and not that which makes one take them as true. The creeds *state* rather than *display* one's faith. One is logically committed to action by one's faith and not causally constrained to act in a way that shows it. One's faith is not an attitude or set of attitudes, but a belief or set of beliefs.

The propositional view is the traditional Catholic view[1]; the attitudinal view has been more favoured by Protestants, though not by them all. John Flavel of Dartmouth, "one of the best of the English Puritans" according to John Baillie, writes: "There be three acts of faith: assent, acceptance, and assurance. The Papists generally give the essence of saving faith to the first, viz. assent. The Lutherans,

G. D. Marshall, "Faith and Assent," reprinted from *Sophia—A Journal for Discussion in Philosophical Theology*, Vol. 5 (April, 1966), pp. 24–34, with the permission of the Author and the Editors.

[1] See Aquinas, *Summa Theologiae*, II, II, 2, 2.

and some of our own, give it to the last, viz. assurance. But it can be neither way so . . . Assent is too low to contain the essence of saving faith; it is found in the unregenerate as well as the regenerate. . . . Assurance is as much too high, being found only in some eminent believers and in them too but at some times . . . Assent widens the nature of faith too much and assurance straitens it too much. But acceptance which saith, I take Christ in all his offices to be mine, this fits it exactly and belongs to all true believers and to none but true believers and to all true believers at all times."[2] And W. Temple writes: "I do not believe in any creed but I use certain creeds to express, to conserve and to deepen by belief in God." And according to Brunner, "Faith is not primarily faith in a truth—not even the truth *that* Jesus is the Son of God; but is primarily trust and obedience towards this Lord and Redeemer Himself." All agree, however, with Flavel that "assent, though it be not in itself saving faith yet is it the foundation and groundwork of it." And no doubt they would also agree with the view that C. H. Dodd attributes to St. Paul: "For Paul faith is that attitude in which, acknowledging our complete insufficiency for any of the high ends of life, we rely utterly on the sufficiency of God. . . . Nor does it mean belief in a proposition, though doubtless intellectual beliefs are involved when we come to think it out."

Whether these two views are mutually exclusive, or whether they may and do involve each other, depends on what an attitude and a belief precisely is. And whether to believe a proposition to be true is altogether too minimal to do justice to the richness of faith, or whether assent is too small a thing to contain and support the degree of confidence and conviction associated with faith, depends on what the assent to a proposition commits one to. Consequently, the question is: what, if anything, does belief add to assent, and what, if anything, does faith add to belief?

One assents to a proposition. By 'proposition' I understand that, *whatever it is*, which is the bearer of truth or falsity. In G. E. Moore's view, a proposition "is not a name for any mere form of words. It is a name for what is *expressed* by certain forms of words—

[2] This and the following citations are given by John Baillie in chapter 5 of *The Idea of Revelation in Recent Thought*, (Oxford, Clarendon Press, 1956).

those, namely, which, in grammar, are called 'sentences'. It is a name for what is before your mind when you not only hear or read but *understand* a sentence. It is, in short, the meaning of a sentence."[3] Now meanings of sentences are neither true nor false, so Moore's view of a proposition cannot be quite right. But there is something important in the contention that a proposition is that, whatever it is, which is capable of truth or falsity and which is before your mind when you understand a sentence. This I want to focus upon, for there is a crucial point here: that which is capable of truth or falsity and is *in fact* before your mind when you think you understand a sentence, may be different in certain respects from that which is capable of truth or falsity and *should* be before your mind when you do understand a sentence. We need, however, propositions as characterised in both of these ways. The latter kind, which I shall capitalise and call a 'Proposition', belongs mainly to pure logic; the former kind, which I shall continue to call a 'proposition', belongs mainly to discussion about ordinary life and discourse, and is more closely associated with making judgments, forming opinions, and beliefs. It may be a question whether sentences used to make value judgments, to declare one's intentions, or to state the attributes of God, express Propositions; but they certainly express propositions. 'P' in 'Probably P' is usually the same Proposition as 'P', but they are, I believe, different propositions. We shall return to this matter later. At this stage, I merely wish to make it clear that our concern is properly with propositions and not Propositions. After all, in ordinary life one knows only what one does know about the meaning of sentences, and not what one should know.

It is obvious from what Moore has said that to assent to a proposition entails that one knows what one is assenting to. It is at least to understand what the sentence means, and what the speaker or writer means to do with it. But, of course, it is also more than this. In giving one's assent to a proposition one is declaring one's agreement with it. To put it very crudely, being in agreement with a proposition is the state out of which one acts intentionally in giving one's assent to it, and one's being in this state can always be given as a

[3] "Belief and Propositions" in *Some Main Problems of Philosophy*, (London, Allen and Unwin, 1953), p. 259.

minimal reason for assenting. Consequently, assent is not purely formal. To lie, or to confess or recant falsely, is to deceive. When form
alone is important, appearances alone are concerned. This shows
the presumption that assent entails the reality of agreement. From
this it follows that one commits oneself to action by assenting to a
proposition. At least one commits oneself to a defence of the proposition and to the denial of any incompatible with it. Assenting, being
necessarily intentional, belongs to the rational mode of proceeding
and therefore admits further relevant rational performances. This is
the case even when one can say no more than *that* one agrees. Such
intuitive claims, while having no logical ground that one is aware of,
are and must be defended by disposing of objections to them. If
the proposition in question is a practical one, that one should cut
down one's expenses, for example, one's assent to it is implicitly a
declaration of a more or less standing intention.

It may be objected that there is a difference between logically
being committed to action and committing oneself to action; or
between what logically commits one to action and what one accepts
as committing oneself to action. But while that is true, we are here
dealing with propositions to which one assents, not with those that
are not asserted and not assented to. So it is as true here as it is
anywhere that if one does not take as committing what one realises
to be logically committing, one is, in the absence of excuses, unreasonable.

If it is true, then, that one commits oneself to action by assenting
to a proposition, it follows that one must be firm and settled enough
in one's mind for there to be a difference between giving assent and
merely entertaining the possibility of doing so. And this entails that
one is sure enough that one is prepared to assent, which itself entails
that one is sure enough about the truth of the proposition for there
to be a difference between giving and withholding assent. But being
sure enough for these is all that *conviction* strictly is. So in assenting to
a proposition, one cannot but be convinced of its truth. This point is
often obscured by our failure to observe the distinction between
being convinced and being persuaded (which is much more a causal
than a logical result), and by our tendency to make conviction shade
first into a feeling of familiarity with a proposition, then into confidence, and then into dogmatism. But the differences between these,

which I hope will become clearer as we proceed, are not differences of degree, but of kind. If this is right, then the agreement one has in assenting, is agreement with the truth of the proposition. It may appear that one sometimes agrees with the assertion of a proposition for reasons quite other than those concerning its truth, but strictly one's assent and agreement concerns the further proposition that it is wise, prudent, necessary or permissible to assert the first proposition. And it is with the truth of that further proposition that one agrees.

It may be objected that if assent entails conviction, such statements as 'I assent to this proposition but I am not convinced that it is true' or 'I assent to it but I am by no means sure of its truth', would be self-contradictory, which they do not appear to be. But if these sentences are not used merely to end an argument or brush aside a position, and if the propositions are *not* self-contradictory, then, if one *can* assent without being at all settled in one's mind, conviction can only be the causal result of assent. But when, therefore, does one properly assent? It would appear that one does so only when one is settled enough in one's mind to preclude the logically possible state of affairs of assent not giving rise to conviction. For otherwise, in giving one's assent, one could only *hope* that the appropriate state of mind would follow, in which case 'I assent' could not contain the implicit declaration of intention that it does contain: the intention to be consistent. And if it does not contain that, it cannot function as it now does in rational discourse. So even if conviction is different from being settled in one's mind as to the truth of a proposition, which it seems quite unnecessary to maintain, assent must still at least guarantee conviction.

If it is true, then, that assent to a proposition entails that one knows its meaning and point, entails that one agrees with it, entails that one commits oneself thereby to action, both verbal and non-verbal, and entails that one is convinced of its truth, what is left then for belief to add to assent?

It may be said, first, that the question does not arise since there is not the essential connection between belief and propositions that there is between assent and propositions. But this is absurd. The object of a belief is most properly a proposition, or, in the material mode, a state of affairs. Belief is conceptual. If it were not, then it would not matter, as of course it does, that a belief could not be declared by words or discriminatory behaviour in non-learning situations, which would remove a large part of the philosophy of perception, to take but one consequence. The intentional enactment of practical beliefs would not be standard, which it is, and it would no longer be always logically appropriate to ask for and give justification of one's own beliefs (which is not to imply that justification is always necessary or useful). It would be possible to believe one knows not what, and impossible to hold that knowledge entails belief. This last would be impossible since if knowledge was not prior to belief, in the sense that one knows that and what one believes, one would be in no position to say that in non-intuitively knowing that P, one must believe that P. In short, if belief were not conceptual, we would deprive ourselves of most of our ways of reflectively dealing with rational discourse and behaviour. It is axiomatic, therefore, in this part of our conceptual scheme, that we must be able to know that and what we believe. As far as ordinary human beings are concerned, this comes to saying that a belief must be avowable or statable. That is, what is believed is a proposition, or a state of affairs that is both indentified and described by a proposition. (This is quite consistent with the possibility of unconscious beliefs, for what is unconscious is possibly avowable; that is, avowable under certain specifiable circumstances.) The object of belief is a proposition, and to believe it, is to accept it as true. The same is true of assent.

Secondly, it may be thought that belief adds a *degree* of conviction to assent. It may be true that in assenting to a proposition one is convinced to some degree of its truth, but when one comes to believe it, one's conviction is stronger. And conviction does seem to admit of degree. We are more convinced about some things than others; we are prepared to take different odds on the truth of different propositions; and we speak about being half-convinced, fully convinced, or not very convinced of the truth of the matter. But, first, this seems to be a misinterpretation of the point that some beliefs are more important to us than others. We are just as convinced about something we do not hold very important, when considered by itself, as we are about something we do hold to be important. But since the beliefs of a rational man cannot be kept isolated from each other, and since they naturally conflict on various occasions, and since they cannot be thought to be of equal importance without reducing an agent to impotence, they are, equally naturally, evaluatively graded. It is understandable, perhaps, that those deemed to be most important should be declared to be those about which one is most convinced; but this is elliptical. There are two propositions here: the first, that one is convinced of the truth of P, Q, and R, and the second, that one is convinced of the truth of the proposition that P is more important, useful, basic, or significant than Q, and Q than R. What is true is that one is not committed to action to the same extent by all one's beliefs (or by assenting to all of a range of propositions). But it is false to say that the degree of commitment is exactly the degree of conviction. It is not, for commitment is a function both of conviction and importance. The question is still open as to whether conviction admits of degree. Secondly, we cannot immediately determine this last point completely by simply translating 'varying degrees of conviction' into 'conviction of the truth of varying degrees of the sum of what is to be believed'. For while that can be done quite often, we are still left with the puzzling case of half-belief where the translation is implausible. But half-belief is either a matter of genuine conviction for half the time in all relevant circumstances, or a matter of genuine conviction in only some of all the relevant circumstances. The beliefs of a mildly superstitious man, and the beliefs of a man who genuinely believes what he says and sings and does on Sunday in worship but not for the rest of the week,[4] are half-beliefs. But such cases are puzzling, not because they show that there can be degrees of conviction but because they seem to show that the genuine beliefs of a rational man can be unworryingly inconsistent. This is of considerable interest, but not in the present argument.

A possible rejoinder to these replies is that belief is, to use one of Newman's formulae,[5] assent to assent. So belief must be distinguished from simple assent. Now it is often true that we assent to an earlier assent. One's first assent may be qualified, or guarded, or

---

[4] Professor Price's examples. See H. H. Price and R. B. Braithwaite, "Half Belief", *Proceedings of the Aristotelian Society*, Supplementary Volume 38 (1964) pp. 149–174.

[5] *A Grammar of Assent*, (London, Burns Oates, 1870), p. 188.

hesitant, or it may be made with reservations. It may be thought that it requires a second assent to remove the qualifications and declare a belief. But it is not at all clear that we thus acquire a belief for the first time. It is surely less confusing to say that where one first believed that probably P was true, one now believes that P is true. Belief has not been added to the assent to P; rather, the object of the assent has changed. In the other alternative, we are left with the notion of a guarded assent, which is as curious as that of a guarded assertion. Unless the manner of assent is being referred to, in which case it is irrelevant to either assent or belief, a guarded assent to or assertion of 'P' can only be expressed as the assent to or assertion of 'Probably P' (or 'Perhaps P' or 'P is plausible'). It will not do to say that one is assenting with reservations to P, for reasonable doubt about the truth of P is incompatible with assent to its truth. Therefore, if one both gives one's assent and expresses one's doubts, there must be two propositions in question. To assert 'Probably P' is to express some doubt about the truth of P, but not enough to make one withhold one's assent entirely from P. One therefore assents to 'Probably P', for that is what one accepts. One certainly understands and means something different by the two propositions. On this depends, indeed, the truth of the Rule of Candour: that one must not assert 'Probably P' if one can assert 'P'[6]. And this is an essential principle of discourse. It may be true that 'P' in 'Probably P' and 'P' *are* the same *Proposition*, but we must not be concerned with that. If one's assent is to the Proposition P, there would indeed be degrees of assent or belief. But since we assent only to what we *do* understand, we do not ordinarily assent to Propositions. So we may deny both that there are degrees of assent and that belief adds anything to assent.

However, it may be thought that this takes no account of the fact that we are able, and sometimes need, to confirm our assent. But if it is true to say that one only assents to a proposition in so far as one understands it, and if what one understands by it is *different* at different times, then, of course, the proposition one first assents to is different from that one later assents to. But they are the same

---

[6] "The Rule of Candour" is Professor D. A. T. Gasking's term. Cf. H. P. Grice, "The Causal Theory of Perception", *Proceedings of the Aristotelian Society*, Supp. Vol. 35 (1961), pp. 121–152.

Proposition. A sentence cannot mean something different at different times unless it is possible to say it means the same. Both points are important. Unless the second is true, one could not say at a later time that if one had realised earlier what P involves, one would not then have assented to it. But that one now retracts one's earlier assent entails that what one then thought one assented to, is different from what one now realises one cannot assent to. This is not the case of merely changing one's mind about P, but of a change in what one takes P to be. If this happens in the case of retraction, it could happen in that of confirmation. When on mature consideration one confirms one's assent to P, one may not be assenting to one's earlier assent to P; one may be assenting to a further proposition Q which is that one's earlier assent to P is correct. If this is not the account to give, the confirmation is a matter either of still being prepared to assent to the original proposition, or of being prepared now to assent to 'Very probably P' when one earlier was prepared to assent to 'Probably P'. This last possibility has already been dealt with. In this case and in the other cases as well, belief adds nothing to assent, since simple assent alone is in question. And in order to have security or weight, simple assent does not logically require further assent, as Newman's formula seems to suggest it does.

Thirdly, it may be thought that while belief adds nothing to assent in simple cases, other cases reveal some difference. These are those in which one's assent is, in Newman's phrase, notional: that is, assent to a notional or abstract proposition. The propositions of faith are exactly of this kind. The implications and significance of these propositions are more difficult to grasp, and action in accordance with them, if possible or appropriate, requires additional judgements about their application to specific situations that occur in one's experience. This might be taken to suggest that one only believes a proposition to which one has assented, when one is familiar with its application and range. But this does not appear to be right. While the application and range of such propositions is restricted, it is also practically inexhaustible. So one cannot become familiar with *it*. One may become more adept at making the relevant judgements, but it is too arbitrary to say that this is what it is to believe. And if this account were true, notional assent would be ignorant folly and more worthless than it is. The implication is that it is easy to give notional assent. But the ease of assent is inversely proportional to the realised implicative power of a proposition. Consequently, for most of us notional assent is difficult. And action in accordance with the proposition we thus assent to, is a series of experiments with its limits and limitations which show us what, more precisely, we can assent to: what practical situations demand a declaration of our beliefs. Therefore, assent to notional propositions does not show a difference between assent and belief; what it does show is that assent can be difficult, complex and open to revision.

Something, however, is added to assent. One becomes confident in one's beliefs and one's feelings mostly fall into sympathy with them. Patterns of reaction and behaviour become established, and a certain style of life may become more evident. That is, assent gives rise to characteristic attitudes. It is these which lag sluggishly behind a conversion or change of mind and belief. But attitudes are different in kind from beliefs. A belief has an essential connection with propositions and their truth, but an attitude has not. An attitude is a causal product and not immediately manipulable by rational procedures. The latter point at least is not true of a belief. An attitude is a causal product because one can only discover, in a third person way, that one has this or that attitude. One may formulate, but not form, one's own attitudes, unless, of course, one forms or comes to a belief from which they causally follow. To formulate an attitude is to state what precisely one's feelings are about something. But this is not and ought not to be the same as stating one's position on the question. If it were, the belief would be as intellectually disreputable as an emotive theory of truth. One may allow or take the statement of one's attitude to be an intuitive claim, but that is to commit oneself to the possibility of giving it up, should sound argument be produced against it. Merely declaring one's attitudes contains no such commitment. An attitude may be the product of all sorts of psycho-physical conditions and material circumstances of the past, as well as of thought and consideration. So may a belief, but if it is a belief, it cannot remain that way, whereas an attitude does. Consequently, an attitude can be changed by brainwashing, drugs, and surgery, but a belief is changed by education, reflection and argument. An attitude is changed in this way only indirectly. So an attitude is not the proper subject for justification. One is neither praiseworthy nor blameable for possessing them. They may be apologised for, but not defended. Of course, what they are products of may be the proper subjects of justification. Depending on one's view of the truth or falsity of determinism, one may say that we are always responsible for our attitudes because, no matter what their aetiology is, they are under the control of our will. Or one may say that we are so only when they spring from our judgements and decisions. It is true that a rational man cannot, and no doubt should not, keep his non-rationally caused attitudes isolated from his beliefs. But it is not by virtue of his attitudes alone that he can be held responsible for them; it is rather by virtue of his being a rational and responsible man, in so far as this entails that he could change them, or allow them to persist, or control the circumstances which occasion their display.

Now, if belief adds nothing to assent, but if an attitude is usually added to either a belief or an assent, then what, if anything, does faith add to belief? It cannot add understanding and acceptance, for assent already encompasses these. It cannot add conviction for the same reason. So having faith adds either confidence, or importance to the object of belief. The latter is a matter of judgement; the former, an attitude. If to have faith is to hold that certain beliefs are of considerable importance, then faith is the assent to certain credal propositions, and the assent to the further proposition that those propositions are of greater moment than others to which one also assents. So faith is no more than assent. But if to have faith is merely, or even essentially, to have a certain attitude or cluster of attitudes towards oneself, others, the universe, God, or whatever its object may be deemed to be, then faith, in itself, loses all connection with truth. This must surely be objectionable. A purely attitudinal view of faith makes it a mere causal product of anything at all, and it thus requires neither justification nor support. One is responsible for it, and therefore praiseworthy in possessing it, only if it is consequent upon the intentional acquisition or fostering of a belief. And even that is not something we can intentionally guarantee. One's assent to a proposition rests upon agreement with its truth, which itself is consequent upon the realisation of its truth. Realisation is something that happens, not something we can intentionally or unintentionally achieve. We can however, desire it, and intentionally place ourselves and others in the best position for it to occur. Whether or not it does, is not in our hands, and neither faith nor hope can make it so.

It may, finally, be objected that the *point* of distinguishing faith from assent is to avoid the purely intellectualist position that religious belief is merely a metaphysical belief and therefore of no practical importance. I do not believe that this is true of metaphysical beliefs, but let us suppose that it is. And let us suppose further that the belief in question is that although God is as the creeds state him to be, this makes absolutely no difference to the way one lives. Then, in the first alternative, this is not a religious belief at all, for it patently is not a belief in God as meet to be worshipped, which, by definition, God at least is. In the second alternative, one who assents to the above propositions is misinterpreting them. He does not realise their necessary implications, which, if he were to, would commit him to action. This *sort* of belief does commit one to action. In the third alternative, his other beliefs prevent him from acting upon his religious belief, and prevent it having any practical bearing upon his life. Now, such a person is not *obviously* wrong. It requires an argument to show that he is. And the argument would turn on the issues raised in the second alternative. Therefore, the point of the distinction between assent and faith may be taken without identifying faith in a misleading way with a mere set of mostly practical attitudes.

It may be replied, however, that this answer does nothing to show that belief *in* . . . is secured by belief *that* . . ., which is the point of the objection. But this is not so. Either belief *in* . . . is a disposition to assent to a certain range of propositions, or it is merely another term for the set of attitudes which arise from the belief that certain propositions are true. In the first case, to believe in my friend, for example, is to be disposed to assent to propositions such as 'He is reliable', 'He will not let me down', 'He will be understanding and loyal'. The disposition to assent to such a range of propositions is *logically* consequent upon the belief *that* he is a friend, and the belief *that* he has certain personal qualities. In the second case, my confidence and trust in him is *causally* consequent upon the belief *that* he is honest, pleasant, and good, and the belief *that* we share an essential sympathy. If belief *in* . . . is interpreted in the first way, belief *that* . . . does guarantee it since it entails it. If the second interpretation is given, the guarantee is as strong as a well-established causal law. If the latter is not good enough in this case, it can never be better in so far as the purely attitudinal view is adopted in order to make it so.

The uniqueness of faith, therefore, lies not in its differences from belief and assent, but in the object of belief. Faith is governed by performances in the rational mode, and reason cannot be denied in order to make room for faith. This raises, of course, the question of whether religious faith is reasonable, or proper for a rational man. But that, fortunately, is quite another question.

2

Religious language describes religious experiences, I

Rudolf Otto

Rudolf Otto's famous book *The Idea of the Holy* is a classic statement of the attempt to ground religious language in religious experience, so that the meaning of religious language is made clear by reference to certain special experiences that the religious believer—indeed, every man at least potentially—has. In this sense religious statements refer to or describe what happens in these special experiences.

Although by reason we may form conceptions of God's characteristics—His immateriality, His personality, His benevolence, His omnipotence—these conceptions *about* God presuppose that we can apprehend God as He is in Himself, otherwise, so Otto rather oddly argues, we would not know *what* the conceptions were about, the *subject* of which the characteristics are predicated. What we mean by *God* as He is in Himself (apart, so to speak, from the characteristics attributed to Him) is given in a quite special kind of experience in which we become aware of what Otto calls the *Holy* or the *Numinous.* In this experience we "feel" or experience some mysterious, overpowering yet immensely attractive reality (*mysterium tremendum et fascinans*) existing objectively outside of ourselves and our subjective states. We do not *infer* from some kind of subjective feeling or experience to some external objective cause of that feeling-state; rather it is *through* the experience itself that we are brought into direct acquaintance with the religious object or numinous reality. This experience is not expressible in rational categories (though we may be able to give more or less helpful analogies of it) and so is nonrational or, better, suprarational. Again, this experience is *sui generis* and cannot be reduced to other "natural" experiences, so that, in this sense, it is indefinable. It follows from this that we cannot argue another person into having the experience by purely rational means; the best we can do is to try indirectly to evoke the experience in him, very much as we do with aesthetic experiences. Otto suggests that every man is at least capable of having these experiences of the numinous, or "intrinsically religious feelings"— indeed he suggests later that the numinous is an *a priori* category of the human consciousness—but of course not every one attends to them and cultivates them, just as everyone is capable of aesthetic experiences but not everyone actually attends to and cultivates them.

Rudolf Otto (1869–1937) was a celebrated German philosopher of religion. *The Idea of the Holy* was first published in 1917, and the following extract comprises the first three chapters of the book.

THE RATIONAL AND THE NON-RATIONAL

It is essential to every theistic conception of God, and most of all to the Christian, that it designates and precisely characterizes deity by the attributes spirit, reason, purpose, good will, supreme power, unity, selfhood. The nature of God is thus thought of by analogy with our human nature of reason and personality; only, whereas in ourselves we are aware of this as qualified by restriction and limitation, as applied to God the attributes we use are 'completed', i.e. thought as absolute and unqualified. Now all these attributes constitute clear and definite *concepts*: they can be grasped by the intellect; they can be analysed by thought; they even admit of definition. An object that can thus be thought conceptually may be termed *rational*. The nature of deity described in the attributes above mentioned is, then, a rational nature; and a religion which recognizes and maintains such a view of God is in so far a 'rational' religion. Only on such terms is *belief* possible in contrast to mere *feeling*. And of Christianity at least it is false that 'feeling is all, the name but sound and smoke';[1]—where 'name' stands for conception or thought. Rather we count this the very mark and criterion of a religion's high rank and superior value: that it should have no lack of *conceptions* about God; that it should admit knowledge—the knowledge that comes by faith—of the transcendent in terms of conceptual thought, whether those already mentioned or others which continue and develop them. Christianity not only possesses such conceptions but possesses them in unique clarity and abundance,

Reprinted from *The Idea of the Holy*, by Rudolf Otto, translated by John W. Harvey, translation originally published by the Oxford University Press in 1923.

[1] Goethe, *Faust*.

and this is, though not the sole or even the chief, yet a very real sign of its superiority over religions of other forms and at other levels. This must be asserted at the outset and with the most positive emphasis.

But, when this is granted, we have to be on our guard against an error which would lead to a wrong and one-sided interpretation of religion. This is the view that the essence of deity can be given completely and exhaustively in such 'rational' attributions as have been referred to above and in others like them. It is not an unnatural misconception. We are prompted to it by the traditional language of edification, with its characteristic phraseology and ideas; by the learned treatment of religious themes in sermon and theological instruction; and further even by our Holy Scriptures themselves. In all these cases the 'rational' element occupies the foreground, and often nothing else seems to be present at all. But this is after all to be expected. All language, in so far as it consists of words, purports to convey ideas or concepts—that is what language means—and the more clearly and unequivocally it does so, the better the language. And hence expositions of religious truth in language inevitably tend to stress the 'rational' attributes of God.

But though the above mistake is thus a natural one enough, it is none the less seriously misleading. For so far are these 'rational' attributes from exhausting the idea of deity, that they in fact imply a non-rational or supra-rational Subject of which they are predicates. They are 'essential' (and not merely 'accidental') attributes of that subject, but they are also, it is important to notice, *synthetic* essential attributes. That is to say, we have to predicate them of a subject which they qualify, but which in its deeper essence is not, nor indeed can be, comprehended in them; which rather requires comprehension of a quite different kind. Yet, though it eludes the conceptual way of understanding, it must be in some way or other within our grasp, else absolutely nothing could be asserted of it. And even mysticism, in speaking of it as τὸ ἄρρητον, the ineffable, does not really mean to imply that absolutely nothing can be asserted of the object of the religious consciousness; otherwise, mysticism could exist only in unbroken silence, whereas what has generally been a characteristic of the mystics is their copious eloquence.

Here for the first time we come up against the contrast between rationalism and profounder religion, and with this contrast and its signs we shall be repeatedly concerned in what follows. We have here in fact the first and most distinctive mark of rationalism, with which all the rest are bound up. It is not that which is commonly asserted, that rationalism is the denial, and its opposite the affirmation, of the miraculous. That is manifestly a wrong or at least a very superficial distinction. For the traditional theory of the miraculous as the occasional breach in the causal nexus in nature by a Being who himself instituted and must therefore be master of it—this theory is itself as massively 'rational' as it is possible to be. Rationalists have often enough acquiesced in the possibility of the miraculous in this sense; they have even themselves contributed to frame a theory of it: whereas anti-rationalists have been often indifferent to the whole controversy about miracles. The difference between rationalism and its opposite is to be found elsewhere. It resolves itself rather into a peculiar difference of *quality* in the mental attitude and emotional content of the religious life itself. All depends upon this: in our idea of God is the non-rational overborne, even perhaps wholly excluded, by the rational? Or conversely, does the non-rational itself preponderate over the rational? Looking at the matter thus, we see that the common dictum, that orthodoxy itself has been the mother of rationalism, is in some measure well founded. It is not simply that orthodoxy was preoccupied with doctrine and the framing of dogma, for these have been no less a concern of the wildest mystics. It is rather that orthodoxy found in the construction of dogma and doctrine no way to do justice to the non-rational aspect of its subject. So far from keeping the non-rational element in religion alive in the heart of the religious experience, orthodox Christianity manifestly failed to recognize its value, and by this failure gave to the idea of God a one-sidedly intellectualistic and rationalistic interpretation.

This bias to rationalization still prevails, not only in theology but in the science of comparative religion in general, and from top to bottom of it. The modern students of mythology, and those who pursue research into the religion of 'primitive man' and attempt to reconstruct the 'bases' or 'sources' of religion, are all victims to it. Men do not, of course, in these cases employ those lofty 'rational'

concepts which we took as our point of departure; but they tend
to take these concepts and their gradual 'evolution' as setting the
main problem of their inquiry, and fashion ideas and notions of
lower value, which they regard as paving the way for them. It is
always in terms of concepts and ideas that the subject is pursued,
'natural' ones, moreover, such as have a place in the general sphere
of man's ideational life, and are not specifically 'religious'. And
then with a resolution and cunning which one can hardly help
admiring, men shut their eyes to that which is quite unique in the
religious experience, even in its most primitive manifestations. But
it is rather a matter for astonishment than for admiration! For if
there be any single domain of human experience that presents us
with something unmistakably specific and unique, peculiar to itself,
assuredly it is that of the religious life. In truth the enemy has often
a keener vision in this matter than either the champion of religion
or the neutral and professedly impartial theorist. For the adversaries
on their side know very well that the entire 'pother about mysticism'
has nothing to do with 'reason' and 'rationality'.

And so it is salutary that we should be incited to notice that
religion is not exclusively contained and exhaustively comprised in
any series of 'rational' assertions; and it is well worth while to
attempt to bring the relation of the different 'moments' of religion
to one another clearly before the mind, so that its nature may
become more manifest.

This attempt we are now to make with respect to the quite
distinctive category of the holy or sacred.

'NUMEN' AND THE 'NUMINOUS'

'Holiness'—'the holy'—is a category of interpretation and valuation
peculiar to the sphere of religion. It is, indeed, applied by trans-
ference to another sphere—that of ethics—but it is not itself derived
from this. While it is complex, it contains a quite specific element
or 'moment', which sets it apart from 'the rational' in the meaning
we gave to that word above, and which remains inexpressible—
an ἄρρητον or *ineffabile*—in the sense that it completely eludes

apprehension in terms of concepts. The same thing is true (to take a quite different region of experience) of the category of the beautiful.

Now these statements would be untrue from the outset if 'the holy' were merely what is meant by the word, not only in common parlance, but in philosophical, and generally even in theological usage. The fact is we have come to use the words 'holy', 'sacred' (*heilig*) in an entirely derivative sense, quite different from that which they originally bore. We generally take 'holy' as meaning 'completely good'; it is the absolute moral attribute, denoting the consummation of moral goodness. In this sense Kant calls the will which remains unwaveringly obedient to the moral law from the motive of duty a 'holy' will; here clearly we have simply the *perfectly moral* will. In the same way we may speak of the holiness or sanctity of duty or law, meaning merely that they are imperative upon conduct and universally obligatory.

But this common usage of the term is inaccurate. It is true that all this moral significance is contained in the word 'holy', but it includes in addition—as even we cannot but feel—a clear overplus of meaning, and this it is now our task to isolate. Nor is this merely a later or acquired meaning; rather 'holy', or at least the equivalent words in Latin and Greek, in Semitic and other ancient languages, denoted first and foremost *only* this overplus: if the ethical element was present at all, at any rate it was not original and never constituted the whole meaning of the word. Anyone who uses it to-day does undoubtedly always feel 'the morally good' to be implied in 'holy'; and accordingly in our inquiry into that element which is separate and peculiar to the idea of the holy it will be useful, at least for the temporary purpose of the investigation, to invent a special term to stand for 'the holy' *minus* its moral factor or 'moment', and, as we can now add, minus its 'rational' aspect altogether.

It will be our endeavour to suggest this unnamed Something to the reader as far as we may, so that he may himself feel it. There is no religion in which it does not live as the real innermost core, and without it no religion would be worthy of the name. It is preeminently a living force in the Semitic religions, and of these again in none has it such vigour as in that of the Bible. Here, too, it has a name of its own, viz. the Hebrew *qādôsh*, to which the Greek ἅγιος, and the Latin *sanctus*, and, more accurately still, *sacer*, are the corresponding terms. It is not, of course, disputed that these terms in all three languages connote, as part of their meaning, *good, absolute goodness*, when, that is, the notion has ripened and reached the highest stage in its development. And we then use the word 'holy' to translate them. But this 'holy' then represents the gradual shaping and filling in with ethical meaning, or what we shall call the 'schematization', of what was a unique original feeling-response which can be in itself ethically neutral and claims consideration in its own right. And when this moment or element first emerges and begins its long development, all those expressions (*qādôsh, ἅγιος, sacer*, etc.) mean beyond all question something quite other than 'the good'. This is universally agreed by contemporary criticism, which rightly explains the rendering of *qādôsh* by 'good' as a mis-translation and unwarranted 'rationalization' or 'moralization' of the term.

Accordingly, it is worth while, as we have said, to find a word to stand for this element in isolation, this 'extra' in the meaning of 'holy' above and beyond the meaning of goodness. By means of a special term we shall the better be able, first, to keep the meaning clearly apart and distinct, and second, to apprehend and classify connectedly whatever subordinate forms or stages of development it may show. For this purpose I adopt a word coined from the Latin *numen. Omen* has given us 'ominous', and there is no reason why from *numen* we should not similarly form a word 'numinous'. I shall speak, then of a unique 'numinous' category of value and of a definitely 'numinous' state of mind, which is always found wherever the category is applied. This mental state is perfectly *sui generis* and irreducible to any other; and therefore, like every absolutely primary and elementary datum, while it admits of being discussed, it cannot be strictly defined. There is only one way to help another to an understanding of it. He must be guided and led on by con-sideration and discussion of the matter through the ways of his own mind, until he reach the point at which 'the numinous' in him perforce begins to stir, to start into life and into consciousness. We can cooperate in this process by bringing before his notice all that can be found in other regions of the mind, already known and familiar, to resemble, or again to afford some special contrast to, the particular experience we wish to elucidate. Then we must add:

This X of ours is not precisely *this* experience, but akin to this one and the opposite of that other. Cannot you now realize for yourself what it is?' In other words our X cannot, strictly speaking, be taught, it can only be evoked, awakened in the mind; as everything that comes 'of the spirit' must be awakened.

THE ELEMENTS IN THE "NUMINOUS"

Creature-feeling

The reader is invited to direct his mind to a moment of deeply-felt religious experience, as little as possible qualified by other forms of consciousness. Whoever cannot do this, whoever knows no such moments in his experience, is requested to read no further; for it is not easy to discuss questions of religious psychology with one who can recollect the emotions of his adolescence, the discomforts of indigestion, or say, social feelings, but cannot recall any intrinsically religious feelings. We do not blame such a one, when he tries for himself to advance as far as he can with the help of such principles of explanation as he knows, interpreting 'aesthetics' in terms of sensuous pleasure, and 'religion' as a function of the gregarious instinct and social standards, or as something more primitive still. But the artist, who for his part has an intimate personal knowledge of the distinctive element in the aesthetic experience, will decline his theories with thanks, and the religious man will reject them even more uncompromisingly.

Next, in the probing and analysis of such states of the soul as that of solemn worship, it will be well if regard be paid to what is unique in them rather than to what they have in common with other similar states. To be *rapt* in worship is one thing; to be morally *uplifted* by the contemplation of a good deed is another; and it is not to their common features, but to those elements of emotional content peculiar to the first that we would have attention directed as precisely as possible. As Christians we undoubtedly here first meet with feelings familiar enough in a weaker form in other departments of experience, such as feelings of gratitude, trust, love, reliance humble submission, and dedication. But this does not by any means exhaust the content of religious worship. Not in any of these have we got the special features of the quite unique and incomparabl experience of solemn worship. In what does this consist?

Schleiermacher has the credit of isolating a very importan element in such an experience. This is the 'feeling of dependence' But this important discovery of Schleiermacher is open to criticisn in more than one respect.

In the first place, the feeling or emotion which he really has in mind in this phrase is in its specific quality not a 'feeling of depend ence' in the 'natural' sense of the word. As such, other domains o life and other regions of experience than the religious occasion the feeling, as a sense of personal insufficiency and impotence, a con sciousness of being determined by circumstances and environment The feeling of which Schleiermacher wrote has an undeniable analogy with these states of mind: they serve as an indication to it, and its nature may be elucidated by them, so that, by following the direction in which they point, the feeling itself may be spontaneously felt. But the feeling is at the same time also qualitatively different from such analogous states of mind. Schleiermacher himself, in a way, recognizes this by distinguishing the feeling of pious or re ligious dependence from all other feelings of dependence. His mistake is in making the distinction merely that between 'absolute' and 'relative' dependence, and therefore a difference of degree and not of intrinsic quality. What he overlooks is that, in giving the feeling the name 'feeling of dependence' at all, we are really employ ing what is no more than a very close analogy. Anyone who com pares and contrasts the two states of mind introspectively will find out, I think, what I mean. It cannot be expressed by means of anything else, just because it is so primary and elementary a datum in our psychical life, and therefore only definable through itself. It may perhaps help him if I cite a well-known example, in which the precise 'moment' or element of religious feeling of which we are speaking is most actively present. When Abraham ventures to plead with God for the men of Sodom, he says (*Gen.* xviii. 27): 'Behold now, I have taken upon me to speak unto the Lord, which am but dust and ashes.' There you have a self-confessed 'feeling of dependence', which is yet at the same time far more than, and something other than, *merely* a feeling of dependence. Desiring to give it a name of its own, I propose to call it 'creature-consciousness' or creature-feeling. It is the emotion of a creature, submerged and overwhelmed by its own nothingness in contrast to that which is supreme above all creatures.

It is easily seen that, once again, this phrase, whatever it is, is not a *conceptual* explanation of the matter. All that this new term 'creature-feeling' can express, is the note of submergence into nothingness before an overpowering, absolute might of some kind; whereas everything turns upon the *character* of this overpowering might, a character which cannot be expressed verbally, and can only be suggested indirectly through the tone and content of a man's feeling-response to it. And this response must be directly experienced in oneself to be understood.

We have now to note a second defect in the formulation of Schleiermacher's principle. The religious category discovered by him, by whose means he professes to determine the real content of the religious emotion, is merely a category of *self*-valuation, in the sense of self-depreciation. According to him the religious emotion would be directly and primarily a sort of *self*-consciousness, a feeling concerning oneself in a special determined relation, viz. one's dependence. Thus, according to Schleiermacher, I can only come upon the very fact of God as the result of an inference, that is, by reasoning to a cause beyond myself to account for my 'feeling of dependence'. But this is entirely opposed to the psychological facts of the case. Rather, the 'creature-feeling' is itself a first subjective concomitant and effect of another feeling-element, which casts it like a shadow, but which in itself indubitably has immediate and primary reference to an object outside the self.[2]

[2] This is so manifestly borne out by experience that it must be about the first thing to force itself upon the notice of psychologists analysing the facts of religion. There is a certain naivete in the following passage from William James's *Varieties of Religious Experience* (p. 58), where, alluding to the origin of the Grecian representations of the gods, he says: "As regards the origin of the Greek gods, we need not at present seek an opinion. But the whole array of our instances leads to a conclusion something like this: It is as if there were in the human consciousness a *sense of reality*, a *feeling of objective presence*, a *perception* of what we may call '*something*

Now this object is just what we have already spoken of as 'the numinous'. For the 'creature-feeling' and the sense of dependence to arise in the mind the 'numen' must be experienced as present, a *numen praesens*, as is in the case of Abraham. There must be felt a something 'numinous', something bearing the character of a 'numen', to which the mind turns spontaneously; or (which is the same thing in other words) these feelings can only arise in the mind as accompanying emotions when the category of 'the numinous' is called into play.

The numinous is thus felt as objective and outside the self. We have now to inquire more closely into its nature and the modes of its manifestations.

---

there', more deep and more general than any of the special and particular 'senses' by which the current psychology supposes existent realities to be originally revealed". (The italics are James's own.) James is debarred by his empiricist and pragmatist standpoint from coming to a recognition of faculties of knowledge and potentialities of thought in the spirit itself, and he is therefore obliged to have recourse to somewhat singular and mysterious hypotheses to explain this fact. But he grasps the fact itself clearly enough and is sufficient of a realist not to explain it away. But this "feeling of reality", the feeling of a "numinous" *object* objectively given, must be posited as a primary immediate datum of consciousness, and the "feeling of dependence" is then a consequence, following very closely upon it, viz. a depreciation of the *subject* in his own eyes. The latter presupposes the former.

3

Religious language describes religious experiences, II

H. J. N. Horsburgh

Three main objections may be made against the thesis that religious experience is the basis of religious belief. First, all statements about our experiences are psychological statements about our feelings, sensations, mental states, etc., and from them no inference to the existence of objective realities is possible. Just because I have certain subjective experiences I cannot conclude that there are real objects corresponding to them. Thus, no experience, however special, can possibly establish that God or any other religious object exists.

Second, claims that anything exists are always subject to verifying tests and checks of a public kind. But claims that one has had direct experiences of God or the *numinous* cannot be verified in this way. Therefore it is not possible to decide whether or not anyone has an authentic (as opposed to an illusory) experience of God.

Third, religious experiences are said to be ineffable in that they cannot be described in the terms of ordinary language. But if this is so then they must be unintelligible.

Horsburgh expounds these three objections and attempts to defend the claims of religious experience against them. Thus, as against the first objection, he admits that *ordinarily* experiential statements are psychological or subjective statements from which no existential conclusions can be inferred. But Horsburgh argues that there is no reason to assume that *all* experiential statements must *necessarily* be of this kind. Indeed, for the mystic or practitioner of religious experience, his special experiences are precisely *not* purely psychological or subjective; rather they provide direct access to some specifically religious reality that transcends his subjective states. Again, Horsburgh admits that religious experiences are not verifiable in the same way that we verify the existence of material objects, but so he claims, they are self-verifying or self-authenticating in that the believer knows when he has found God "by the overwhelming significance of the encounter." Just as, in a community of blind people, one who suddenly finds that he can see will not be able to verify his claim of having visual experiences to his blind fellows, so also the religious believer will not be able to verify his claim of having religious experiences to those who have never had similar experiences or who are not prepared to put themselves into a position to have such experiences.

Finally, although the object of religious experience eludes description in ordinary concepts, this is not because it cannot be identified *at all,* but because it can only be identified in a *special nonconceptual* way. That religious experience is not unintelligible or vacuous is shown by the fact that, although the believer cannot give a positive characterization of his experiences, he can nevertheless give a negative characterization of them. In other words, he can at least say what his experiences and the ineffable religious objects they disclose are *not* like.

H.J.N. Horsburgh is a philosopher at the University of Glasgow, Scotland. This article, "The Claims of Religious Experience," first appeared in the *Australasian Journal of Philosophy*.

At one time the believer could rest securely on religious experience. The sceptics might nibble at the doctrinal frills of his religion; but they could not touch his seamless inner garment of truth, which was freshly woven in every generation by the experience of the Church's saints, and, to a lesser extent, even by the experience of the most vacillating and sinful Christian. But in our own century the sceptics have tried to set their teeth in this seamless garment. Psychologists have carried out what are commonly thought of as damaging researches into the nature of religious experience, and more recently philosophers have joined them in making difficulties for the believer—and not only the neanderthalers of the linguistic age in philosophy (the early logical positivists), but also *Homo sapiens* at his highest power, as represented by the followers of the later Wittgenstein. It is with this recent philosophical onslaught that I am concerned in this article.

An attempt to estimate its force should be prefaced by a close study of what has actually been claimed for religious experience—particularly by the mystics, since it is with them that I am primarily concerned. But such an investigation is clearly impossible, as even the classics of Western mysticism form a literature of very considerable bulk. I shall therefore confine myself to the examination of some of the claims that might be made. These claims will be considered as they are suggested by the objections themselves.

My paper, then, has two aims: (*a*) to give a brief account of the main objections which have recently been brought against religious experience as either a source of, or as a means of confirming, religious beliefs; and (*b*) to consider what important claims

H. J. N. Horsburgh, "The Claims of Religious Experience," *Australasian Journal of Philosophy*, Vol. 35 (December, 1957), pp. 186–200; reprinted by permission.

they dispose of (if any). The first of these aims is rendered difficult by the fact that as the attack comes from a single school of philosophy the objections tend to run into one another. The three parts into which I divide it are therefore somewhat artificial. I shall call these (1) the psychological objection, (2) the verificationist objection, and (3) the objection from the ineffable nature of religious experience. These labels are mere conveniences: I claim no special aptness for them.

I.

The psychological objection is the most popular at the present time. One can therefore find many accounts of it. I shall quote from three writers who have recently put it forward. ". . . I want to argue", says Mr. Alasdair MacIntyre, "that neither feeling-states nor mental images could provide evidence for religious belief. . . . The reason for this is that the point of the experience is allegedly that it conveys information about something other than the experience, namely, about the ways of God. Now an experience of a distinctively 'mental' kind, a feeling-state or an image cannot of itself yield us any information about anything other than the experience."[1] A much more elaborate account of the same objection is to be found in Mr. C. B. Martin's article, "A Religious Way of Knowing".[2] But at one place it is succinctly stated: "The only thing that I can establish beyond correction on the basis of having certain feelings and sensations is that I have these feelings and sensations".[3] Finally, an account of essentially the same objection is to be found in Professor R. B. Braithwaite's Arthur Eddington Memorial Lecture.[4] "If it is maintained", says Braithwaite, "that the *existence* of God is

[1] *New Essays in Philosophical Theology*, ed. A. Flew and A. MacIntyre (London, S.C.M. Press, 1955), pp. 255–56.

[2] *Mind*, Vol. 61 (October, 1952), pp. 497–512; reprinted in *New Essays*, pp. 76–95.

[3] *New Essays* . . . p. 79.

[4] *An Empiricist's View of the Nature of Religious Belief*, (Cambridge University Press, 1955), p. 4.

known by observation in the 'self-authenticating' experience of 'meeting God', the term 'God' is being used merely as part of the description of that particular experience." At first sight this seems to be quite a different argument. But this impression is mistaken; for what Braithwaite is saying is that the term "God" can only be used, in such contexts, as part of one's description of a particular experience, for one is only referring to one's own feelings, images, etc., and these cannot be used to establish an existential claim.

In the above I have given pride of place to MacIntyre's statement of the objection because it reveals the nature of the argument most clearly. It is also the purest form of the argument, since both the other versions contain intrusive references to other issues. (I shall have something to say about these issues later without referring back explicitly to the passages I have quoted.)

I think it must be agreed that if mystical experiences consist merely of unusual feelings or peculiar sensations or images, i.e., if they are experiences of "a distinctively 'mental' kind" in MacIntyre's sense, they do not establish the existence of God or support any belief concerning His nature. Indeed, no massive apparatus of logic is needed to appreciate this point; it might be expected to lie within the range of even a mystic's mundane intelligence. But to say that mystical experiences are any of these things is to beg the most vital question at issue, namely, the nature of mystical experience. Admittedly, mystics do frequently use the words "feeling", "image", and "sensation" in connexion with their experiences. But linguistic philosophers are aware that the logical topography of these terms is most involved and should therefore be the first to appreciate that mystics may sometimes use them in different senses from those illustrated by such sentences as "I have a prickly sensation", "I am haunted by the image of Britannia", or "I have a numb feeling in my toe". In fact, it is obvious that more is claimed by mystics for their experiences than is allowed by those who urge the psychological objection; they would refuse to agree that their visions are visionary in the same sense as the dagger of Macbeth, or that their moments of ecstasy or illumination are ecstatic or illuminating in the same senses as the experience of a gardener confronted by a perfect rose or of a logician suddenly conscious of an interesting distinction. And their claim to have experienced something other than bizarre or beguiling feelings is borne out by the fact that their conduct in no way resembles the conduct of those who have devoted their lives to the cultivation of such feelings.

Braithwaite and MacIntyre do not even dismiss these claims; they ignore them. And Martin summarises the psychological objection in the sentence I have quoted before he has examined them. However, he later attempts to show that the logic of such statements as "I have direct experience of God and therefore know He exists" is "very, very like" the logic of such admittedly psychological statements as "I have a queer feeling and therefore know I have a queer feeling". I shall contend that Martin is wrong in this logical assertion. But at the moment I wish to make a different point, namely that even if these statements have a similar logic one can only rule out the existential claim with assurance by falling back (as all the writers quoted do, at least implicitly) on cast-iron assertions as to the possibilities of experience. Thus Martin says:[5] "Because 'having direct experience of God' does not admit the relevance of a society of tests and checking procedures it places itself in the company of the other ways of knowing which preserve their self-sufficiency, 'uniqueness', and 'incommunicability' by making a psychological and not an existential claim". In brief, the existential claim must be withdrawn. But it is quite conceivable that the world should be such that only some people can (in the empirical sense) discover certain things about it. For all that Braithwaite, MacIntyre and Martin know to the contrary this may describe the actual situation of the mystics. In other words, the existential claim can only be ruled out by applying logical distinctions (e.g., those between thoughts, feelings, sensations, images, etc.) that have arisen out of ordinary experience. But mystical experience is not ordinary experience; and therefore, it remains an open question whether the distinctions that we ordinarily make would require either to be modified or changed altogether if account were to be taken of it. There seems to be something scholastic in its rigidity about this whole mode of argument. One can imagine, for example, the plight of a present-day scientist pitch-forked without books or apparatus into the middle ages and forced to engage in

[5] *New Essays* . . . p. 85.

discussion with philosophers who applied 20th century techniques to the elucidation of 13th century speech. At every turn he would be accused of unwarrantably extending the meanings of words, using misleading analogies, falling into mislocations and distortions of logical geography, etc., etc. What could he do if these philosophers stood on their logic and refused to enlarge their experience in the way that he might suggest?[6]

But in any case it is quite wrong to speak of the logic of statements concerning religious experience as "very, very like" the logic of psychological statements. There are several important differences. But, at the moment, so as not to trespass on the ground of the next section, I shall mention only one. This difference arises out of the fact that, whereas psychological statements are always made with the same assurance, claims based on religious experience are made with varying degrees of assurance. Thus, it does not make sense to ask: "Is A less sure he has the sensation x than B is sure he has the sensation y?" On the other hand it makes perfectly good sense to ask: "Which of them is the more sure that he has had direct experience of God, A or B?"

To point out further differences would be to pass on to the verificationist objection. Indeed, the psychological objection is to be regarded as a special or disguised form of the verificationist objection, in that, if subjected to sufficient scrutiny, it turns into that objection. Thus, when someone claims to have intuitive or clairvoyant powers and refuses to admit that his "hunches" are mere feelings, images, etc., we test his claims, and the retention or withdrawal of the word "mere" turns on the results of these tests. In advancing the psychological objection, therefore, one is maintaining either that such tests have been applied to the mystic and his claims shown to be unfounded or that (as Martin suggests) no tests can be applied to him and therefore his claims *must* be unfounded.

---

[6] The cult of failing to understand one's opponents has reached such proportions in some quarters that it gives rise to curious flickers of apprehension. Thus, I have never heard a philosopher complain that he cannot understand those stories of Edgar Allan Poe's in which the spirit of someone dead returns to inhabit or share the body of someone living. Yet in discussions of immortality many philosophers fail to understand similar notions. One can only grieve when the hallmark of philosophical acumen becomes an incapacity to understand.

II.

Martin raises the verificationist objection in as telling a way as any when he asks: "How do we know that someone has had direct experience of God or that we ourselves have had such an experience?" In other cases in which existential claims are made "a whole society of tests and checking up procedures are available"; in this case, according to Martin, it does not exist. He sharpens the objection by drawing attention to two interesting possibilities. The first of these is the possibility of a full description of an alleged direct experience of God. He writes:[7] ". . . the theologian discourages[8] any detailed description of the required experience ('apprehension of God'). The more naturalistic and detailed the description of the required experience became, the easier would it become to deny the existential claim. One could say, 'Yes, I had those very experiences, but they certainly did not convince me of God's existence'. The only sure defence here would be for the theologian to make the claim analytic—'You *couldn't* have those experiences and at the same time sincerely deny God's existence'." The second possibility is that those who used to make the existential claim should cease to do so, while maintaining that their experiences have not changed. "Perhaps they still attend church services and pray as often as they used to do, and perhaps they claim to have the same sort of experiences as they had when they were believers, but they refuse to accept the conclusion that God exists."[9]

I want to begin what I have to say by way of comment on this objection with some remarks on the subject of self-authentication, the topic raised by the question "How do I know that I have had direct experience of God?"

---

[7] *New Essays* . . . p. 80.

[8] Martin produces no evidence whatsoever to justify the use of the word "discourage". This would seem a peculiarly disingenuous attack, coming from one who would probably also wish to urge the objection from the ineffable nature of mystical experience.

[9] *New Essays* . . . p. 87.

Martin and Braithwaite pay no heed to the most remarkable feature of self-authentication in religious experience, namely, that it is not self-authenticating in the same way as it has sometimes been claimed that moral intuitions are self-authenticating. Thus, if asked "Why is murder wrong?", the ethical intuitionist would reply "One just *knows* that it is". This is not a slowly dawning moral perception; it is something that strikes one as soon as one thinks about it. But mystical experience does not seem to be self-authenticating in its beginnings; or, at any rate, not so self-authenticating as to be destructive of doubt. Many religious people can set themselves the question, "Have I had direct experience of God?" and be forced to answer either "I don't know" or "I think so, but I'm not sure". Only the experiences of the greatest mystics would seem to be fully self-authenticating. As I have already shown, this growth of self-authentication serves to distinguish the logic of statements about mystical experience from the logic of ordinary experimental statements. It is also important in connexion with the testing of the mystic's claims, as I hope to show.

Nobody who emphasises the importance of religious experience would wish to deny that this self-authentication is mysterious; indeed, for different reasons from those of the sceptic he would wish to stress its mystery. Nevertheless, something can be said to dispose us more favourably towards it. For example, it can be pointed out, many everyday assertions are mysterious in a somewhat similar way. Thus, when looking for a friend's house one may be told: "Keep straight on and you can't miss it". Painfully aware of one's capacity to miss the obvious, one may fail to be reassured by this prophecy. Yet it may be justified; and when one sees one's friend's house one may appreciate why it could be made. Similarly, one must have had certain experiences to appreciate why some experiences have been called self-authenticating.

It can also be pointed out that at least an element of self-authentication attaches to many of our cognitive experiences. Thus, we may set out to look for something without knowing what it is, impelled by an indeterminate longing. Yet faced by an object, an occupation, or an activity we may instantly recognise that it is what we have been looking for. Our response to what we find guarantees that it is the true object of our search. The religious man goes in quest of God, either alone or supported by the beliefs and practices of a religious community; and he knows when he has found Him by the overwhelming religious significance of the encounter. He has met God when it is only God Whom he could have met, i.e., when he has met the Being in Whom he can find his fulfilment.[10] This may sound like the perfect vindication of the psychological objection, since it can at once be suggested either that the mystic's voyage is one of disguised self-discovery (similar to that which reaches its completion when a man suddenly discovers that what he really wants to do is to paint), or that the whole voyage is a self-deception like that of an ancient mariner setting sail in his dreams for the wonderful port that he has never visited. The response of the mystic, it will be said, is like that of the dying man to the mirage; God is the oasis that should, that must exist—that would exist if thought really had the omnipotence that children and primitives ascribe to it. But just as the ordinary romantic youth is prepared to trade in his dreams for any pretty girl of flesh and blood, discovering that his response to the pretty girl is very different from, and goes far beyond, his response to any figure of fantasy; so the overwhelming power of the mystic's final encounter argues the Presence of a Being Who is more than a figment of his own imagination. Moreover, it is not the sickly and highly emotional who, in contemplative orders, have sometimes reached the level (as they claim) of fully self-authenticating experience; the greatest mystics appear to have been eminently sane men with a handsome disrespect for the phenomena of hysteria, self-hypnosis, and the like. Nobody, for example, can read St. John of the Cross with an open mind without being checked between facile explanations. Indeed, it may be asserted more generally that one can turn to the writings of the mystics after forty years of Freudian investigation without receiving an impression of psychological naivety. In brief, the mystery of self-authentication is more than sheer mystification, and a comparison of the mystic's claims with those of a man who is pronouncing on the peculiarities of his after-images is simply fatuous.

---

[10] As P. T. Geach says, "in 'God exists' we are not predicating something of God, but predicating the term 'God' itself; 'God exists' means 'something or other is God'". See *Proceedings of the Aristotelian Society*, Vol. 55 (1954–55), p. 266.

Finally, it is instructive to consider other cases in which the hideous cry of "Self-authentication" would echo just as deafeningly among the ivory towers of philosophy. Let us suppose that there is a community consisting of three people, A, B, and C. They are all blind but otherwise normal. Their scientific knowledge has reached a very high level so that they have been able to develop scientific aids which fulfil all the functions of eyes with a single exception. Let us now suppose that A suddenly discovers that he can see. He tries to tell B and C about his extraordinary experiences but finds them intransigently sceptical when it is discovered that his alleged new sense gives him no predictive advantages that can be appreciated by the others. Thus as his visual experience increases he can predict colour changes that they cannot predict; but they are unimpressed by these predictions, since they question the existence of colours in A's sense. (However, they discover that his alleged colour predictions are correlated with predictable changes in what we call light waves. Thereafter they are inclined to say in the manner of Braithwaite that A's colour words function as parts of his descriptions of the anomalous experiences caused by these changes.) Inevitably, A becomes a target for the psychological and verificationist objections. He then discovers that he can often make the same predictions as the others with fewer scientific aids. After protracted tests B and C agree that he can. But when he makes existential claims on the basis of his visual experiences they immediately look stern and warn him against "self-authentication". He insists that looking at things is itself a way of verifying that they exist and have certain properties, but this they refuse to admit; and the logic of use supports them since, in this community, verification has nothing whatever to do with seeing. I suggest that the objection to mystical experience on the ground that it is self-authenticating may be as pointless as this objection to A's "self-authenticating" visual experiences.

The same point can be brought out by considering another case—the impact of a stranger with extraordinary clairvoyant powers on a community of normal men. P, Q, and R—the local intellectuals—are forced to admit after extensive tests that Z can describe things which are out of sight as accurately as a normal man describes things that are fully visible and close at hand. Nevertheless, they refuse to allow him to make existential claims on the basis of these powers alone, on the ground that this would mean that his clairvoyant experiences were to be regarded as self-authenticating. Z points out that he "makes sure" before asserting anything, "looking" again and again as a man might look at something near him; but they insist that what Z "sees" in this way must be checked by what he and others see in the ordinary way. But surely P, Q, and R are being unreasonable? A community in which men had reliable clairvoyant powers would have a logic that permitted them to test existential and all other cognitive claims by the use of those powers. Indeed, clairvoyant perception might count for more than seeing, since it might give rise to fewer errors, e.g., those caused by the refraction of light, etc.[11]

To all this it may be objected, however, that A and Z do not claim certainty for the statements they make on the basis of their visual or clairvoyant experiences, whereas the mystic does. But such a criticism fails to distinguish between logical and empirical certainty. A and the mystic both say they are certain; but neither is making his claims analytic—as Martin suggests. Thus, the mystic does not say "You *couldn't* have these experiences and at the same time sincerely deny God's existence". It remains logically possible for the mystic to stop short of the existential claim. But it appears to be empirically impossible. In this it is similar to the run of everyday assertions. Thus, a man may have smelt, felt, and seen hundreds of lampreys, yet his dying words, having eaten a surfeit of them, may still be—"there's no such animal". This is logically possible; but in a sincere, sane man with a good knowledge of the language it is empirically impossible.

Turning now to the charge that there are no tests in the field of religious experience, I first wish to point out that one can only reasonably ask for those tests which take account of the general nature of the field in which a claim is being made. The claims that A can see, that he is less anxious as a result of psychotherapeutic treatment, that he loves B, and that he has added a column of

---

[11] To this it might be objected that my use of the word "reliable" refers back to such tests as creatures like myself are able to employ. But this criticism misses a big point in order to make a small one. The big point is that one's native constitution might be such that clairvoyance provided one with part of one's criteria of reliability.

figures correctly are all different in important ways; and therefore the procedures by which they are tested must also be significantly different. Philosophers, in recent times, have often been unreasonable in what they have said about verification, insisting on paradigm procedures that they knew to be inapplicable to the field in which certain claims had been made. Some, for example, impugned the objectivity of history because its hypotheses could not be shown to be objective in the same ways or in the same sense, as the hypotheses of science. But history was too respectable a study to be safely attacked for long, particularly by those with the built-in conventionality which comes from basing oneself on the ordinary usages of language. Religion has therefore become a popular object of old-style attack—even although nobody has ever supposed that the methods of verification used in scientific work can also be used to test religious claims.

But are there any tests whatsoever in the field of religious experience? In my view there are. Something can be done to understand these tests by returning to A, B and C. A is clearly extending the meaning of the term "exist" when he claims that it should have no closer connexions with what we hear than with what we see. He is unimpressed by C's ingenious objections to this extension, knowing that they represent "the empiricism of one who has had little experience".[12] Let us now suppose that the blindness of A, B and C has been due to some psychological disorder and that A does not suddenly develop the power of sight but accidentally undergoes some mildly therapeutic experience as a result of which he manages to detect the faintest glimmerings of light. He then slowly develops a therapeutic technique which eventually enables him to achieve normal vision. B and C can now test A's claims by using the technique that A has developed. With his assistance they may also improve it, so that, if we now suppose the community to be a larger one in which this form of blindness is endemic, a greatly improved therapeutic technique may eventually come into general use. Much may also be learnt about the stages in which correct vision is developed and the steps which have to be taken to ensure

---

[12] J. S. Mill's criticism of Bentham. See *Mill on Bentham and Coleridge*, ed. F. R. Leavis, (London, Chatto, 1950), p. 62.

that misleading visual phenomena, such as "seeing stars", etc., are not cultivated instead of those which A, and other competent judges, know to be desirable.

The position of the mystic is somewhat similar to A's. His claims can only be tested if others, observing the changes in him or recognising that he has travelled further along the same road as themselves, are induced to follow him. But following the mystic is a very much more complex and arduous undertaking than following A. To begin with, he insists that the religious quest is one in which progress is only made by those who give it pride of place in their lives. It therefore involves a commitment with pervasive and sometimes distasteful implications. Furthermore, one requires to have faith not only in those things which bear some resemblance to a technique, i.e., religious exercises and forms of worship, but also in the creeds and codes of behaviour which are also deemed essential.[13] It is not to be wondered at, therefore, that few who live outside the religious communities make a sustained and intensive effort to test these claims. Within the religious communities, on the other hand, they have been continuously tested over the centuries, and the stages through which the believer must pass—which vary with the nature of his religious gifts, etc.—have been very fully charted in relation to his goal. At the same time, experience has exposed the pitfalls and cul-de-sacs which he must avoid and the dangerous places where he must travel with special care. As a result, a spiritual director can make confident judgments regarding the extent and depth of the experience of those whom it is his duty to guide, basing them partly on what they have to tell him about their religious life and partly on how they behave.

---

[13] The "experiment" has certain features which are not fully paralleled in any other. Thus, one has to commit oneself not only to making a certain experiment but to believing that it will have a certain outcome; one must have faith in the mystic and in the God Whom he is inviting one to seek. Of course, men have often staked their lives on the result of an experiment. But the same experiment might have been successfully conducted—or another experiment designed to test the same claims—with less at stake. When the stakes are less than this in the religious experiment its results are invariably negative. Some "experiments" in the field of human relations are somewhat similar. I am indebted to Mr. Arthur Burns for stressing this vital difference to me in discussion.

All this would seem to be a perfectly adequate system of testing—one that can be studied in a very extensive literature which shows a continuous interest in, and awareness of, the problems of verification.

NOTE. There are other points which I might make about testing that I do not feel justified in elaborating in this paper. The most important of these is that verification is affected not only by the nature of the field in which claims are to be tested but also by the dominant concepts and interests of the society in which they are made. The whole subject is therefore much more complex than it has sometimes been made to seem in the more parochial pronouncements of the logical positivists and their successors.

III.

The objection which bases itself on the ineffable or inexpressible nature of religious experience is even more important than it is common, not least because the mystics and their followers are concerned to stress the same facts as the critics and sceptics. The objection is as trenchantly stated by A. J. Ayer as by any other contemporary writer. ". . . . To say that something transcends the human understanding," he writes, "is to say that it is unintelligible. And what is unintelligible cannot be significantly described. . . . If one allows that it is impossible to define God in intelligible terms, then one is allowing that it is impossible for a sentence both to be significant and to be about God. If a mystic admits that the object of his vision cannot be described, then he must also admit that he is bound to talk nonsense when he describes it."[14]

It would seem to be obvious that this objection is likely to have more force against some claims than against others.

* * *

I propose briefly to consider its impact on the following sorts of claims so far as they rest on religious experience:

[14] *Language, Truth and Logic*, 2nd. ed. (London, Gollancz, 1946) p. 118.

(i) That God exists.

(ii) That God has certain attributes.

(iii) That one's religious experiences provide one with reasons for conceiving God in certain ways rather than in others.

The objection strikes at the second sort of claim with greater force than at either of the others. In fact, at first sight it seems quite fatal to claims of this kind. But a second look may dispose one to think otherwise. Thus, it might be maintained that such claims are risky but possible inductions. Consider A's claim that B loves him. "What makes you think so?" someone asks. "Because with her I've felt—well, I can't describe it." "If you can't describe it, how does it help?" "But that's just it—you can be sure when you feel like that that they really love you." It might be said that the claim that God loves us is founded on experience in just the same way as A's claim. But such an answer is inadmissible since it overlooks the fact that A can only use his indescribable feelings as a test of B's love because there are many women and he has been able to establish the reliability of this test by first using other tests of women's feelings for him. The mystic cannot make such inductions, first, because there is only one God, and secondly because, *ex hypothesi*, he has no non-experiential methods of establishing God's love for him.

But what if it should be said—perhaps by someone who recalls the abundance of negations in the writings of the mystics—that ineffable experiences may be negative guides to what something is like? Suppose we say that the position of the mystic is similar to that of B when something brushes against her in the darkness and she finds she cannot describe it. "Did it seem hard?" A asks. "No." "Then did it seem soft?" "No, it didn't seem soft either. Oh, I can't describe it. It just felt—funny." But while such cases show that one can reject a description without being able to offer another in its place, one's disavowals are useless if they extend to every possible description—and it is certainly the case that the mystic refuses to accept any description of his experiences. (He writes about them in ways which prove to be evocative to his fellow mystics.) Therefore, this defence must also be rejected. However, experiences such as B's are useful because they help to remind us that when one says that x is indescribable one is not saying that it is featureless;

for that which cannot be described may still be recognised when it recurs. Thus, although mystics insist that their experiences are ineffable they do classify them to some extent and are sometimes prepared to say that they have had a certain kind of experience a definite number of times.

It seems, therefore, that the ineffable character of mystical experience rules out claims of the second kind. But I fail to see how it can be used against the assertion that God exists. As I have already tried to show, experience may give us sufficient warrant for extending the meaning of the word "exist" (or any other word); and even in ordinary life existential claims are made when one cannot describe what it is that one is affirming the existence of. Thus, when B says "something bumped into me", she will not withdraw the existential claim when she finds she can neither identify the object nor accept any suggested description of it. But to make such a comparison is calculated to stir the critic. "Yes", he may say, "B persists in making an existential claim. But she only does so — and other people are only interested in her claim — because she thinks that something unidentified is present and wishes to enlist other people's assistance in identifying it, lest it should prove to be dangerous or otherwise important. If, after repeated efforts, it cannot be identified she will either withdraw the existential claim or say combatively, 'Well, I know that *something* bumped into me'. In either case other people will cease to take an interest in it; and if B often has such experiences they will quickly come to the conclusion that she is mentally deranged. The mystic, on the other hand, is asserting the existence of something and at the same time insisting that it cannot be identified. This is very different." Much of what I am supposing the critic to say about B's experience seems to me sound. But he is neglecting certain possibilities. Thus, it might transpire that other people had had experiences similar to B's when walking in the same locality and that in no case had it been found possible to identify what it was that bumped into them. In such circumstances an existential claim might continue to be made without any description being given of what it is that is being asserted to exist. "But", I will be told, "this claim will only be made for the same reason as before, namely, the possibility that further investigation will uncover the nature of this mysterious something-

or-other. If no amount of investigation serves to advance our knowledge the claim will be withdrawn and the experience will be regarded as of a 'distinctively mental kind'." I should agree that this is the probable course of events; but I should want to stress its unsatisfactoriness. However, even if one ignores this unsatisfactoriness an alternative remains, namely, that which is embodied in the mystic's claims. Thus, it might be found that the unknown x, which bumps into people, eludes description not because it cannot be identified but because it can only be identified in a special way. This is what mystics have said about God. Thus, it is not pointless for them to say that God exists even when they admit that He cannot be described, since they also affirm that He can be apprehended in a special way by those who seek Him. Of course, one can rule out the special non-conceptual form of apprehension spoken of by mystics as nonsensical. But if one does one is denying the meaningfulness and appositeness of an expression without having had the experiences which give it meaning and establish its appositeness — a procedure that puts one in reach of the criticism which J. S. Mill levelled at Bentham.

Again, I do not think the objection has any force against claims of the third kind, e.g., against the claim that it is best to think of God as a loving God. The mystic, in his highest spiritual flights, does not require a conception of God: at such times (if we believe him) he enjoys direct communion with God, and the special form of consciousness to which he has attained is one that has no use for concepts. But for the ordinary course of his life, and for the instruction of others, the mystic requires a conception of God. Clearly, it is a good reason for conceiving God in this way rather than in that, that it has been found that this way is the more conducive to spiritual progress, i.e., to more profound and indubitable encounters with God. Of the conceptions and descriptions that are the most useful of all it can be said that they are as true as truth can be, the point of this unfashionable statement being that they are the best spiritual ladders available, but that one comes to the end of the longest ladder and must therefore eventually discard them. Ayer simply ignores the possibility of claims of this kind.

In my view, therefore, the force of the objection which Ayer raises depends on the nature of the claim against which it is directed.

It is as fatal to claims of the second variety as it is harmless when brought against claims of the first and third. But it is these latter sorts of claims which are vital to mysticism. Claims of the sort which cannot be sustained in the face of this attack are precisely the sort of claims which are clearly inconsistent with even the most obvious and familiar features of mysticism.

It has become obvious that I do not think the recent philosophical critics of mysticism have succeeded in dislodging the believer from what I take to be his ultimate stronghold. But I recognise that my rebuttals are most unlikely to convince those who are not sympathetically inclined towards mysticism. This is partly due to such factors as my own intellectual deficiencies. But it is also due to the difficulty of bringing critic and believer into effective touch with one another. One feels this in the course of reading even *New Essays in Philosophical Theology*, although the contributors (Christian and non-Christian) have a common philosophical method; and it is still more obviously true when the believer is either a mystic or one who follows him from afar. In such a case the critic is like an elephant, the believer like a whale, and their combat is apt to have the unreality of a schoolboy frolic in which "dead" and "living" dispute as to which is which. In a disagreement of this kind there must come a point when the whale can only tempt the elephant by hinting at the marvels of underwater life, and the elephant can only stamp his feet, indicating that it is he who stands on solid ground. But there is a vital difference between them; for Leviathan, the father of the whales, will only be found—if he is found at all—by those who venture from the land.

4

Religious language is analogously descriptive

G. H. Joyce

One traditional way of meeting the problem of how religious statements may have meaning is to hold that these statements describe God in an *analogical* way. The term "analogy" is used here in a special technical sense and has nothing to do with ordinary arguments by analogy—for example, Plato's argument that governing a political society is analogous to captaining a ship. The theory of analogical predication, as it might better be called, was sketched out first by Aristotle in the *Categories* and *Metaphysics* and was later developed by Aquinas. It is Aquinas's version of the theory that G.H. Joyce presents here.

When we say "God exists," or "God is the cause of all that exists," or "God is good," the terms "exists," "cause," and "good" are not being used in exactly the same way as when we say, for example, "The sun exists," "The sun is the cause of all the energy in the world," "Sunlight is good for plants." What we mean by "exists" with respect to a material thing like the sun is that it is perceivable by our senses, that it is spatio-temporally measureable, etc. But clearly we do not mean this when we say "God exists." Again, what we mean by "good" with respect to mundane things like sunlight is that they are efficient means to some end—for example, enabling plants to grow. But we do not mean this when we say "God is good."

But, on the other hand, neither are these terms being used

purely metaphorically, as though we meant, "God *as it were* exists," or "God is *so to speak* good." When we say "God is angry" it is obvious that "angry" is being used metaphorically and that we mean "God is *as it were* angry," for "angry" is a term that can only be applied properly or literally to human beings capable of psycho-physical states such as emotions and feelings. But, Aquinas claims, "exists," "cause," "good," etc. are not terms that apply only to a determinate class of things, for there is no determinate class of things that exist, or that are causes, or that are good in the way in which there is a class of things that are alone capable of being angry in the strict sense. Thus, although we ordinarily learn the use of these terms from their ordinary mundane applications, their use is not restricted exclusively to those applications, and there is no logical impropriety in stretching or extending them to supramundane applications as when we say "God exists" etc. In these latter applications they are not used univocally or meta-phorically but analogically. Aquinas claims that a number of other terms are similar to "exists," "good," and "cause" and so may also be used to describe God. He also emphasizes that when we use such terms of God we are using them in a way that is beyond our ken. We know *that* God exists and *that* God is good but we do not know, save negatively, *how* God exists or *how* God is good.

This explanation of Aquinas's theory of analogy is taken from *Principles of Natural Theology* by the English Jesuit philosopher G.H. Joyce.

1 THE ATTRIBUTES OF GOD

Before commencing our discussion of the attributes of God it is necessary first to consider whether anything save the mere fact of His existence is not by the very nature of the case beyond the reach of our faculties. Kant is not by any means alone in maintaining this. Other thinkers also confidently assert that the attempt to attain to any positive knowledge regarding the Divine Being can bear no fruit except to entangle the mind in a series of contradictions, inasmuch as the conditions under which we exercise the faculty of reason put such knowledge altogether out of our reach. They assure us that the traditional theistic teaching according to which man, unaided by revelation and relying on reason alone, can establish that God is infinite, immutable, omnipresent, all-wise, and all-good, is grounded on palpable fallacies: that although in order to account for the world of experience we are compelled to postulate an unknown ground of being, reason will carry us no further than this. No attribute can be affirmed of this ultimate ground except that it is unknown and unknowable. It is asserted that the so-called attributes of God are all of them perfections known to us from the world of experience and involving limitations proper to finite beings alone. If the theist will but scrutinize them, he will soon recognize that they are incompatible with the infinity which he is constrained to affirm of God: and that reason thus compels him to the admission that he knows nothing regarding God's nature. He attributes to Him intelligence, will, causality. Do not all of these of their very nature imply the determination of a substance by accidents? Is it,

From G. H. Joyce, *Principles of Natural Theology* (London, Longmans, 1922), pp. 236–261; reprinted by permission.

then, seriously contended that the Divine nature is a composite structure composed of diverse elements!

Kant raises this difficulty in his *Prolegomena to Every Future System of Metaphysics*, §§ 57, 58. Reason, he says, leads us to hold the existence of a Supreme Being, the ground of all reality: and this may be done, provided we confine ourselves to the "deistic conception, . . . which, however, only represents a thing containing all reality, without our being able to determine a single one of its qualities, because for this an instance would have to be borrowed from the sense-world, in which case I should always have to do with an object of sense, and not with something completely heterogeneous, which cannot be an object of sense." We are compelled, he admits, to judge that the world is related to the Supreme Being as a watch is to its maker or a ship to its builder, thus viewing it "as though it were the work of a supreme understanding and will." But we must not imagine that we thus arrive at any knowledge of the nature of the Supreme Being. We certainly cannot attribute reason and will to Him: for "I have no conception whatever of any understanding but of one like my own, namely of one to which intuitions must be given through the senses": and the same difficulty holds good as regards a will. All that our judgment implies is that the Supreme Being is in some way the source of the reason inherent in the world of experience. "Here," he says, "only the form of reason everywhere met with in the world is considered, and to the Supreme Being so far as it is the ground of this form of reason in the world, Reason is attributed." In other words, we may judge that there is in the Supreme Being *something* in virtue of which He adapts means to ends, very much as our intelligence enables us to employ for various purposes the materials which nature provides. But what that *something* is we cannot tell. We have no ground for holding it to be intelligence: for intelligence, in the only form in which it is known to us, supposes conditions which belong essentially to the sense-world.

It must not be supposed that these objections are altogether new and that the philosophers of the eighteenth and nineteenth centuries discovered difficulties for which theism was wholly unprepared. The agnostic controversy had in fact been fought out long before and by champions of the first rank. The famous Jewish doctor, Moses Maimonides, raised precisely the same issue in the twelfth century in his treatise, *Moreh Nebukim (Ductor Dubitantium)*.[1] His objections are substantially the same as those which we have been considering. He, too, appeals to God's essential simplicity and to the impossibility of the Divine substance being conditioned by relations. His conclusion is that the attributes which we affirm of God are most frequently to be understood metaphorically. When we say "God is intelligent," we signify no more than that God acts *as though* He were intelligent: just as when we speak of God as being angry, we understand the word metaphorically and not literally. In other cases the terms applied to Him are to be taken as signifying a causal relation. God may be called intelligent or good as signifying that He is the cause of goodness and intelligence in creatures. Lastly, they can be understood negatively. We say God is intelligent to indicate that He is not inanimate matter or possessed of merely sensitive life like the animals. It is manifest that these conclusions hardly differ from those of Kant. It is to be regretted that neither Kant himself nor his English successors were acquainted with St. Thomas Aquinas's reply to the Jewish doctor. The greatest of the Scholastic thinkers was perfectly alive to the importance of the issue, and deals with it in more than one of his works.[2] He gives, it may safely be said, a full and final solution of the arguments advanced in the *Ductor Dubitantium*.

2 THE ANALOGICAL KNOWLEDGE OF GOD

St. Thomas bases his refutation on the certain principle that no cause can confer any perfection which it does not in some manner possess. The perfection is the result of the cause's action. And an agent must possess a perfection before its action can be of such a

---

[1] Moses Ben Maimon, born at Cordova, 1135; died at Cairo, 1204. He was the greatest of the medieval Jewish thinkers.

[2] *Summa Theologiae*, I, 13; *Contra Gentiles*, I, 31; *De Potentia*, VII, 4–7.

kind as to confer it. As a thing *is,* so does it act. If, then, it be admitted that God is the cause of created perfections, we must of necessity admit that in some way these perfections must be found in Him. It does not follow that the mode in which God possesses them is identical with that in which a creature enjoys them: it may be very different.[3] The artist could not carve the statue unless the form which he is giving to the marble were to be found in him. But its mode of existence in his mind differs from that which it has when realized in stone. In him it has a nobler and more spiritual manner of being: for it is not limited by material conditions. So, too, in regard to the creature and the Creator. The perfections of the creature are not merely referable to God in the sense that He has power to produce them, but the same perfections are actually in some way intrinsic to Him. Here, however, a distinction must be drawn. Among created perfections some there are, which involve in their concept no imperfection at all, as, *e.g.,* life, intelligence, existence. These are termed 'pure' perfections. The mode in which they are found in creatures may be an imperfect mode. Indeed, it must be so, for it is necessarily finite and limited. But the perfection expressed by the definition in each case, as distinguished from the particular manner of its realization, connotes no imperfection. These perfections may be affirmed of God in strict and literal truth. The perfection is really found in Him, though in a far higher manner than in creatures. To use Scholastic terms which we have already explained, it is in Him both *formally* and *eminently.* There are other endowments of the creature which in their very notion involve imperfection. Such are all those which imply material conditions. The faculties of sense, and all forms of physical beauty, will serve as illustrations. These are termed 'mixed' perfections, and these, it is manifest, are not found in their proper nature (*formaliter*) in God, though whatever there is in them of goodness belongs to Him in some sublimer way. Terms denoting such perfections as these can only be predicated of God metaphorically. Thus when He is declared to be 'merciful' and 'just,' the attributes signified are understood to be predicated of Him in their literal sense. But when

[3] *De Pot.,* VII, 5.

God is spoken of as 'angry' with sinners, the term is employed metaphorically, and simply denotes that His action is comparable to that to which a just judge may be moved by a righteous indignation with crime.[4]

The agnostic objections, which we considered in the previous section, were one and all based on the supposition that inasmuch as our knowledge is derived from our experience of creatures, our concept of any perfection found in them necessarily includes the imperfect mode in which the creature possesses it: and that, consequently, if we predicate it of God we are implicitly attributing this mode to Him also. Thus Kant, as we have seen, urges that we cannot say that God is intelligent without thereby implying that He gathers information from the perceptions of sense. Mansel takes it for granted that the divine attributes must denote accidental determinations distinct one from another: and that since in efficient causality as we know it, not merely is the effect related to the cause, but the cause to the effect, we must necessarily imply the same when we say that God is the First Cause. Yet this is not the case. When we attribute to God a perfection which is found in the created world, we understand that in Him it has none of the limitations which adhere to it as it belongs to the creature. In other words, we employ the word not univocally, but *analogously*. A term is univocal if its signification is precisely the same in regard of all the subjects of which it is predicated. The senses of an analogous term, on the other hand, are not absolutely identical. They are similar: there is a proportional resemblance between them. If the attribute 'intelligent' were, indeed, univocal, it could not be predicated of God in any literal sense. For in the form in which we are familiar with intelligence, its activity is accidental: whereas in the Infinite a distinction between substance and accident is inconceivable. Every term which is predicated both of the finite and the Infinite, of creatures and of God, is analogous. And this being so, there is absolutely no ground for assuming that the limitations which condition the perfection as it is found in the creature, adhere to it in the Divine Being: or that the multiplicity and variety of the

[4] *Ibid*, VII, 5, ad 2.

attributes predicated are incompatible with the simplicity of the Godhead. It will indeed appear that the Divine attributes, many though they be, all signify one and the same Supreme Perfection, in whom there is no distinction; but that by reason of the infinitude of that Perfection the human mind can only represent it under a diversity of aspects and by means of concepts differing one from another.

That the terms signifying those 'pure' perfections, which seen first in the creature are then attributed to God, are all analogous, is easily shewn. The transcendentals themselves—Truth, Goodness and Unity—are analogous and not univocal, and since they are not restricted to any one of those divisions of being which we term the Categories, and in consequence do not connote the limitations which such a division involves, there is no reason why they should not be found in Infinite Being itself, existing in a different mode, but the same as regards their essential character. God is said to be One and True and Good, without it being in any way implied that His Being is limited, or qualified by accidents. This is equally the case as regards His intelligence, His will, His life, His causality, etc., etc. Intelligence is not, like sense-perception, a knowledge restricted in its scope to certain particular aspects of reality, and essentially proportioned to these limited aspects. It embraces all being in its range. It is the power to know being as such. It is related to being in so far as it is true. In man it may be hedged in by limitations. But intelligence as such connotes no limitation: it is a knowledge no less appropriate to an Infinite than a finite nature. The same is true of will. Will is related to being in so far as good. It is the propension of a rational agent towards being apprehended by the intellect as good. Life is implied in intelligence and in volition. There are modes of life which are finite: but life as such, i.e., being in so far as endowed with the power of immanent action, does not involve finiteness. Efficient causality is the origination of being: final causality the purpose and end of being. All these terms, then, are, in the nature of things, analogous. And the same will be seen to be true as regards all other such attributes. We say that God is all-beautiful. Beauty is goodness, the contemplation of which brings delight to the mind. The moral virtues which we predicate of God (justice, mercy, etc., etc.) are the goodness of the Divine will in its various aspects.

Infinity, immutability, immensity, eternity, are attributes of an altogether different class. Here we are not concerned with something which is found, though in but a limited degree, in creatures also. These are perfections proper to God alone: and there is no call that the terms should be analogous. In the sections in which they are severally discussed it will appear clearly that they none of them involve any distinction in God. Here it is sufficient to note that infinity is simply the mode of being proper to God, just as finiteness is proper to creatures. It is not something additional to and distinct from that being. The other three are direct deductions from infinity, and are, in fact, but aspects under which infinite Being is apprehended in relation to creatures.

To understand the sense in which the same term may be employed of God and of the creature, it will be necessary to examine with some care the notion of analogy.

There are, as St. Thomas points out, two kinds of analogy, distinguished the one from the other by important differences. They are designated *analogy of attribution* and *analogy of proportion*[5] respectively.

We have analogy of attribution when a term is employed in a secondary sense (or senses) to denote things because of some relation which they bear to the reality which it signifies in its primary sense. Thus the term "healthy" primarily signifies a quality proper only to a living body. But it is likewise used of food, of medicines, of the complexion, etc., etc., by reason of their respective relations to the health of the body. For food may be such as to promote health, medicine such as to restore it, a complexion such as to manifest it. These are, therefore, denominated healthy by *attribution*. The healthy body is known as the 'prime analogate': the things which receive the name in virtue of their relation to this are the 'secondary analogates.' It is characteristic of this species of analogy that the quality or 'form' properly signified by the term is found in the primary analogate alone. Secondary analogates receive the name by extrinsic denomination. Otherwise it would not be predicated

---

[5] St. Thomas terms them *analogia proportionis* and *analogia proportionalitatis* respectively. The employment of names so similar could only be productive of confusion. Hence the term *analogia attributionis* has been commonly used in place of *analogia proportionis*.

of them by 'attribution.' Analogy of proportion arises when two different things display distinct but similar relations. Thus we speak of a man as being 'a pillar of the state' by analogy of this kind, because the relation which the man bears to his country is similar to the relation of a pillar to the building which it supports. So, too, we speak of a landscape as 'smiling,' when the beauty and fertility of a district makes Nature seem kindly and attractive in the same way that a smiling face will do, where persons are concerned. These are mere metaphors. But analogy of proportion may be *real* as well as *metaphorical*. It is real when the quality designed by the term is intrinsic to both analogates. Thus, we speak of 'sex' in regard both of animals and plants. The thing signified in the two cases is very different. But proportionally they are the same. There is a true analogy between sex in a vertebrate and sex in a dicotyledonous plant. So, too, we speak of the soul of a man, and the soul of a dog. It is only by analogy of proportion that the same term is employed of the indestructible spirit of man and the perishable vital principle of the brute. But, again, the analogy is real, not metaphorical.

When we affirm of God some perfection which is found in creatures, we do so by this second kind of analogy—analogy of proportion. If the perfection is a 'mixed' perfection, including in its concept some imperfection, then we can only employ the analogy of metaphor. In this way we say that God is 'angry' with the wicked, that he 'lends an attentive ear' to the prayers of the just. The term employed denotes something which is intrinsic only to men. It is applied to God metaphorically because of a certain similarity of relations. But it is otherwise as regards 'pure' perfections. In this case the analogous term is predicated in a real not a metaphorical sense. When we say that God *lives*, that He created the world by *intelligence* and *will*, that He is *just* and *merciful*, we are well aware that in Him life, intelligence, will, etc., are something different to what they are in ourselves. Nevertheless, in each such case we hold that He veritably possesses the perfection signified. Although God's intelligence differs from our own, we are not wholly ignorant of its character: we know it as having the same relation to the Divine nature which our intelligence has to our nature. Kant saw correctly that our concepts of God must be analogical, and his explanation of the analogy here employed is in its general lines accurate.[6] But since he erroneously held that we neither have nor can have any knowledge whatever of God, he concludes that the fourth term of our proportion must likewise remain wholly unknown to us. In this he was mistaken. The mind has the power to form concepts which are truly, though of course inadequately representative of God. This is best seen in the most fundamental of such concepts, that of self-existent Being. We derive the concept of 'being' or 'thing,' in the first place, from created objects. We apprehend the objects of sense in a confused way as 'things.' But we recognize that this concept is absolutely universal: that there can be nothing to which it does not apply. The perfection expressed is one which is present everywhere—in qualities, relations, etc., as well as in substances. Yet a substance is a 'thing' in a very different sense from that in which an accident is so termed: and a quality again in a different sense from a relation. Thus we realize that the term is analogous, not univocal. It expresses a perfection which is found in different degrees, between which there is only a proportional resemblance. It has not always, like the univocal term, exactly the same meaning. Its precise signification only appears when it is actually predicated of a particular subject.

But if the term "being" is analogous, it is applicable, not merely to contingent created being, but to self-existent being: and, as thus understood, is truly representative of its object, God. God, then, is not a mere name, for which the mind has no corresponding idea, and to which in consequence it attaches a number of notions which are mutually repugnant. Our power of forming analogous concepts gives us ideas which are truly applicable to Him. Reason compels us to admit the existence of a First Cause, the originating principle of the contingent beings which experience manifests: and the mind

---

[6] After stating that we are "obliged to regard the world *as though* it were the work of a supreme understanding and will", he says in the next section: "Such a cognition as this is one according to analogy, which does not signify an imperfect resemblance of two things, as the word is commonly taken to mean, but a perfect resemblance of two relations between totally dissimilar things." Kant here makes the conditions of an analogy somewhat too strict. It is not necessary that the resemblance between the relations should be perfect. It is sufficient that there should be a real, even though in some respects, an imperfect resemblance. In the same way the things in question need not be 'totally' dissimilar.

conceives that supreme source as self-existent being. The whole series of our deductions regarding the perfections of God is ultimately based on concepts of this character.

Kant was wholly mistaken when he declared that we have no means of forming any idea whatever of the unknown *x* which is to the Supreme Being what our intellect is to us. Analogy enables us to conceive a perfection related to the Divine nature as reason is related to human nature. There is, of course, between the two an immeasurable difference. The one is finite: the other infinite. The one, a mere faculty sometimes producing an act, sometimes not so: the other is identical, not merely with the Divine Being Itself, but with its own activity and its own act. We cannot express the two by a concept which, like our specific and generic notions, is identical in its reference to all its subjects. But the concept of intelligence is analogous, and as such is referable, in different but proportionate applications, to both.

In the same manner the terms, beauty, goodness, justice, unity, causality, etc., are none of them, any more than intelligence or will, univocal. Not one of these expresses a generic or specific nature, as do, *e.g.*, such terms as colour, extension, corporeity. We cannot by means of abstraction form concepts of them such that whenever and wherever they are predicated, they always mean the same. It is only when they are actually predicated of a particular subject that we know the particular kind of goodness or beauty, etc., that is signified. Hence all these terms can be applied in their proper sense not merely to creatures, but to God as well.

It may, perhaps, be said that if there be a similarity of relations between human nature and its attributes on the one hand and the divine nature and its attributes on the other, a way is open to us to attain a full and perfect knowledge of God and to solve the riddles not merely of human, but of the divine being. So, indeed, it is contended by some. Thus, Principal Caird, when engaged in denying the possibility of mysteries, in the sense of truths revealed by God but impenetrable to human reason, enquires whether such truths may not be made known by analogies, and replies: "If a representation is a true representation, it must belong to the same order as the thing represented. The relation between them is a thinkable relation, and one which, though immature individual intelligence may not apprehend it, thought or intelligence in general is capable of apprehending."[7] Such reasoning would appear to view analogy after the fashion of a sum in proportion, in which, if the data are sufficient, we can readily arrive at an absolutely accurate knowledge of the unknown term. The resemblance of relations in an analogy is not of this kind. There is, for instance, a true proportional analogy between the perceptions of sense and the conceptions of reason in regard of their respective objects. But a knowledge of only one of these relations would not enable its possessor to attain a full and adequate idea of the other. How much more is this the case where one of the two relations involves an infinite nature. Do those who thus argue really believe that the human intellect is capable of forming an adequate mental representation of infinite being? The fallacy is patent.

From a very different point of view it has been objected that in contending for a real, though analogical, knowledge of God, Scholasticism is inconsistent with itself. St. Thomas is express in asserting that while we can know God's existence, we cannot know *what* He is. We can know *quia est* but not *quid sit*. And the same teaching is common to the Schoolmen generally. How, then, can it be maintained consistently that we are able by analogy to acquire a very considerable measure of knowledge regarding God's nature? This difficulty has been recently urged by some modernist writers in defence of their own position. Yet the inconsistency is only apparent. In the terminology of St. Thomas, on the one hand, knowledge of the essence of a thing (*quid res sit*) requires far more than the analogical knowledge which we have described, and, on the other, knowledge *quia est* may include a good deal besides the bare fact of existence. We know *quid res sit* when our mind can form a concept accurately representing its constitutive principle, the form which makes the thing what it is. Such is the knowledge we have, *e.g.*, of a mathematical figure, when we are able to give its definition. This, manifestly, is impossible in regard of God. We cannot form a concept expressing His essential nature as it is in itself. We represent Him by a series of concepts, which either remove from Him some limitation proper to creatures, *e.g.*, infinite, immutable, or else

[7] J. Caird, *Philosophy of Religion*, (Glasgow, Maclehose, 1889) p. 73.

signify some perfection, which we know as found in finite creatures, and which, inasmuch as it is analogous and not confined to its finite mode of realization, is attributable to God. These, however, give us only an imperfect and confused knowledge of Him. But when our knowledge of anything, though real as far as it goes, is thus obscure, and falls short of an apprehension of that essential nature which makes it what it is, it is still classed by the Schoolmen, following the Aristotelian terminology, as knowledge *quia est*.

In this connection St. Thomas cites with approval the teaching of the pseudo-Dionysius to the effect that those perfections which are common to God and creatures are predicable of Him in three ways, termed respectively the way of *affirmation*, the way of *negation*, and the way of *eminence*.[8] The way of affirmation is exemplified when, *e.g.*, we say that God is just and wise and merciful. In such predications we have regard to the perfections signified by the terms wisdom, justice and mercy. But as we have explained at length, these attributes are not in God after the manner in which our minds are constrained to conceive them: for we can only conceive them as they are found in creatures, viz., as accidental forms distinct one from another. In God there can be nothing of this kind. His plenitude of being can receive no accidental determination: nor can there be in Him any composition of diverse elements, but only the one simple and supreme perfection which is Himself. From this point of view it may be said that God does not possess wisdom or mercy or justice. This is the way of negation. But these negations do not arise from any deficiency in God. They do not imply that He is devoid of these perfections, but on the contrary, that He possesses them in a mode which exceeds our power of comprehension. This brings us to the way of eminence: and we say that God is superlatively wise, superlatively just, etc., etc. He is, in the words of the Areopagite, "the affirmation of all things, the negation of all things, that which is above all affirmation and all negation."[9]

---

[8] *De Pot.*, VII, 5, ad. 2. Cf. Dionysius, *De Divinibus Nominibus*, II, 3; VII, 3.
[9] *De Div. Nom.*, II, 4.

3 SOLUTION OF THE DIFFICULTIES

In the analogical character of our knowledge of God lies the solution of the agnostic arguments enumerated at the beginning of this chapter. This is manifest as regards Kant's contention that we cannot attribute reason or will to God, inasmuch as both intelligence and appetition, as we know them, are dependent for their exercise on sensible data. We shall shew that it is no less true of the other objections there mentioned. It will be convenient to treat first the difficulty urged by Mansel that a plurality of attributes is altogether inconsistent with the simplicity which the consentient voice of theistic philosophers declares to be a characteristic of the Divine nature.

In accordance with the doctrine of analogy we reply that the perfections which in creatures are found as distinct determinations, as, *e.g.*, justice and mercy, or even as separate faculties, as, *e.g.*, intellect and will, exist in God as one simple Reality, infinite perfection, containing within itself, but in a higher manner which our minds cannot conceive, all those aspects of goodness which in creatures are found distinct from one another. That supreme and simple Reality is the Divine essence. The limited powers of the human intellect on the one hand, and on the other the infinitude of the object under consideration, compel us to represent it by a number of different concepts drawn from those created perfections of which it is the source. These we call divine attributes. They are justly affirmed of God, and, notwithstanding their plurality, do not in any way, if rightly understood, imply any distinction in the Godhead.

Yet here a new problem awaits us. If the divine attributes are but one and the same reality, have they not one and all the same signification. When we speak of justice and mercy in a man, we speak of different things. But in God the thing is ever the same. How, then, can we avoid the conclusion that the divine attributes are synonymous one with another: that we may say with equal truth, God pardons by His justice and punishes by His mercy, as that He pardons through mercy, and punishes through His justice? Yet to admit this would be to own that those terms which designate the divine attributes are not analogous in their reference to God and creatures, but equivocal.

The objection overlooks the fact that speech is immediately significative, not of things as they are in themselves, but as mentally conceived. The word denotes the thing, not the concept; but it denotes the thing as known by the mind. Now, since we do not know God directly, but only through the effects which He produces in the created world, we form concepts of Him viewed as the source of this or that created perfection. We conceive Him as merciful, as just, as wise, etc., thereby signifying that the plenitude of the Divine substance contains, in the mode proper to it, the perfections expressed by these terms. In Him, it is true, these perfections coalesce: they are one with the Divine substance and one with each other: but the terms are not interchangeable. Our minds can form no single concept to express that all-embracing unity of being: our only resource is to form partial concepts, each of which exhibits some aspect of the Divine fullness.

On this point the Scholastic logic provided, as usual, a clear and precise terminology. Between the divine attributes there is, it was said, 'a conceptual distinction grounded on the reality (*distinctio rationis cum fundamento in re*).' The attributes, that is, are not distinct determinations in God, as are justice and mercy in man: the distinction is the work of the mind. But it is grounded on the reality, because the fullness of the Divine being contains all that is involved in these terms.

We may now direct our attention to the difficulties connected with causation. It was asserted that the notion of causality is wholly incompatible with the concepts of the Infinite and the Absolute. We pointed out that the causes with which our experience makes us familiar are such as can only exercise causality in virtue of a change in themselves. Until this change takes place they remain causes in potency only. To pass from potency to act they must receive a new accidental determination which we term 'action,' and which constitutes them as 'agents.' Moreover, so far as the physical order is concerned, all causation involves corporeal action. But the term cause is analogous, as the term being is analogous. As being is predicated alike of those finite essences which are called out of nothingness, and of the self-existent essence which is in act from all eternity, so, too, the term cause is applicable, not merely to causes which are to begin with causes in potency and only subsequently causes in act, but to that Cause which needs no ulterior determination, but is a cause in the full sense of the term, a cause in act, from all eternity. God is the *motor immobilis*; in Him causation involves no change. He does not cause by external corporeal activity: nor does He need any internal change in order to produce His effects.

Section B

RELIGIOUS LANGUAGE AS NONDESCRIPTIVE

5

Religious language is meaningless

Rudolf Carnap

As we saw before, G.D. Marshall attempted to show by a purely formal analysis that if religious statements are to have certain desirable logical properties, then they must be descriptive in function. In the following essay Rudolf Carnap tries to show, likewise by purely formal logical analysis, that religious statements cannot be descriptive, for like all metaphysical statements they fail to satisfy the logical conditions that every statement has to satisfy if it is to have descriptive meaning. As we have just said, Carnap's thesis here is a general one about the whole class of metaphysical statements of which, he supposes, religious statements are a subclass.

It is important to notice that Carnap is claiming that we can eliminate metaphysics, and the central concepts of religion, by purely neutral logical analysis, that is, simply by examining the logical conditions that any word or set of words must satisfy if they are to be bearers of meaning, and then by remarking that typically metaphysical and religious words and statements do not, as a matter of fact, satisfy these conditions. For Carnap, it is not as though the metaphysician and religious believer is making *false* statements; rather he is not really making any meaningful statements at all, either true or false.

For Carnap, the main condition of meaningfulness is that every word or set of words be *verifiable,* that is, we must be able to specify what criteria govern the legitimate or illegitimate use of a word, or what evidence would count toward establishing that a given proposition were true or false. As a matter of fact, only empirical or scientific propositions satisfy this condition and so they alone are meaningful. Religious statements, despite their grammatical form, are meaningless, they lack intelligible content or sense and in this way are "nonsense."

Rudolf Carnap (1891–1972) was one of the leading figures in the so-called Vienna Circle of the 1920s from which the movement of Logical Positivism or Logical Empiricism emerged. The article from which the following excerpt is taken bears the title "The Elimination of Metaphysics Through Logical Analysis of Language." It was first published in *Erkenntnis,* and in an English translation by Arthur Pap, in *Logical Positivism.*

I. INTRODUCTION

There have been many *opponents of metaphysics* from the Greek skeptics to the empiricists of the 19th century. Criticisms of very diverse kinds have been set forth. Many have declared that the doctrine of metaphysics is *false*, since it contradicts our empirical knowledge. Others have believed it to be *uncertain*, on the ground that its problems transcend the limits of human knowledge. Many antimetaphysicians have declared that occupation with meta-physical questions is *sterile*. Whether or not these questions can be answered, it is at any rate unnecessary to worry about them; let us devote ourselves entirely to the practical tasks which confront active men every day of their lives!

The development of *modern logic* has made it possible to give a new and sharper answer to the question of the validity and justifica-tion of metaphysics. The researches of applied logic or the theory of knowledge, which aim at clarifying the cognitive content of scientific statements and thereby the meanings of the terms that occur in the statements, by means of logical analysis, lead to a positive and to a negative result. The positive result is worked out in the domain of empirical science; the various concepts of the various branches of science are clarified; their formal-logical and epistemological connections are made explicit. In the domain of *metaphysics*, including all philosophy of value and normative theory, logical analysis yields the negative result *that the alleged statements in*

From Rudolf Carnap, "The Elimination of Metaphysics Through Logical Analysis of Language," *Erkenntnis*, Vol. II (1932); English translation by Arthur Pap. Reprinted with permission of The Macmillan Company from "Religious Language is Meaningless" by Rudolf Carnap in *Logical Positivism*, edited by A. J. Ayer. Copyright The Free Press, a Corporation, 1959. Pp. 60–81.

this domain are entirely meaningless. Therewith a radical elimination of metaphysics is attained, which was not yet possible from the earlier antimetaphysical standpoints. It is true that related ideas may be found already in several earlier trains of thought, e.g. those of a nominalistic kind; but it is only now when the development of logic during recent decades provides us with a sufficiently sharp tool that the decisive step can be taken.

In saying that the so-called statements of metaphysics are *meaningless,* we intend this word in its strictest sense. In a loose sense of the word a statement or a question is at times called meaningless if it is entirely sterile to assert or ask it. We might say this for instance about the question "what is the average weight of those inhabitants of Vienna whose telephone number ends with '3'?" or about a statement which is quite obviously false like "in 1910 Vienna had 6 inhabitants" or about a statement which is not just empirically, but logically false, a contradictory statement such as "persons A and B are each a year older than the other." Such sentences are really meaningful, though they are pointless or false; for it is only meaningful sentences that are even divisible into (theoretically) fruitful and sterile, true and false. In the strict sense, however, a sequence of words is *meaningless* if it does not, within a specified language, constitute a statement. It may happen that such a sequence of words looks like a statement at first glance; in that case we call it a *pseudo-statement.* Our thesis, now, is that logical analysis reveals the alleged statements of metaphysics to be pseudo-statements.

A language consists of a vocabulary and a syntax, i.e. a set of words which have meanings and rules of sentence formation. These rules indicate how sentences may be formed out of the various sorts of words. Accordingly, there are two kinds of pseudo-statements: either they contain a word which is erroneously believed to have meaning, or the constituent words are meaningful, yet are put together in a counter-syntactical way, so that they do not yield a meaningful statement. We shall show in terms of examples that pseudo-statements of both kinds occur in metaphysics. Later we shall have to inquire into the reasons that support our contention that metaphysics in its entirety consists of such pseudo-statements.

2. THE SIGNIFICANCE OF A WORD

A word which (within a definite language) has a meaning, is usually also said to designate a concept; if it only seems to have a meaning while it really does not, we speak of a "pseudo-concept." How is the origin of a pseudo-concept to be explained? Has not every word been introduced into the language for no other purpose than to express something or other, so that it had a definite meaning from the very beginning of its use? How, then, can a traditional language contain meaningless words? To be sure, originally every word (excepting rare cases which we shall illustrate later) had a meaning. In the course of historical development a word frequently changes its meaning. And it also happens at times that a word loses its old sense without acquiring a new one. It is thus that a pseudo-concept arises.

What, now, is *the meaning of a word?* What stipulations concerning a word must be made in order for it to be significant? (It does not matter for our investigation whether these stipulations are explicitly laid down, as in the case of some words and symbols of modern science, or whether they have been tacitly agreed upon, as is the case for most words of traditional language.) First, the *syntax* of the word must be fixed, i.e. the mode of its occurrence in the simplest sentence form in which it is capable of occurring; we call this sentence form its *elementary sentence*. The elementary sentence form for the word "stone" e.g. is "x is a stone"; in sentences of this form some designation from the category of things occupies the place of "x," e.g. "this diamond," "this apple." Secondly, for an elementary sentence S containing the word an answer must be given to the following question, which can be formulated in various ways:

(1.) What sentences is S *deducible* from, and what sentences are deducible from S?

(2.) Under what conditions is S supposed to be true, and under what conditions false?

(3.) How is S to be *verified*?

(4.) What is the *meaning* of S?

(1) is the correct formulation; formulation (2) accords with the phraseology of logic, (3) with the phraseology of the theory of knowledge, (4) with that of philosophy (phenomenology). Wittgenstein has asserted that (2) expresses what philosophers mean by (4): the meaning of a sentence consists in its truth-condition. ((1) is the "metalogical" formulation; it is planned to give elsewhere a detailed exposition of metalogic as the theory of syntax and meaning, i.e. relations of deducibility.)

In the case of many words, specifically in the case of the over-whelming majority of scientific words, it is possible to specify their meaning by reduction to other words ("constitution," definition). E.g. "'arthropodes' are animals with segmented bodies and jointed legs." Thereby the above-mentioned question for the elementary sentence form of the word "arthropode," that is for the sentence form "the thing x is an arthropode," is answered: it has been stipulated that a sentence of this form is deducible from premises of the form "x is an animal," "x has a segmented body," "x has jointed legs," and that conversely each of these sentences is deducible from the former sentence. By means of these stipulations about deducibility (in other words: about the truth-condition, about the method of verification, about the meaning) of the elementary sentence about "arthropode" the meaning of the word "arthropode" is fixed. In this way every word of the language is reduced to other words and finally to the words which occur in the so-called "observation sentences" or "protocol sentences." It is through this reduction that the word acquires its meaning.

For our purposes we may ignore entirely the question concerning the content and form of the primary sentences (protocol sentences) which has not yet been definitely settled. In the theory of knowledge it is customary to say that the primary sentences refer to "the given"; but there is no unanimity on the question what it is that is given. At times the position is taken that sentences about the given speak of the simplest qualities of sense and feeling (e.g. "warm," "blue," "joy" and so forth); others incline to the view that basic sentences refer to total experiences and similarities between them; a still different view has it that even the basic sentences speak of things. Regardless of this diversity of opinion it is certain that a sequence of words has a meaning only if its relations of deducibility to the protocol sentences are fixed, whatever the characteristics of the protocol sentences may be; and similarly, that a word is significant only if the sentences in which it may occur are reducible to protocol sentences.

Since the meaning of a word is determined by its criterion of application (in other words: by the relations of deducibility entered into by its elementary sentence-form, by its truth-conditions, by the method of its verification), the stipulation of the criterion takes away one's freedom to decide what one wishes to "mean" by the word. If the word is to receive an exact meaning, nothing less than the criterion of application must be given; but one cannot, on the other hand, give more than the criterion of application, for the latter is a sufficient determination of meaning. The meaning is implicitly contained in the criterion; all that remains to be done is to make the meaning explicit.

Let us suppose, by way of illustration, that someone invented the new word "teavy" and maintained that there are things which are teavy and things which are not teavy. In order to learn the meaning of this word, we ask him about its criterion of application: how is one to ascertain in a concrete case whether a given thing is teavy or not? Let us suppose to begin with that we get no answer from him: there are no empirical signs of teavyness, he says. In that case we would deny the legitimacy of using this word. If the person who uses the word says that all the same there are things which are teavy and there are things which are not teavy, only it remains for the weak, finite intellect of man an eternal secret which things are teavy and which are not, we shall regard this as empty verbiage. But perhaps he will assure us that he means, after all, something by the word "teavy." But from this we only learn the psychological fact that he associates some kind of images and feelings with the word. The word does not acquire a meaning through such associations. If no criterion of application for the word is stipulated, then nothing is asserted by the sentences in which it occurs, they are but pseudo-statements.

Secondly, take the case when we are given a criterion of application for a new word, say "toovy"; in particular, let the sentence "this thing is toovy" be true if and only if the thing is quadrangular. (It is irrelevant in this context whether the criterion is explicitly stated or whether we derive it by observing the affirmative and the negative uses of the word.) Then we will say: the word "toovy" is synonymous with the word "quadrangular." And we will not allow its users to tell us that nevertheless they "intended" something else by it than "quadrangular"; that though every quadrangular thing is also toovy and conversely, this is only because quadrangularity is the visible manifestation of toovyness, but that the latter itself is a hidden, not itself observable property. We would reply that after the criterion of application has been fixed, the synonymy of "toovy" and "quadrangular" is likewise fixed, and that we are no further at liberty to "intend" this or that by the word.

Let us briefly summarize the result of our analysis. Let "a" be any word and "S(a)" the elementary sentence in which it occurs. Then the sufficient and necessary condition for "a" being meaningful may be given by each of the following formulations, which ultimately say the same thing:

1. The *empirical criteria* for "a" are known.

2. It has been stipulated from what protocol sentences "S(a)" is *deducible*.

3. The *truth-conditions* for "S(a)" are fixed.

4. The method of *verification* of "S(a)" is known.[1]

3. METAPHYSICAL WORDS WITHOUT MEANING

Many words of metaphysics, now, can be shown not to fulfill the above requirement, and therefore to be devoid of meaning.

Let us take as an example the metaphysical term "principle" (in the sense of principle of being, not principle of knowledge or axiom). Various metaphysicians offer an answer to the question which is the (highest) "principle of the world" (or of "things," of "existence," of "being"), e.g. water, number, form, motion, life, the

---

[1] For the logical and epistemological conception which underlies our exposition, but can only briefly be intimated here, cf. Wittgenstein, *Tractatus Logico Philosophicus* (London, Routledge and Kegan Paul, 1922), and Carnap, *Der logische Aufbau der Welt* (1928).

spirit, the idea, the unconscious, activity, the good, and so forth. In order to discover the meaning of the word "principle" in this metaphysical question we must ask the metaphysician under what conditions a statement of the form "x is the principle of y" would be true and under what conditions it would be false. In other words: we ask for the criteria of application or for the definition of the word "principle." The metaphysician replies approximately as follows: "x is the principle of y" is to mean "y arises out of x," "the being of y rests on the being of x," "y exists by virtue of x" and so forth. But these words are ambiguous and vague. Frequently they have a clear meaning; e.g., we say of a thing or process y that it "arises out of" x when we observe that things or processes of kind x are frequently or invariably followed by things or processes of kind y (causal connection in the sense of a lawful succession). But the metaphysician tells us that he does not mean this empirically observable relationship. For in that case his metaphysical theses would be merely empirical propositions of the same kind as those of physics. The expression "arising from" is not to mean here a relation of temporal and causal sequence, which is what the word ordinarily means. Yet, no criterion is specified for any other meaning. Consequently, the alleged "metaphysical" meaning, which the word is supposed to have here in contrast to the mentioned empirical meaning, does not exist. If we reflect on the original meaning of the word "principium" (and of the corresponding Greek word ἀρχή"), we notice the same development. The word is explicitly deprived of its original meaning "beginning"; it is not supposed to mean the temporally prior any more, but the prior in some other, specifically metaphysical, respect. The criteria for this "metaphysical respect," however, are lacking. In both cases, then, the word has been deprived of its earlier meaning without being given a new meaning; there remains the word as an empty shell. From an earlier period of significant use, it is still associatively connected with various mental images; these in turn get associated with new mental images and feelings in the new context of usage. But the word does not thereby become meaningful; and it remains meaningless as long as no method of verification can be described.

Another example is the word "God." Here we must, apart from the variations of its usage within each domain, distinguish the linguistic usage in three different contexts or historical epochs, which however overlap temporally. In its *mythological* use the word has a clear meaning. It, or parallel words in other languages, is sometimes used to denote physical beings which are enthroned on Mount Olympus, in Heaven or in Hades, and which are endowed with power, wisdom, goodness and happiness to a greater or lesser extent. Sometimes the word also refers to spiritual beings which, indeed, do not have manlike bodies, yet manifest themselves nevertheless somehow in the things or processes of the visible world and are therefore empirically verifiable. In its *metaphysical* use, on the other hand, the word "God" refers to something beyond experience. The word is deliberately divested of its reference to a physical being or to a spiritual being that is immanent in the physical. And as it is not given a new meaning, it becomes meaningless. To be sure, it often looks as though the word "God" had a meaning even in metaphysics. But the definitions which are set up prove on closer inspection to be pseudo-definitions. They lead either to logically illegitimate combinations of words (of which we shall treat later) or to other metaphysical words (e.g. "primordial basis," "the absolute," "the unconditioned," "the autonomous," "the self-dependent" and so forth), but in no case to the truth-conditions of its elementary sentences. In the case of this word not even the first requirement of logic is met, that is the requirement to specify its syntax, i.e. the form of its occurrence in elementary sentences. An elementary sentence would here have to be of the form "x is a God"; yet, the metaphysician either rejects this form entirely without substituting another, or if he accepts it he neglects to indicate the syntactical category of the variable x. (Categories are, for example, material things, properties of things, relations between things, numbers etc.).

The *theological* usage of the word "God" falls between its mythological and its metaphysical usage. There is no distinctive meaning here, but an oscillation from one of the mentioned two uses to the other. Several theologians have a clearly empirical (in our terminology, "mythological") concept of God. In this case there are no pseudo-statements; but the disadvantage for the theologian lies in the circumstance that according to this interpretation the statements of theology are empirical and hence are subject to the judgment of empirical science. The linguistic usage of other theologians is clearly metaphysical. Others again do not speak in any definite way, whether this is because they follow now this, now that linguistic usage, or because they express themselves in terms whose usage is not clearly classifiable since it tends towards both sides.

Just like the examined examples "principle" and "God," most of the other *specifically metaphysical terms are devoid of meaning*, e.g. "the Idea," "the Absolute," "the Unconditioned," "the Infinite," "the being of being," "non-being," "thing in itself," "absolute spirit," "objective spirit," "essence," "being-in-itself," "being-in-and-for-itself," "emanation," "manifestation," "articulation," "the Ego," "the non-Ego," etc. These expressions are in the same boat with "teavy," our previously fabricated example. The metaphysician tells us that empirical truth-conditions cannot be specified; if he adds that nevertheless he "means" something, we know that this is merely an allusion to associated images and feelings which, however, do not bestow a meaning on the word. The alleged statements of metaphysics which contain such words have no sense, assert nothing, are mere pseudo-statements.

6

Religious language is symbolic and "impressive"

J. H. Randall, Jr.

Signs represent or stand for something else, but symbols are functional. In other words, according to Randall, symbols are neither true nor false but are more or less useful or effective in bringing about certain kinds of activity. Some symbols may be cognitive (for example, mathematical and logical symbols) in that they are means of bringing about cognitive activity. Other symbols (for example, artistic and religious symbols) are noncognitive in that they are means of bringing about artistic and religious responses. Thus religious symbols (i) provoke emotional responses and so stimulate appropriate action; (ii) provoke a common or group response; (iii) communicate "ineffable" experiences that are difficult to express in ordinary representative language; (iv) make us "see" the world and ourselves in a new light.

Religious language is therefore not "significant," or representative, or descriptive, or true or false. Rather it is "impressive" in function, that is to say, its function is to create certain impressions and to function as a means of imaginative "revelation" or "vision" or "insight." As Randall puts it: "The *religious* function of religious beliefs is to strengthen religious faith and commitment —it is not to give 'knowledge' but rather 'salvation'—it is to express, strengthen, enhance and clarify a practical commitment, to one's 'ultimate concern,' in Tillich's phrase, or to 'faith in God.'"

J. H. Randall, Jr. is Professor of Philosophy at Columbia University, New York. The following section is taken from his book *Nature and Historical Experience*.

At the outset it is necessary to draw a sharp distinction between a "symbol" and a "sign." A "sign" we have defined as something which provokes the same human response as some other thing, for which it can stand as a kind of surrogate or substitute. A "sign" hence "stands for" or "represents" something other than itself: it is always the "sign of" something else, and can hence serve as evidence for that other thing. In contrast, a "symbol" is in no sense representative: it never stands for or takes the place of anything other than itself. Rather, a "symbol" *does* something in its own right: it operates in its own characteristic way. On this point the terminology is as yet hardly settled; but though the particular way of expressing it is in the present state of usage arbitrary, the distinction is fundamental. It is important to realize that social, artistic, and religious symbols are not "signs"; they are all non-representative symbols which function in various ways in both intellectual and practical life.

Symbols fall into two main classes, cognitive and non-cognitive, which have quite different specific functions, and quite distinctive ways of operating—so distinctive that the two classes might well be called by different names. Both classes of symbols agree, however, in (1) performing the general functions of all Connectives: they serve to relate and connect and organize; in (2) having the ontological status of Connectives: their reality is functional, and consists in what they do; in (3) being built upon the functioning of linguistic signs, of language, though each of the two classes is made possible by different traits of language.

Cognitive symbols function in various ways in the knowing-process, in inquiry. They include mathematical and logical symbols, which, in Dewey's words, are "artificially instituted and freely

From J. H. Randall, Jr., *Nature and Historical Experience* (New York, Columbia University Press, 1958), pp. 263–270. Reprinted by permission.

manipulable." Such cognitive symbols operate in activities that are themselves cognitive and that eventuate in knowledge and truth. The body of scientific concepts, hypotheses, and theories is full of such non-representative but cognitive symbols. An instance is the notion of "velocity at an instant."

In contrast, non-cognitive symbols, including those that play a role in social processes, in art, and in religion, do not have as their function to participate in activities that eventuate in knowledge and truth. Their function is to lead to other kinds of consequences than knowledge. Such non-cognitive symbols can be said to "symbolize" not some external thing that can be indicated apart from their operation—they are not evidence—but rather what they themselves *do*, their proper functions. Socials symbols include legal systems, moral codes, and ideals. Artistic symbols are symbols functioning in the artistic situation, in the Situation functioning artistically. Such artistic symbols are often drawn from other fields: thus religious symbols, or social symbols, can on occasion function artistically. Religious symbols are symbols functioning in a distinctive way as instruments or means in the religious situation.

The third major type of Connectives is made up of myths. One established usage of the term makes "myth" synonymous with Connectives in general, and I should personally find no objection to thus generalizing the concept. If "myth" be more narrowly restricted, it might be well to keep it to its original meaning of μῦθος, or story, as in Plato, for example. This would make "myth" an especially appropriate term for the instruments of historical unification, historical myths. These include origin or creation myths, like the myth of a Golden Age, or of a primitive Communism: and also outcome or eschatological myths, like the Stoic final conflagration, or like the myth of a classless society. Such an historical myth would be defined as a "story," the historical accuracy or inaccuracy of which is irrelevant to its functioning as a myth, that is, as an instrument of historical unification. The term "historical myth" should not be limited to mean an "historically false story." Evolution, for instance, is a unifying "myth," whether or not our theories and knowledge of the process can be warranted.

There is a second, non-temporal kind of intellectual unification which might well be called metaphysical myths—close to what Kant called "regulative ideas." These instruments of unification would include the metaphysical myths of the "Unmoved Mover," the "Unconditioned," the "Universe as a Whole," the "Ultimate Context," the "Principle of Concretion," and such other generalizations and unifications of factors found by metaphysical analysis in every particular process. Metaphysical myths of unification of this sort are widely used by rational or philosophical theology, which could hardly dispense with them. Occasionally they even manage to function religiously as well. And in the Western religions, like Judaism, Christianity, or Communism, historical myths have always played a central role.

I should like to conclude with a few observations as to the functions and the standards of adequacy of non-representative, non-cognitive symbols, social, artistic, and religious. Just what is it that such non-cognitive symbols do? In the first place, all of them, including religious symbols, provoke in men an emotional response, and stimulate appropriate human activities. In traditional terms, they act on the will rather than on the intellect. They act as motives, they lead to action on the part of the men who are influenced by them. They do not, like signs, merely lead the mind to other things: they produce results in conduct.

Secondly, they provoke in a group of men—the community for whom they serve as symbols—a common or shared response. They stimulate joint or cooperative activity. This response can become individualized; but even then its individualized form is derivative from what is fundamentally a social or group response. The response is common or shared, although the "meaning" of the symbol—that is, its relation to other elements of men's experience—would receive a different intellectual interpretation from different members of the symbol-community. Thus a physical "social symbol," like the flag, or an intellectual "social symbol," like "the state," or "liberty," would be fitted in quite differently with other ideas by different men, though all would be stimulated to patriotic emotions and activities, or to libertarian feelings and attitudes.

Thirdly, non-cognitive symbols are able to communicate qualitative or "shared" experience, experience that it is difficult to put into precise words or statements, and may well be "ineffable." This is particularly clear with artistic symbols: they act powerfully in men's experience, but it is notoriously almost impossible to state exactly what they "mean." Needless to say, such artistic "symbols" must be carefully distinguished from what are often indeed *called* "symbols" in works of art, but what are in fact really representative "signs"—signs of something else. It is just that element in a poetic metaphor that is lost through translation into common prose that distinguishes the "symbol" that is at work from the element of mere "sign."

Religious symbols share with other non-cognitive symbols these three characteristics. But in addition, and fourthly, religious symbols in particular can be said to "disclose" or "reveal" something about the world in which they function. Religious symbols thus have a very intimate relation to what is usually called religious "knowledge," one that is peculiarly close in the case of those intellectual religious symbols that are religious beliefs or ideas.

Religious symbols are commonly said to "reveal" some "Truth" about experience. But it is clear that this "Truth" is not what we should call in the ordinary sense "knowledge." This revelation can be called "knowledge" or "truth" only in a sense that is equivocal or metaphorical. It is more like direct acquaintance than like descriptive knowledge: it resembles what we call "insight" or "vision." Such religious symbols do not "tell" us anything that is verifiably so; they rather make us "see" something about our human experience in the world.[1]

Non-cognitive symbols resemble linguistic signs in many ways. Like linguistic signs, they are factors in the human social situation to which the members of a group have been conditioned to respond. Like them also, they seem to have their foundation in the process of signification on the lower, organic level. This resemblance is so striking, indeed, that these symbols are often dealt with in terms of "language." By a certain extension men have talked as though they constituted a distinctive "language" of their own, and have tried to explore them in terms of the "language of art" or of the different arts, or of "the language of religion." They have approached these

---

[1] For a fuller development of religious symbols, and what they can make us "see," see the author's *The Role of Knowledge in Western Religions* (Boston, Beacon Press, 1958) chapter 4: "Knowledge, Intelligence, and Religious Symbols."

symbols as though their function could be easily identified with certain of the functions of language, like expression and communication. Such symbols, it has been assumed, must "express" and "communicate" something. What is it that they express and communicate? Such questions have led to theories of "artistic truth," and to a new version of the ancient "religious truth."

It is very doubtful whether the extension of "language" to cover the functioning of non-cognitive symbols, for all its suggestiveness, and for all the illumination it brings, does not also introduce so much confusion as to make the game not worth the candle. To be sure, the very same question can be raised about treating cognitive symbols—all postulate systems of "artificial signs"—likewise on the analogy of language. The ensuing confusions, though very different, are probably just as great. Each of these extensions of the notion of language complements the other. Each seizes upon certain functions of language in the narrower sense, while disregarding other functions. Hence, in terms of this general analysis, it might be better to say, that while both such systems of artificial and manipulable signs on the one hand, and such non-cognitive symbols and their functioning on the other, are founded upon and made possible by different traits of language, it would be clarifying to distinguish both of them from the functioning of language in any strict sense.

A symbol, we have made clear, signifies not something else that might function in its place, but rather it signifies what it does, the response it provokes, in the primary mode of signification. It points to what it does, not to anything else that can do the same thing. Now this is certainly one of the functions which the use of language performs, one of the directions in which the functioning of language tends. It has been said that language oscillates between mathematics and music. It might also be said that language oscillates between performing the function of mathematics and performing the function of "symbols". The former is the exact and precise statement of and expression of certain relations; the latter is the poetic or artistic use of language. In much recent literature, the use of language to convey information in precise and exact statements has been contrasted with its use to "express emotions"—its so-called "emotive" use. This way of stating a significant contrast seems to go at the matter from the wrong end. One use of language is certainly to make exact statements—to "express" certain relations. But the poetic or artistic use of language is hardly "expression" as contrasted with "statement"—it is rather "impression"—its use to create certain "impressions." Many individual words are "impressive" in this way: that is, they can function as *symbols* to provoke a response, without standing for anything as *signs*. Santayana has remarked on the "awful" impression which can be made in English by the word "God." But it is generally certain combinations of words—certain unforgettable phrases or lines—which thus function as symbols.

It is just at this point that we go wrong, when we extend the notion of language to deal with the arts. We go wrong, if we conceive that the arts share with language the function of expressing and communicating in exact statement some proposition or truth—or some dubious "artistic truth"—in the case of the art of religion, some "religious truth"—that might be—perhaps better, at any rate more clearly—stated in words. The arts, including religion, do not significantly employ "signs" of anything else. Their resemblance to language lies not in their "expressive" function; it lies in their "impressive" function. They resemble language to the extent that it employs *symbols*, not to the extent that it uses *signs*. They are not, except incidentally, "significant," in the secondary mode of signification, of anything else for which they stand. They are "significant" in the primary mode—like all symbols, they point to what they do. Those who emphasize the autonomy of the arts, including religion, and regard as incidental the "expression" of culture, social conflicts or trends, ideas, or what have you, seem clearly to be right. A "Bible in stone" like the cathedral of Chartres, overladen as it is with innumerable *signs* of the Christian faith, becomes, according to Paul Tillich, for that reason at least, no more "significant" than, to use his favorite example, a teacup by Cézanne. With all due deference to Paul Tillich, this is an obvious prejudice. It is a prejudice which, very regretfully, I must confess, I share with him completely. Of course, the cathedral of Chartres itself, being the work of inspired artists, is also an artistic symbol—like the teacups of Cézanne.

The various arts differ greatly in the extent to which to which they do employ signs. Some types of poetry and literature, some kinds of plastic art, use signification in the secondary mode for a large part of their material. On the other hand, it has always been exceedingly difficult to treat music in such terms. The point I am suggesting here is this: no matter how extensive its employment of signs, that belongs to the materials and techniques, to the procedures of the art—that is not the art's primary function, which is to create "impressive" symbols. One of the main problems in the analysis of the arts is to inquire in detail just how they manage to transform the signs they use into symbols. I have elsewhere examined in some detail how in the art of religion religious symbols function as instruments of imaginative "revelation"—which is something quite different from what the signs of theology may possibly "signify" as truth.

If non-cognitive symbols function, not to produce knowledge and truth, but something else, and their products cannot therefore be judged by their truth or falsity, what are the standards of the adequacy and the validity of such non-cognitive symbols—moral, social, artistic, and religious? All Connectives are used to *do* certain definite things, to perform certain determinate functions. Their "adequacy" and "validity" can only be judged and appraised by *how well* they perform their respective functions. A functional test is alone possible, and such a test will of course vary with the specific function. Moreover, the appraisal of the validity of Connectives must always be *comparative*—in comparison with how well another Connective performs the same function—as in the case of theories or organizing hypotheses in the sciences.

Can the standard of the functioning of non-cognitive symbols be properly said to be "truth"? It is well to remember that Connectives, even cognitive symbols, though they play a part in all knowledge, are not themselves "true." Though they are used in formulating "true statements," neither language nor systems of measurement are "true" themselves. Ideals, like Democracy or Liberty, are hardly "true." Mathematics is formally "valid," and strictly speaking should not be called "true." Scientific theories and hypotheses are not "true," in contemporary philosophies of science, but rather "warranted" or "tested."

This is especially important in the case of religious symbols of, which so many are "intellectual" symbols, that is, religious "beliefs" and "doctrines." Stated very briefly, it can be said that the *religious* function of religious beliefs is to strengthen religious faith and commitment—it is not to give "knowledge" but rather "salvation"—it is to express, strengthen, enhance, and clarify a practical commitment, to one's "ultimate concern," in Tillich's phrase, or to "faith in God," the more traditional intellectual religious symbol. The "truth" of religious beliefs is quite irrelevant to their performing their *religious* function. They can do it just as well if they are not "literally" true; and they do it no better if they are. This may be disconcerting to the "rationalist," but it seems to be a fact of life.

Intellectual consistency between "scientific" and "religious" beliefs—if the latter are taken as giving an intellectual explanation of anything—is a very great value. But it is an intellectual and philosophical value, not a "religious" value. From a living religion, most men continue to want other things more than they want intellectual consistency and clarity. The appeal of intellectual consistency between religious and philosophic beliefs seems to be limited to those whose religious interests are severely intellectual and philosophical. In any event, there is a basic distinction between religious beliefs that are "fundamental," and perform a religious function—that are religious symbols—and those that give intellectual understanding, that construe and interpret religious insight in terms of some particular philosophy, and adjust it to the rest of a man's knowledge and experience. The latter beliefs are the basis of a "rational" or "philosophical" theology. Their function is very important, and not to be lightly discarded. But it is a philosophical, not a religious, function, though certain terms in such a philosophical theology can *become* religious symbols in time, like the Logos, or the Trinity.

But these interesting questions I have dealt with more fully elsewhere.

7

Religious language is paradoxically evocative

I. T. Ramsey

Religious language is unavoidably paradoxical in that it has to use words, originally devised to talk about spatiotemporal objects, to speak about nonspatiotemporal objects and states of affairs. But, Ramsey argues, all religious paradoxes are not cases of self-contradiction, or conceptual confusion, or "category mistake," for some at least of them may be illuminating or revealing, that is, when we see that their point is not a descriptive one but an *evocative* one. Their function, Ramsey claims, is to effect a "disclosure" of "what's seen and more"—or, in more general terms, that reality is "not restricted to observables." However, while religious language is not itself "verifiably descriptive," it nevertheless relies upon and uses ordinary descriptive language, otherwise we would not be able to understand the meaning of religious statements at all outside specifically religious situations. The relationship between "I" or the self seen ("nonobjectively") by myself, and, on the other hand, seen ("objectively") by another person, provides an analogy with the relationship between religious language and ordinary language. Language about the "I" is often paradoxical, but illuminatingly so, and while it is nonempirical and nondescriptive, it nevertheless has an "empirical anchorage" in descriptive language.

The Rt. Rev. I. T. Ramsey, Lord Bishop of Durham, England, was formerly Nolloth Professor of the Philosophy of the Christian Religion at the University of Oxford. This present essay, "Paradox in Religion," was first published in the *Proceedings of the Aristotelian Society.* Bishop Ramsey died in 1972.

I.

In *Reasons and Faiths* my fellow symposiast Mr. Ninian Smart, after quoting a characteristic assertion from the *Īśa Upaniṣad:* "It is both far and near; It is within all this and It is outside all this," remarks that such "paradoxical pronouncements fulfil such a number of functions that by understanding the gist of them one can penetrate to the heart of the philosophy of religion."[1] In *Christianity and Paradox* Dr. Ronald Hepburn, considering more particularly theism, comments that "paradoxical and near-paradoxical language is the *staple* of accounts of God's nature and is not confined to rhetorical extravaganzas."[2] It seems then as if religious discourse not only revels in paradox but considers it illuminating. Here seem to be, if anywhere, what Professor John Wisdom would call revealing improprieties.[3]

But such reflections lead directly to the question with which I shall be concerned in this paper: can we do anything to distinguish illuminating and revealing improprieties from those which merely bewilder and confound us? It is a question which Hepburn himself raises early in his book: "When is a contradiction not a *mere* contradiction, but a sublime Paradox, a mystery?"[4] Though Hepburn has a number of constructive suggestions to make I think he would say that for the most part the religious discourse he examines

---

I. T. Ramsey, "Paradox in Religion," *Proceedings of the Aristotelian Society*, Supp. Vol. 33 (1959), pp. 195–218. Reprinted by courtesy of the Editor of the Aristotelian Society. Copyright 1959, The Aristotelian Society.

[1] Ninian Smart, *Reasons and Faiths*, (London, Routledge and Kegan Paul, 1958) p. 20.

[2] R. W. Hepburn, *Christianity and Paradox*, (London, Watts, 1958) p. 16.

[3] John Wisdom, *Philosophy and Psycho-Analysis*, (Oxford, Blackwell, 1953) p. 112.

[4] *op. cit.* p. 17.

displays vicious muddle rather than revealing improprieties, so we are still left with the question on our hands. What Hepburn has done is to make the question all the more urgent and challenging. If certain paradoxes preserve and reveal something, what do they reveal, and how? Can we give any clues by which to recognise illuminating improprieties, revealing absurdities?[5] For our present purpose and without claiming that our classification is either definitive or exhaustive but merely an attempt to bring some sort of order into a vast and complex topic, let us begin by distinguishing the following brands of paradox: First, there is what we might call *avoidable paradox* which spotlights some confusion or other, as for example when a blunder in argument leads to a plain and obvious self-contradiction. Since the muddle can often be cleared up by retracing the steps of our argument, and since (at best) it may have a useful negative point to make, we might speak of this brand of avoidable paradox as *retrospectively negative*.

On the other hand, there is paradox which, while it is avoidable, is only avoided when we are led forward to a new assertion which somehow arises out of the two original assertions. Since there thus arises some positive significance from the paradox, as and when it is resolved, we may say that it is *subsequently significant*. This is the case with any antimony (as with Kant) and with dialectic in general, but not, I think with Hegelian dialectic in particular. For with Hegel, while any paradox of thesis and antithesis was resolvable in a synthesis, this immediately generated another paradox waiting to be resolved. So the Hegelian dialectic would be a better example of unavoidable paradox claiming to have some sort of rational structure.

This brings us to our second group: *unavoidable paradox*. The significance of such paradox (it would be claimed) arises from and is bound up with its permanence and unavoidability. But within this group there arises the possibility of an important sub-division. Such unavoidable paradox may have a discernible, if curious, structure in virtue of which it becomes revealing; alternatively, the

---

[5] Cf. Prof. Gilbert Ryle who concludes his article "Categories", in *Logic and Language*, 2nd. series, ed. A. Flew (Oxford, Blackwell, 1959) p. 81, with the question: "What are the tests of absurdity?"

paradox may permit of no such structure being discerned. The paradox will then be permanent without permitting of any logical examination or assessment and we might call it (*b*) *logically inaccessible*, to distinguish it from the former brand which we might call (*a*) *logically explorable*.

What I propose to do in this paper is to examine cases of paradox in religion which fall into each of these two categories and their two sub-divisions.

II.

Let us look first at what we have called avoidable paradox which is retrospectively negative, and begin with two examples from non-religious discourse.

1.   An example which Ryle gives: the child finding it a paradox that "the Equator can be crossed but not seen",[6] for whatever can be crossed, like roads, bridges, hills, can generally be seen. Here paradox arises because of a failure to distinguish cartographical language and physical object language. But the paradox might also arise as a declaration that, having distinguished these two languages, we are at a loss as to how to relate them.

2.   As a second example take the assertion: "Since all roots inevitably benefit from treatment with ammonium nitrate, so then must the roots of quadratics." But obviously the roots of quadratics cannot be treated with nitrate. Here is self-contradiction which arises from failing to recognise that here are two different uses of the token "root". Once we recognise this, it is clear that the paradox is sheer absurdity, and its negative point of little value.

Now religious discourse includes examples of paradox which may be regarded as of this negative and resolvable kind, and we will try to give parallel examples to the two we have just given.

---

[6] *op. cit.* p. 81.

1.   As an example of religious paradox closely similar to the Equator case, let us recall an aphorism of William Temple's 'I believe in the Holy Catholic Church, and sincerely regret that it does not at present exist.'[7] Compare: "I believe I can cross the Equator, but regret that it does not exist to be seen." Here is paradox all right. But once again it has only a negative point to make, *viz.* that the word "Church" used in a credal profession, and the word "Church" used of a visible community, belong to two different logical areas. The problem of their relationship it leaves on our hands.

2.   As with our second general example, let us now take a case of religious paradox which displays sheer confusion and utter muddle. I am bold to say that this seems to me to occur at a certain stage in the development of Trinitarian doctrine as H. A. Wolfson describes it.[8] He argues that in Judaism there was a pre-existent Wisdom and a pre-existent Messiah, though (he says) the two were never identified. We might have expected that to be a merit, for how could we ever *identify* the ideas of Wisdom and Messiah? We could point at a Messiah once he appeared, but could we ever point in the same way at Wisdom? A Messiah exists in time and might pre-exist before birth, but how can we talk in the same way about existent and pre-existent wisdom? However, nothing daunted, it was to Paul's credit (says Wolfson) to identify pre-existent Wisdom with the pre-existent Messiah and to use these terms interchangeably. Nor was that all. "While there is no explicit identification in Paul of the Holy Spirit and the pre-existent Messiah, he undoubtedly identified them."[9] Further, in the Fourth Gospel, the pre-existent Messiah was identified with the *Logos* of Philo's philosophy. So we then had:

[7] F. A. Iremonger, *Life of William Temple*, (Oxford, University Press, 1948) p. 387: quoted by P. Harthill, *The Unity of God* (London, Mowbray, 1952), p. 139 and called (rightly) "a paradoxical bit of rhetoric intended to focus attention on the sin of disunion".

[8] H. A. Wolfson, *The Philosophy of the Church Fathers*, (Cambridge, Harvard U.P. 1956).

[9] *ibid*, pp. 164–5.

pre-existent Wisdom = pre-existent Messiah = Holy Spirit
                                                  (St. Paul)
                                              = pre-existent
                                                  Logos (Philo)

But from all this "identification" arises the question: Is the Holy Spirit then pre-existent like *Logos*, or is it not?" which (since there was a one-stage and a two-stage account of this *Logos* pre-existence) develops into the question: "Was there a Trinity before, as well as after, the Incarnation?" But how can God who is beyond change, undergo a radical constitutional upheaval? Here is paradox all right, and it arises (at any rate in part) from a failure to recognise that "pre-existence" like "root" in our general example, is being used interchangeably between vastly different logical areas. Utterly different uses of "pre-existence" have been illegitimately "identified." It only needed "pre-existent" to be then taken in all cases as straightforwardly descriptive (which presumably it might be in the case of a Messiah) and confusion was even worse confounded. Here is utterly unrevealing paradox generating bogus questions, which men were more anxious to answer than to examine. The overall result is the kind of increasingly profitless muddle which characterises not a little doctrinal speculation.

III.

Let us now pass to the second brand of paradox we distinguished above: paradoxes which are avoidable but, in contrast with these last examples, positively significant.

Starting once again with a non-religious illustration, let us recall the familiar example of wave and particle theories in contemporary scientific method. To bring out the paradoxical character of this example, I think we have to formulate it as follows. Certain physical phenomena are best treated in terms of particle mechanics which presupposes that matter is discontinuous; at the same time, other physical phenomena are best treated in terms of wave mechanics which presupposes that matter is continuous. The world, therefore, is both continuous and discontinuous; a plain self-contradiction.

It might be said that this paradox belongs really to the first group, for "matter" and the "world" do not obviously belong to the same logical areas. But let us set that possibility aside and for the purpose of our present example notice only that the scientist working with this paradox does so with the intention that it must somehow and eventually be overcome in a more comprehensive and therefore more illuminating hypothesis. Whether or not this has been attained in the present instance by Bohm and others who talk about hidden parameters uniting the areas, I am not competent to say, but the possibility of their being right is enough to record for our purpose.

Granted that such paradox and procedure is not only justified but illuminating in science, what of possible theological parallels? Hepburn, who takes the example as a paradigm for understanding religious paradox, has no difficulty in showing that whether in assuming a parallel ontology, or some kind of similarity between a theological and scientific "hypothesis", the scientific near-parallel at crucial points breaks down. But could we ever expect it to be otherwise? If the theological case were identical with the scientific, theology, like science, would be concerned with no more than observables. But—to raise already a major point to which I return presently—can there be any distinctively *religious* language which talks of nothing more than observables?

Even so, let us agree with Hepburn so far as to admit that *some* religious paradox has a *prime facie* affinity with the scientific case and I may take specifically an example from Christology. The doctrine of the *Communicatio Idiomatum*, sponsored by Cyril of Alexandria and receiving Conciliar authority in the Tome of Leo, argued that while the human and divine natures of Jesus Christ were separate, the attributes of the one could be predicated of the other becauxe of their union in the one person of Christ. Here is paradox indeed. Natures supposedly wholly separate are found to be united. On one interpretation it would certainly be a vicious muddle, *i.e.*, if it was supposed that a thing called a "person" united two other things called "natures" which were nevertheless utterly separate. Further, when the doctrine has been taken in this descriptive way, it has certainly led to what I would say is pointless controversy, *viz.*, as between Luther and the orthodox. But if the doctrine means to assert that while words about "human nature" and "God" are logically diverse, yet they have to be mixed to talk about Jesus Christ, so that as used of Jesus, words like "union" or "Person", or Cyril's phrase "hypostatic unity", are logical peculiars whose behaviour awaits elucidation—it may be right or wrong but it is not necessarily sheer muddle, and we may agree that some sort of encouragement for this task of elucidation can be derived from the scientific case. In this way the development of Christological doctrine can provide us with something close to the scientific parallel. But let us notice that it only does this by appealing in the end to crucial words and phrases which still await a logical placing. The original paradox may have been avoided, but only in a way which reveals more clearly than ever the characteristically pre-posterous core. In this way we are pushed on to the unavoidable paradox which is peculiarly religious.

It will be useful at this point to take an example from Nuer religion, for it leads us to the same sort of conclusion. In the religious discourse of the Nuer can be found assertions such as these: "The twin is a bird"; "The cucumber is an ox". Professor Evans-Pritchard elucidates these assertions as follows:

"When a cucumber is used as a sacrificial victim Nuer speak of it as an ox. In doing so they are asserting something rather more than that it takes the place of an ox. They do not, of course, say that cucumbers are oxen, and in speaking of a particular cucumber as an ox in a sacrificial situation they are only indicating that it may be thought of as an ox in that particular situation; and they act accordingly by performing the sacrificial rites as closely as possible to what happens when the victim is an ox. The resemblance is conceptual, not per-ceptual. The 'is' rests on qualitative analogy. And the ex-pression is asymmetrical, a cucumber is an ox, but an ox is not a cucumber. A rather different example of this way of speaking is the Nuer assertion that twins are one person and that they are birds."[10]

10 E. Evans Pritchard, *Nuer Religion*, (Oxford, University Press, 1956) p. 128.

Professor Evans-Pritchard continues a little later:

> "It seems odd, if not absurd, to a European when he is
> told that a twin is a bird as though it were an obvious fact, for
> Nuer are not saying that a twin is like a bird, but that he is a
> bird. There seems to be a complete contradiction in the
> statement. . . . But, in fact, no contradiction is involved in the
> statement, which, on the contrary, appears quite sensible, and
> even true, to one who presents the idea to himself in the Nuer
> language and within their system of religious thought. He does
> not then take their statements about twins any more literally
> than they make and understand themselves. They are not
> saying that a twin has a beak, feathers, and so forth . . . when
> Nuer say that a twin is a bird they are not speaking of either
> as it appears in the flesh . . . . they are speaking of the associa-
> tion birds have with Spirit through their ability to enter the
> realm to which Spirit is likened in metaphor and where Nuer
> think it chiefly is, or may be. The formula does not express a
> dyadic relationship between twins and birds but a triadic
> relationship between twins, birds, and God. In respect to God,
> twins and birds have a similar character."[11]

In such a case it is clear that what started as paradox concludes
as a group of more transparent assertions, *viz.*, that in respect of
God or Spirit, twins, birds, cucumber and oxen have a similar
symbolic function. The paradox only arises if, in Evans-Pritchard's
words, we mistake the rules governing the assertions and think of
the formulae as expressing a dyadic relationship rather than a
triadic relationship. But this does not mean that the example falls
into the negative class of avoidable paradox which we considered
above. For while it is true that the paradox has disappeared when
the correct structure of the formula has been recognised, it has only
disappeared on the introduction of another concept, *viz.*, God or
Spirit, whose logical behaviour remains unmapped. All we can
gather is that such a concept, while it somehow refers to observables

[11] *ibid.* pp. 131–2.

such as beaks, twin births, cucumber skin, oxen, refers to more than observables as well.

The same conclusion might be drawn from a less obviously religious example: "Hail to thee blithe spirit, bird thou never wert".[12] Bird, obviously the skylark is. Shelley is therefore saying that here we have something which is both a bird and not a bird. Paradox indeed. Yet he might say it was justified in so far as what has a beak, feathers and so forth, is a symbol of what is beak, feathers and more than any number of such items, *i.e.*, spirit. But, to reiterate our earlier point, the logical behaviour of "Spirit" is still on our hands.

Let us conclude this section with a further note on the Nuer tribe which will lead us conveniently to our next group of para-doxical assertions. Much earlier in the book Evans-Pritchard has remarked that Nuer prayers

"as is the case among other peoples, are often repetitions, but rather in the form of parallelisms than of tautologies, for they are variations of meaning within the same general meaning. Different images are used to express the same general idea, each stressing a different aspect of it."[13]

The important question which arises out of this remark is: Is the variegated and often conflicting discourse displayed by prayers only paradoxical and complex in so far as it contrives to bring together all kinds of ideas in curious concatenations,[14] thereby producing striking and unusual effects—the grotesque can often be the exciting and memorable—or does the discourse of prayer somehow contrive so to combine words and evoke images as to tell some new kind of story altogether, a story about what can never be cashed in terms of such words and images taken at their face value, a story

---

[12] P. B. Shelley, *To a Skylark*, lines 1–2.
[13] *op. cit.* pp. 26–7.
[14] Cf. J. Newton's hymn (*English Hymnal* 405)
Jesus! my Shepherd, Husband, Friend
My Prophet, Priest and King
My Lord, my Life, my Way, my End . . .

about something which is not merely observable, a story for which the rules (if there are any) still need to be elucidated? This brings us to what is most characteristically religious paradox: paradox claiming to be of the unavoidable kind.

IV.

Let us begin with two typical examples of irreducible religious paradox arising as I shall try to make clear, from the attempt to describe what is both "seen and unseen" in language primarily suited to observables:

(1) "Religion is the vision of something which stands beyond, behind, and within, the passing flux of immediate things."[15]

(2) God is impassible yet loving, timeless yet purposive, both transcendent and immanent.

(1) Let us notice that if we take this sentence at its face value it is plainly self-contradictory. What is "beyond" cannot be "within". But the sentence has a religious point to make because it can be given (as I shall try to show) a different logical structure altogether, a structure which from the point of any descriptive language, is odd.

Let us begin with the "passing flux" of what's seen: the replacement of one noise by another, one view by another, night following day. From this beginning the writer hopes to evoke a "vision" said to be, preposterously enough, "of the unseen". To do this he offers us certain prepositions as operators or directives. "*Within*": try to sub-divide and sub-divide, ever to penetrate more and more closely into what's seen. "*Beyond, behind*": without leaving the "passing flux" extend our view, add, develop, continuously.

[15] A. N. Whitehead, *Science and the Modern World*, (Cambridge, University Press, 1933) p. 238.

Now here it will be recognised, is a technique very similar to that which Bradley set forward for evoking what he called "immediate experience"[16]—something which "is not intelligible .... in the sense of being explicable" but something which breaks in on us and satisfies us when no "relational addition from without (or) relational distinction from within" produces anything but "a sense of defect".

Whitehead's assertion likewise must be understood by reference to a situation which is "the passing flux" and more, a situation which breaks in on us (we must hope) as we practice the technique of sub-division and continuous expansion.

Further, the example supplies us, I suggest, with a general clue to the structure of *some* unavoidable religious paradox at any rate. Religious discourse in its most characteristic areas arises, we see, from the claim that there is something to be talked about which is not only spatio-temporal, but more than spatio-temporal as well.[17] Now supposing that we agree on this basic claim, what should we expect to be appropriate currency for such discourse? How should we expect to talk, in terms of observables, about what is observables and more, a "more" never compassed by observables however far these are enumerated?

One answer—and I do not claim it is the only answer—will be that we may properly speak of a characteristically religious situation in terms of an infinite series of observables, and this suggestion may help to illuminate another sort of paradoxical utterance which follows immediately on the assertion from Whitehead quoted above. He continues: (Religion is) "something which is real, and yet waiting to be realised .... something whose possession is the final good, and yet is beyond all reach."[18] We may conveniently take with this, such Christian assertions as "Salvation is both attained and yet not attained;" "The kingdom of God has come and yet is to come." "Revelation is both final and progressive".

[16] F. H. Bradley, *Essays on Truth and Reality*, (Oxford, University Press 1914) chapter VI, esp. pp. 188–9.

[17] Christian paradox is a special case which arises when an attempt is made to use the historical to talk about what is historical and more. While Christian assertions are in part "about history", they do not stand or fall on historical criteria alone; nor is their historical reference always very determinate.

[18] *op. cit.* p. 238.

In all these cases there is on the one hand a characteristically religious situation which is the topic of the utterance, something called merely "Religion" or more specifically "Salvation", "The Kingdom of God", or "Revelation". From this standpoint religion is "real" and "the final good", Salvation is a "state", the Kingdom of God is "here and now", Revelation is "final". But if we talk about such a situation we must talk of it in terms of a never-ending series of observables. So *our talk* will be of religion as "waiting to be realised", "beyond all reach", of Salvation as a "process", of the Kingdom of God as "yet to come", or Revelation as "progressive". But the paradox is not that there are, so to say, two different and incompatible kinds of religion, salvation, kingdom, revelation. The paradox merely calls our attention to the fact that *our* talk about what we are given in the characteristically religious situation discourse in terms of observables will never be finite and complete. The situation will be talked about in terms of language and imagery whose span is in principle infinite.

It is with such a background that I have used, and I think justifiably used, on more than one occasion[19] mathematical parallels for religious paradox. For in mathematics, too, we meet unavoidable paradox. A series can "have" an "infinite sum" (or a "sum to infinity") which at some point or other in a mathematical argument we "see", without the series ever having a sum which is given by straight addition. It is sometimes said that a circle is a regular polygon with an infinite number of sides, even though no polygon, however many its sides, is a circle. This second paradox is specially illuminating because it gives us a technique for developing a sides story until we "see" what a circle is. The mathematical case thus resembles the theological in so far as we have unavoidable paradox which (if the formalists will allow me to say so) is significant and illuminating in so far as it grounds characteristic phrases in a discernment and a disclosure, and gives them a logical structure of an unexpected kind.

A further point: on this background we may usefully take some theological phrases—I do not say all—as phrases generative of an

---

[19] I. T. Ramsey, *Religious Language*, (London, S.C.M. Press, 1957) pp. 59, 69; "Note on the Paradox of Omnipotence", *Mind*, Vol. 65 (April, 1956) pp. 263–6.

infinite series, and it is this consideration which lies behind my suggestion of models and qualifiers[20] as a guide to the structure of some—I do not say all—religious phrases. It is in terms of 'models and qualifiers' that we shall treat the second example of typical religious paradox.

(2) *God is impassible yet loving, timeless yet purposive, transcendent and immanent.* If these phrases are taken at their face value, if they are given the logic which their grammar suggests, self-contradictions abound. How can what is impassible be loving, how can what is timeless display a purpose, do not immanence and transcendence mutually exclude one another? But suppose that the phrases are not to be taken at their face grammar. Then, while self-contradiction as such disappears, impropriety and unavoidable paradox inevitably remain. What can we do about it? Let me give even in outline, a possible treatment of this paradoxical assertion.

God is impassible yet loving. Take first: *God is impassible.* Read "impassible" as "im-passible", and as such directing us to try to effect a disclosure by operating ("im"-like) on situations displaying "passibility" *i.e.*, in such a way as tries to overcome and deny that feature. In this way the theological word "impassible" first presents us with a model situation, *viz.*, a situation characterised by "passibility", something which everyone, religious or not, can understand. We then operate on this model with the qualifier "im" in the hope that sooner or later a disclosure situation will be evoked. The idea is that starting with something which displays passibility we must endeavour to reach something which is stable, and recalling Bradley's example we may obviously try to do this by relational division from within, or relational addition from without. This technique must continue until (or so we hope) a disclosure situation is evoked.

When this happens the phrase "impassible" has a second point—though a very negative one—to make, a point about language. It suggests that the word "God", used to talk of what is disclosed, must have a logical placing away from all language suited to passible things.

What now of *God is loving?* Here we must notice at the outset, that the sentence as it stands, is already misleading, "incomplete"

---

[20] *ibid*, Ch. II and pp. 175–6.

in a sense not unlike that which Russell[21] introduced. So our first task is to substitute for the original sentence one of the following more complete versions: *God is infinitely loving; God is perfectly loving; God is all-loving*. What we have to do now to understand such an assertion is to construct a series of situations characterised by love (being in this way models) in such a way that there will (or so we hope) dawn on us a situation which includes and is more than them all. "Perfect", "infinitely", "all" are qualifiers directing us to continue such a series along the right lines: to think away any imperfect, finite, limited features of any and all terms in the series. In this way the qualifiers enable the construction to be developed to any length until the disclosure occurs.

Then, and secondly, the qualifier has again a point to make about the logical placing of "God". If, for instance, we have used the qualifier "infinitely", the assertion that "God is infinitely loving" makes the point that the word "God" stands to language about loving somewhat as the "sum" of an infinite series stands to any finite summation of its terms. We may remind ourselves indeed that people have spoken of God as "Infinite Love" which makes the parallel with the infinite series exceedingly close. Alternatively, if we have used a qualifier like "perfect" or "all", I suggest that their claim would be that the word "God" is a unique and ultimate key-word dominating the whole of a theistic language scheme, an "irreducible posit"[22] to which the theist appeals as his end-point of explanation.

The same treatment might be given to "time-less" on the one hand, and to "purposive" on the other. Both are examples of qualified models, though before the last can be developed it must once again be completed by a qualifier—this time by "eternally".

Both elements of each pair of assertions in the original para-doxical utterance are thus harmonised by being tracked back to the same kind of situation. Nor is there any self-contradiction for we do not take the assertions at their face grammar. The logical structure,

---

[21] B. Russell and A. N. Whitehead, *Principia Mathematica* (Cambridge, University Press) Introduction; chapter III, p. 66.

[22] In a sense not unlike that used by W. V. O. Quine in *From a Logical Point of View*, (Boston, Harvard U.P., 1953) p. 44.

for instance, of "God has an eternal purpose" is on our view as much like that of

$$``2 = \mathop{S}_{r=1}^{r=\infty} \left(\frac{1}{2^{r-1}}\right)"$$

as it is like that of "Aneurin Bevan has a long-term purpose". But as often in philosophy, to clear one problem is to make another more prominent, and certainly, a major logical problem remains: how to connect the word "God" with verifiably descriptive words—something about which the theory of models and qualifiers makes only outline suggestions; how to maintain both the logical uniqueness, distinctiveness, and so on of "God" and yet provide some account of its union with descriptive words. And this, I may say (to complete this section) is the theme of the paradoxical assertion that *God is immanent and transcendent*. Here is the crucial theological paradox. But it is for the most part a proposition about the use of words, *viz.:* how can the word "God" be united with words like "table", "human beings", "goodness", "evil", "beauty", and so on ("immanent") and yet be a word of unique logical status different in its logical behaviour from all other nouns? This latter is at one and the same time the claim of "transcendence", and the point of the ontological argument.

So for the theist, at any rate, it looks as if any defence of the preposterous must finish up by facing this logical problem set by the word "God", or "Spirit", a problem which in its Christian version concerns also words and phrases like "Person" and "hypostatic unity". The basic problem in assessing and defending unavoidable religious paradox is how words can be both united with yet distinguished from verifiably descriptive words—however many sorts of "description" there be; what logical behaviour can we give to words which are to be united with verifiably descriptive words, without themselves being verifiably descriptive? Here is the basic problem and it arises from the claim of religion to talk of what is seen and more than what is seen, using as the basis of its currency language suited to observables.

V.

It is at this point that there comes the great divide amongst those who are otherwise united in holding that paradox in religion is unavoidable. For some would say that no sort of reasonable account can be given of this unavoidable paradox; that theological phrases are logically inaccessible; that the problem we have just raised can never arise. Contrariwise, others would say that this unavoidable paradox is logically explorable, and they would try to make some suggestions as to the solution of the problem.

The difference between these viewpoints may be illustrated by reference to what has been called Tertullian's paradox: "The Son of God died; it is by all means to be believed because it is absurd (*ineptum*). And he was buried and rose again; the fact is certain, because it is impossible (*impossible*)."[23] Some, recalling passages in Tertullian where he is critical of philosophers would interpret this to be a rejoicing in paradox which was logically inaccessible. Here (they would say) in the Incarnation was something quite opaque to all examinations of prying philosophers; something calling only for (I suppose, blind) acceptance. Here is an anticipation of views which we find in Kierkegaard and most obviously in Karl Barth. But considering that the treatise is written against Marcion, and that its overall purpose is to reject what Tertullian himself called the "docetic parody" which would have denied the "reality" of Christ's earthly life, it can be argued that what is by contrast *ineptum* and *impossibile* is the original unparodied story which must talk of Incarnation using words about observables like human flesh. And in so far as Tertullian used phrases which anticipated orthodox Christological doctrine, we may say that the paradox which he considered quite unavoidable he also considered logically explorable. Here is the second position with regard to unavoidable paradox. It is the position I would myself wish to defend and among other companions I think I would have at least Professor C. A. Campbell

[23] Tertullian, *De Carne Christi*, chapter 5.

who argues both for a "symbolic" theology and for non-theological clues to it.[24]

But let us look first at some of those who would say that the unavoidable paradox of religion is logically inaccessible. First, Kierkegaard. While all of us may welcome Kierkegaard's insistence that the basis of religion is in some curious empirical situation in which I am "existentially" set, and while we might well agree that super-scientific descriptive metaphysics is not appropriate currency for what the religious man desires to talk about, yet in the end faith for Kierkegaard involves a "leap" which, he would say, is un-bridgeable no matter how peculiar the structure of any proposed bridge. Or perhaps it is fairer to say that in his time nothing was available but metaphysical bridges of super-scientific design, and such bridges he uncompromisingly rejected. Now we may agree that faith involves some sort of "going beyond"; we have ourselves spoken of "more than what's seen" breaking in on us in a disclosure —a discernment to which the religious man responds with an appropriate commitment. But this is not so much a "leap" into some new territory as that we find ourselves being carried over into it, and then retrospectively have the job of mapping the track by which we travelled, peculiar though it be. And since Kierkegaard's time the possibility of very peculiar paths such as he never con-templated has shown itself.

In our own day the most notable representative of this view is undoubtedly Karl Barth, who starts from the position that God is not man. God is "wholly other". Man must not formulate theologies which "rob God of his deity".[25] But then there is Jesus—

---

[24] C. A. Campbell, *On Selfhood and Godhood*, (London, Allen & Unwin, 1957). See esp. lecture XVII *et seq.*

Here, too, I think, would come H. H. Farmer who, with Paul Roubiczek would argue in effect that while paradox is unavoidable in theology—for like all thinking it works by contraries—its oppositions are to be so plotted as to issue in a pro-gressive transformation of our "feelings". Here would be paradox which, if successfully explored, would lead us to "feel" what any assemblage of contrary concepts is bound paradoxically to express. Here, too, perhaps, should be placed Tillich: "Paradox has its logical place" (*Systematic Theology*, Vol. I, p. 64).

[25] Karl Barth, *Church Dogmatics* (Edinburgh, T. and T. Clark, 1936–62) Vol. II, p. 281.

God *and* man—therefore any talk about Jesus will be paradoxical indeed, for it will bridge the unbridgeable. Here, let us notice, is a double degree of paradox. We have first the necessarily paradoxical character of any theology of the "wholly other". An Incarnational theology however has to go even further—and here Barth closely follows Kierkegaard. An Incarnational theology must somehow bring together in one discourse talk about this "wholly other" and about man. Barth's answer is to make such Incarnational discourse unique and inaccessible, and to do this at the cost of declaring that we never understand the "real" meanings of words when these are taken outside a Christian setting. There may be something in such a claim. But how on Barth's severe dichotomy words outside Christian discourse have any meaning whatever is not clear. Granted that it is a blunder to rob God of his deity, is it not also a blunder to rob God of his world, a world which everybody, Christian or not, manages to talk about? If, like Barth, we have paradox which is logically inaccessible, how do we write intelligible books or begin to talk significantly about religion to unbelievers? Perhaps (he would say) we don't. The truth is that Barth can never do with logical links between Christian theology and ordinary discourse; but neither can he do without them; and the only conclusion is that in fact there must be peculiar links whose logical behaviour awaits elucidation.

Meanwhile, from the philosopher's point of view Barth's mistake is at least two-fold:

(1) Recognising the uniqueness of the word "God" whose logical behaviour is indeed (as we are willing to grant) "wholly other", Barth translates this proposition about words into one of supposed facts which the words picture. How much of the paradox and the absurdity in which Barth revels arises from the consequent ontology which sponsors two worlds?

(2) Barth further supposes that with a uniquely distinctive and compelling revelation—"self-authenticating" as he would call it (and let us allow that phrases like this may be apt labels for the exceptionally peculiar religious situation to which the Christian *quâ* Christian makes appeal)—there must necessarily go a unique

and self-guaranteeing theology. Here we have an opposite blunder from (1); in this case we have the characteristics of a situation illegitimately transferred to language. In these ways then we would say that Barth has a mistaken view of the logical character of religious language and of its empirical anchorage, and we need not be put off any logical exploration of paradox by the old-fashioned epistemology which lies behind Barthian theology.

But there have been others less theologically minded who have taken a somewhat similar view of the logical inaccessibility of religious paradox. Mr. Thomas McPherson has spoken of religion as the inexpressible,[26] arguing that the improprieties and paradoxes of religion can never be demonstratively linked with what religion talks about, and this is a point of view very similar to that of Mr. Alasdair MacIntyre. For MacIntyre the religious man becomes religious by a total unquestioning acceptance of some authoritative demand. On this view "belief cannot argue with unbelief: it can only preach to it".[27] But *how* can it preach? *How* can its words manage to "recount the content of its faith"?[28] Have we to say that these are bogus and unanswerable questions? The question is even more serious for MacIntyre because he rightly makes a point of emphasising the extent to which theological language uses ordinary words, "the large degree of resemblance between religious language and everyday speech".[29] Must we never attempt to map these resemblances, however peculiar their logical connexions?

What light has this negative position to shed on the paradoxical character of religious assertions? All its advocates rightly claim that religion deals in unavoidable improprieties; that if religion uses ordinary words it uses them in a very special sort of way; that religious discourse is not somehow high-powered scientific theory offering some kind of scientific explanation; that religion concerns us as persons in a vital total loyalty. But are they right in supposing that no account can be given of the logical structure of the phrases

[26] T. McPherson, "Religion as the Inexpressible", *New Essays in Philosophical Theology*, ed. A. Flew and A. MacIntyre (London, S.C.M. Press, 1955) pp. 131–143.

[27] A. MacIntyre, *Metaphysical Beliefs* (London, S.C.M. Press, 1957) p. 211.

[28] *ibid.* p. 211.

[29] *ibid.* p. 178.

appropriate to this loyalty? There can, I suppose, be only one answer, and that is to try ourselves to do some logical exploration, and look for the results.

Here we may return to the starting point of this present discussion by reflecting that what this group does—apart from the many differences among its members—is to take such a word as "God", and to make it so distinctive and ultimate as to exclude all connexion with non-theological language. We are back with what we called the crucial problem in assessing unavoidable paradox in religion. So let us face the challenge put to us by such as Kierke-gaard and Barth by returning to this crucial problem to see if there is any hope that the unavoidable paradox displayed by religious language can nevertheless be given some kind of recognisable logical structure. Can we do anything—albeit in outline—to suggest that logical exploration of unavoidable paradox may be worth while?

Let us start by taking one of the points which Kierkegaard and others emphasise, *viz.*, that religious loyalty involves the whole of ourselves. In this way they direct our attention to the significance of the word "I" for understanding religious discourse.[30] It is with some reflections on the importance of "I" as a clue to religious paradox that I will end this paper.

Though normally we can ignore the point with impunity, there is in fact a lack of logical fit between my assertion "I am doing x" (a state of affairs not restricted to "objects", for how can 'I' to myself be wholly a matter of objects?) and "He is doing x" said of me by another (wholly a matter of "objects" or what we have called "observables").[31] The difference—and it then gives rise to para-doxical assertions—is revealed in certain unusual cases. "Did you lecture yesterday?" we ask Dr. X, and when in Descartes' phrase he had let his mind go on holiday while he expounded for the eighty-fifth time his favourite theory about the date of *Galatians*,

---

[30] Cf. J. Heywood Thomas, *Subjectivity and Paradox* (Oxford, Blackwell, 1957) esp. chapter VII. C. A. Campbell (*op. cit.*) makes the same kind of point from a quite different direction.

[31] Cf. J. R. Jones and T. R. Miles, "Self-Knowledge", *Proceedings of the Aristo-telian Society*, Supp. Vol. 30 (1956) pp. 120–156; and J. R. Jones, "The Two Contexts of Mental Concepts", *Proceedings of the Aristotelian Society*, Vol. 59, (1958–59) pp. 105–124.

he replies with engaging frankness: "I did and I didn't." Paradox indeed. We say of the athlete coursing round the track: "He is running magnificently to-day"; but the athlete says "Not a bit of it—it's the new B.D.H. drug that is taking my legs round." The athlete runs yet he does not run. Alternatively, on some other occasion the coach and the medical director may say: "We cannot understand how he keeps on running", "He's running and yet he can't be." Whereupon the athlete comments: "Oh yes, I am running—it's something like will-power " And the coach comments more significently than he suspects, "God alone knows what's happening," for the paradox is near-theological. Or there are cases of depersonalization when "I" known to the world as Charlie Bloggs dissociate myself wholly from Charlie Bloggs who is laughing heartily over someone's misfortune. Charlie Bloggs is both laughing and is not laughing. In these ways "I"—somewhat like "God"—gives rise to unavoidable paradox in virtue of having to be both associated with verifiable descriptions, yet distinguished from any or all of them.

Secondly, we might notice that "I" is only given its full—more than "objects"—use in a disclosure. If we ask: "What does "I" talk of?" we shall only know the answer when we come to ourselves, when we are aware of ourselves in a disclosure situation,[32] when according to Hume we "feel a connexion"[33] between all our "distinct perceptions" which is something more than any and all such distinct perceptions or observables—hence Hume's perplexity. The logical behaviour of "I" then, being grounded in a disclosure and ultimately distinct from all descriptive language while nevertheless associated with it, is a good clue to that of "God", and we can expect the paradoxes of "I" to help us somewhat in our logical exploration of unavoidable religious paradox, to help us distinguish the bogus from the defensible.

Incidentally, it may be helpful to summarise these suggestions by reference to the theory of types:

[32] I. T. Ramsey, "The Systematic Elusiveness of 'I'", *Philosophical Quarterly*, Vol. 5 (July, 1955) pp. 193–204.
[33] David Hume, *A Treatise of Human Nature* (London, Everyman, 1956) Vol. II, p. 319.

(1) Many ordinary absurdities—avoidable paradoxes, retrospectively negative—are admittedly species of type-trespass.

(2) The paradoxes most characteristic of religion would also be cases of type-trespass if the key-words of religious discourse such as "God" were native to any one type-distinguished area, to any one language frame.[34] For it is characteristic of such key words to be associated with any and all verifiable descriptions, *i.e.* to be frame-transferable by nature. This incidentally is the linguistic version of the doctrine of creation.

(3) So if religious improprieties are to be revealing and not absurd, they must centre on categories which, while they have freedom of association with all type-distinguished categories, are not themselves native to any one language frame. The crucial question is: are there any categories which in this way fall outside a theory of types, and my suggestion has been that there is at least one word: "I".

(4) "I" and its paradoxes may then provide a paradigm for reasonable paradox in religion, as solipsism is the primitive metaphysics.[35]

If this seems too vague and generalised a note on which to end, let me point to two practical conclusions which follow from our reflections:

(i) Any unavoidable religious paradox will be defensible only in so far as it can be so structured as to be evocative of a disclosure situation comprising "what is seen and more". Failure to do this results in an irreligious theology.

(ii) Any unavoidable religious paradox will be the more

---

[34] Adopting this phrase from Ninian Smart's *Reasons and Faiths*, p. 10, and using it as he does, against the background of Dr Waismann's article "Language Strata", *Logic and Language*, 2nd series, ed. A. Flew (Oxford, Blackwell, 1959) pp. 11–31.

[35] Cf. Wittgenstein, *Tractatus Logico-Philosophicus*, 5.62.

defensible in so far as it can be explored in characteristically personal terms. Paradoxical theism centering on friendship will thus be more reliable than paradoxical theism centering on the Law Courts, on Judges, Generals, or Despots, and much more reliable than that which clusters around wholly impersonal models such as are used in mechanical and hydrodynamical theories of grace.

VI.

Summary

There are presumably countless types of paradox, not least in religious discourse, and what I have tried to do has been to separate out and comment on a few specimens. Some of the paradox in religion may be sheer muddle, and we mentioned some patristic discussions of the Trinity as an example. Other paradox may plead, in a negative sort of way, the oddness of certain religious phrases— Temple's aphorism was a case in point, though here we are left with words whose logical behaviour is still to be elucidated. The same is true about that kind of paradox in religion which we called positively significant, and of which we took the *Communicatio Idiomatum* as our example. What it leaves on our hands is the logical placing of key Christological phrases.

When we came to what we called unavoidable paradox in religion we saw that its basic justification was that religious discourse must contrive to talk about "what's seen and more" in terms of the language suited to observables, and I tried to show how some typically theistic assertions, paradoxical in character when regarded as directly descriptive, could be so structured as to be suitable currency for the religious situations they were meant to evoke and express. But this presented us with what I call the crucial problem of unavoidable religious paradox: How words which are not verifiably descriptive in any way can be linked with words that are.

Some would say that this question is bogus and that the un-avoidably paradoxical character of theological language is logically inaccessible simply as a matter of fact, being revealing to the converted and unrevealing to those who are not. Sheep and goats must be most decisively separated. But part of the logically inaccessible paradox of theological language, at least for Barth, arose (we saw) because of an illegitimate supposition that theological words mirror and picture what they talk about.

On the other hand I suggested that some kind of logical exploration of unavoidable religious paradox was possible, and that we might be encouraged in such exploration by having as our paradigm the word "I", the paradoxes associated with it, and the empirical anchorage it must be given. What I have tried to allow for is genuine mystery in the sense that "what there is" is not restricted to observables, and to suggest that it is as apt currency for such mystery that there arises "mysterious paradox", which is then neither a vicious muddle nor an inaccessible incantation, but paradox whose structure can be investigated and explored under the guidance of the logical behaviour of "I". "I" is the best (perhaps the only) clue to all genuine mystery, all sublime paradox, and all revealing impropriety.

8

Religious language is "practical"

Edouard Le Roy

If "dogmas" or religious statements such as "God is a person," "Jesus is risen," were taken to be speculative or theoretical or "intellectualistic" in function then, so Le Roy claims, it would (i) be impossible to prove that they were true, or even to give them any intelligible content; (ii) it would mean that the believer's commitment to religious beliefs was dependent upon a prior acceptance of abstruse philosophical ideas; so that (iii) religious beliefs would only be accessible to an intellectual elite; and (iv) religious faith would not require any effort of the will and so would not be able to be freely adopted or be a virtue.

The only theoretical meaning that religious statements have is negative, that is, they exclude certain erroneous ways of religious speaking. For example, the theoretical meaning of "God is personal" is "God is *not* to be thought of as an impersonal cosmic force." But the fundamental meaning of religious statements is a *practical* one, that is, their function is to prescribe rules of practical conduct. Le Roy does not mean that they prescribe rules of *moral* conduct, but rules of practice in the most general sense. Thus, "Jesus is risen" means, "Always think of Jesus as a contemporary"; and "Christ is really present in the Eucharist" means, "Always treat the consecrated host as you would treat Jesus if He were visibly present." These practical rules can be justified in a sense, though not by any kind of theoretical proof but by "lived experience." They may also be given theoretical or hypothetical "explanations" by the theologian, but it remains true that their own fundamental meaning is not theoretical but practical.

Edouard Le Roy (1870–1954) was a French Catholic philosopher who played a part of some importance in the so-called Modernist movement in the Catholic Church in the early years of this century. The following text is the main part of an article "What is a Dogma?" ("Qu'est-ce qu'un dogme?") first published in the journal *La Quinzaine*. It has been translated by the editor especially for the present volume.

We are no longer in the age of partial heresies. In those times a purely logical and dialectical kind of argumentation was sufficient because there were common principles that were, on one side and the other, always accepted. But it is not the same, when these principles are no longer accepted, and when the fundamental difficulty is precisely to establish a starting point on which all can agree. Now, this is how things are at the present time. Today agnosticism does not attack one dogma rather than another; it consists above all in a prior and global refusal to accept anything. Whether or not this or that proposition is a dogma is not discussed; it is the very idea of dogma that affronts and gives scandal. Why is this so?

When one examines the commonly held reasons behind this rejection, one finds four main ones which I will summarize briefly, at the same time attempting to present them as forcefully as I can.

1. A dogma is a proposition that is proposed as being neither proved nor proveable.[1] Even those who affirm it to be true declare that it is impossible ever to succeed in grasping the basic reasons for its truth. Now, modern thought, faithful to Leibniz's teaching, tries to prove even the traditional "axioms." At the very least it wishes, with Kant, to justify them by critical analysis which would show them to be necessary conditions of knowledge, implied *a priori* in every act of reason. Modern thought mistrusts those so-called "immediate evidences" that were so facilely multiplied in former times. Most often it finds in them simple postulates that have been adopted for more or less unconsciously recognized reasons of

From Edouard Le Roy, "Qu'ést-ce qu'un dogme?" *La Quinzaine* (16 April, 1905), pp. 495–526. Translated by M. J. Charlesworth and printed by permission.
[1] I mean here, *intrinsic* proof.

practical utility.[2] In short, in each and every case it demands long and detailed discussion before it considers itself justified in coming to a conclusion. And the proofs that it demands are not just any kind of proofs, more or less indirect, but direct and specific proofs. Modern thought does not favor arguments that are too general, that deal *en bloc* with large classes of things, and that proceed by global demonstrations because it has too often had experience of what illusions and errors, what lacunae and half-truths they conceal. It does not, moreover, favor external or extrinsic reasonings that result in proofs of a negative kind, in demonstrations by *reductio ad absurdum*, based on the principles of contradiction or impossibility, because it has too often had experience[3] of how imprudent and risky it is to declare impossible or contradictory something that through force of habit only *appears* to be so. Thus, if it is to be faithful to the tendencies that have assured its success in all spheres, it can do nothing but absolutely condemn the very idea of a specifically dogmatic proposition. In what rationally acceptable system could such a proposition find a place without being at odds with it? Since Descartes, is it not the incontestably first principle of method that we should hold as true only what we see clearly to be so? Whence comes the right then to make an exception when it is a matter of propositions that claim to be the most important, the most profound, and the most peculiar of all? Obviously, it is not proper to be less attentive to the rigor of the rules that are our protection against error, precisely when our affirmations are of the gravest import and refer to objects that are the most difficult and the most hidden of all. On the contrary, it is then that it is right to be all the more demanding, all the more scrupulous and exacting, than usual.

2.   No doubt, it will be said that dogmatic propositions are not really affirmed without proof. In fact, indirect demonstration has been tried many times. A certain kind of Apologetic, which

---

[2] Cf. the "new philosophy" that has emerged from the works of Mr. Bergson.
[3] In the sciences in particular.

considers itself thoroughly traditional,[4] claims to establish that these propositions are true, although it admits that it is not able to manifest the how and the why of their truth with full evidence. There is a kind of analogy, it would seem, between this approach and that of the mathematician who is sometimes restricted to theorems of simple existence, or that of the physicist who often accepts facts of which he does not know how to give any theoretical explanation, or again that of the historian who always gets his knowledge through testimony alone. And so it seems that the first objection fails. True, this would be a very simple solution. But there is one unfortunate thing, namely that the analogy referred to is seen on reflection to be quite inexact. For the difficulty we wish to avoid reappears in its entirety when we come to justify the postulates that the so-called indirect demonstration assumes. When a mathematician is content to establish a theorem of simple existence (I mean a theorem affirming the existence of a solution that is in itself inaccessible to us) he does not reason any less rigorously than in the other parts of his science. But, here (with regard to dogmatic propositions) there is nothing like this. We would need to have proved *directly* that God exists, that He has spoken, that He has said this or that, that today we possess His authentic teaching. And this comes back to saying that we would need to have resolved the problem of God, of Revelation, of biblical inspiration, of the authority of the Church by *direct* analysis. But these precisely are questions of the same kind as properly dogmatic questions, questions *a propos* which it is completely impossible to produce arguments comparable to the mathematician's. In the same way, when a physicist accepts a fact for which he can give no theoretical explanation, at least for him this fact corresponds to precise experiences, to operations that can be carried out practically, in short, to a set of gestures of which he has direct knowledge. But what is there similar to this in the case of dogmas? Finally, the historian only consents to accept the truth through testimony because phenomena of the same kind as those of which he has direct perception are involved. Again, he judges his

[4] This method of *extrinsic* demonstration claims to be traditional. That however is a matter of history on which a good deal could be said. But such a discussion is outside my subject here.

discipline conjectural and uncertain to the extent that it is concerned with causes that are more or less hidden or events that are more or less distant. How much more then must we come to the same conclusion in the case of dogmas where we are faced with facts that are mysterious, extraordinary, baffling—facts to which nothing analogous in our human experience corresponds.

Our solution is all in vain then: so-called indirect demonstration is based inescapably upon an appeal to the transcendence of pure Authority. It claims, or at least appears to claim, to inject the truth into us from outside, just like a ready made "thing" that might enter into us against our will. Any dogma will appear then as an enslavement, as a limit upon the rights of the mind, as a threat of intellectual tyranny, as a shackle and restriction imposed on liberty of inquiry from the outside. All these things are radically contrary to the very life of the mind, to its need for autonomy and sincerity, to its generative and fundamental principle, the principle of immanence. Let me dwell on this last point, for the principle of immanence has not always been properly understood. Often it is made into some kind of a monster, although nothing is simpler nor more evident. It can be said that the essential achievement of modern philosophy is to have become clearly aware of it; anyone refusing to admit it no longer counts as a philosopher; anyone not able to understand it shows by this fact that he has no philosophical 'nous' at all. Here is what the principle consists in. Reality is not made up of distinct pieces juxtaposed alongside each other. Everything is internal to everything else. In the least detail of nature or science, analysis finds again the whole of science and the whole of nature. Each of our states and our acts implicates our whole soul and the whole of its powers. Thought, in a word, is implicated with itself completely in each of its moments or degrees. In short, there is never, as far as we are concerned, a purely external datum, like some kind of brute fact. A datum of this kind would remain absolutely unassimilable, unthinkable; it would be nonexistent for us, for by what would we grasp it? Experience itself is not at all the acquisition of "things" that are first of all completely foreign to us; it is rather a passing from implicit to explicit, a movement in depth revealing to us the latent exigencies and the virtual wealth in any system of knowledge that has been clarified; it is an effort of organic development bringing out what is in reserve or awakening needs that enlarge our action. Thus, no truth enters into us save insofar as it is postulated as a more or less necessary complement by what goes before, as food which to become actual nourishment assumes that the one who receives it has the previous dispositions and preparation, namely the stimulus of hunger and the function of digestion. Even the establishing of a scientific fact has this character in that no fact has a meaning, nor consequently exists for us, save through a theory in whose bosom it is born and into which it is fitted. On these various points, a critical examination of the sciences has recently confirmed the philosophers' reflexions. It is obvious that I cannot enter into detail about this here.[5] But the little that I have said will no doubt suffice to give us a glimpse at least of how what has been called *extrinsicism* is in opposition to modern thought in spirit, attitude and method.

3.   However, despite all that has been said, let us admit the teaching of dogma by simple assertion of a doctrinal Authority that we accept as being above criticism. At least, if these dogmas were to be acceptable they would need to be perfectly intelligible in their formulation, not giving an excuse for any ambiguity in interpretation or any possibility of error about their real meaning. But this is not the case with them. First, their formulas often belong to the language of a particular philosophical system which is not always easily understandable, and which does not always escape the danger of equivocation or even contradiction. It cannot be doubted, for example, that the doctrine of the Word has, both in its origins and in its context, very close links with Alexandrian neo-Platonism; or that the theory of matter and form in the sacraments, or the relations between substance and accident in the dogma of the Real Presence, are closely linked to aristotelian and scholastic ideas. Now, these various philosophies are sometimes doubtful with regard to their bases, and obscure in their expression. In any case, they have long since been discarded and have fallen into neglect among philosophers and scholars. Is it necessary then, in order to be a Christian, to begin by being converted to one of these philosophies?

[5] See *Bulletin de la Société française de philosophie*, February 25, 1904.

This would be a difficult undertaking, in face of which many believers themselves would feel particularly embarrassed. And, moreover, even this would not be sufficient, because the mixture of the several languages deriving from quite heterogenous philosophies causes a further difficulty that is not less embarrassing than the first. And this is not all. In addition, the dogmatic formulas contain metaphors taken from the realm of common sense, as for example when they speak of the divine "fatherhood" or the divine "sonship." It is impossible to give a precise intellectual interpretation of these metaphors and so determine their exact theoretical value, for they are images that cannot be converted into concepts. It would be anthropomorphism to take them literally, and at the same time their deeper meaning cannot be defined. They cannot even be used without reservation nor followed out to the end without landing in ridiculous and absurd consequences. From this derives considerable uncertainty, and this goes to increase the mixture of imaginative symbols with abstract formulas of which we spoke just now. In short, the main difficulty that a number of people these days experience with respect to dogmas is that they do not manage to find in them any meaning to be thought about. These formulations mean nothing to them, or rather they appear to them as indissolubly bound up with a state of mind that they no longer share and that in their view they cannot return to without losing something. Many believers, moreover, implicitly take the same view and prefer to abstain from reflection completely, knowing in advance what obstacles they would meet in thinking out what they believe in the forms proposed to them. As a contemporary philosopher has put it: "What embarrasses the great majority of believers is that, even before we ask them for a *proof* of what they believe, we ask them to *define* precisely what they *affirm* and what they *deny*."[6]

4. Finally, to put things at their best, let us pass over the preceding difficulties. Even after that, there still remains a last objection that seems to be a very serious one. It is that dogmas constitute a body of propositions that is incompatible with the whole body of positive knowledge. They do not belong to the same

[6] Belot: *Bibliothèque du Congrès international de philosophie*, Paris.

level of knowledge as other propositions, either by their content or by their logical character. They cannot then be put together with these latter so as to constitute a coherent system. Whence there follows, if one accepts them, an inevitable disruption of the mind's unity, a disastrous necessity to live in two halves. Being immutable, these propositions appear to be foreign to the progress that is the very essence of thought. Being transcendent, they remain without relationship with any real intellectual life. They do not bring any addition of illumination to any of the problems that concern science and philosophy. The least reproach that can be made against them is that they seem to be without any use, to be vacuous and sterile. This is a very grave reproach in an age when it is being recognized more and more clearly that the value of any truth is mainly measured in terms of the services that it renders, in terms of the new results that it suggests, the consequences with which it is pregnant—in short, to the enlivening influence that it has on the whole body of knowledge.

Such are, briefly summarized, the main reasons why the very idea of dogma is repellent to modern thought. I have tried hard to present them as forcefully as possible, putting myself, in order to expound them, in the position of those who judge them to be decisive, and speaking not in my own name, as it were, but in theirs. It remains to inquire now what conclusions and what lessons we must draw from all this.

* * *

For my part, with my own intellectual upbringing, I cannot but acknowledge that these reasons are perfectly valid. I see no legitimate way to refute the above reasoning. The principles that it involves appear incontestable to me, as do the conclusions it draws from them. In fact, I do not see that it has ever been answered, save by invalid sophistries or by rhetorical tricks.[7] But eloquence is not proof, and neither is diplomacy. I am then led to ask myself whether

---

[7] The discussion in detail of these replies would be a very interesting task; but it cannot be done here.

the only solution might be to show that the notion of dogma that is condemned and castigated by modern thought *is not* the Catholic notion of dogma.

It may perhaps be thought that in speaking in this way I am renouncing the role to which I had promised to limit myself and that I am now definitely asserting theses and no longer just posing questions. This would be a misunderstanding. No doubt, I am affirming something here. But what am I affirming? Nothing but *facts*. It is a fact that today's unbelievers are brought up short before dogmas by the objections mentioned before. Again, it is a fact that anyone (even among believers) who has understood the mentality and the methods of science and contemporary philosophy cannot but agree with these objections. Let it be clearly understood, even those who submit most wholeheartedly and enthusiastically to an Authority placed over them cannot be influenced by it with regard to the question at issue. No Authority can make me find, or prevent me from finding, a train of reasoning solid or weak, nor that such and such a notion has or has not meaning for me. I am not saying merely that it does not have the right to do so, but that it is something radically impossible, for in the last resort it is I who think and not the Authority who thinks for me. Nothing can override this fact. Even I myself cannot make myself, or prevent myself, encounter the conviction the evidence gives in this or that case. No doubt, I admit that Authority imposes such and such a belief on me, and that this leads me to adopt such and such a line of conduct; but how would it impose a belief on me in virtue of a kind of demonstration that I judge to be unconvincing? And how would I obey the Authority if it should impose on me that I should understand a given formulation that I do *not* understand? One might just as well ask me not to think any more at all. No *reason* can be *of faith*; this is a matter of *identity* pure and simple. There is no such thing as a *revealed logic*.

So I come back to what I said just now. And, *speaking as a philosopher*, I declare that I am unable to think any differently from our adversaries on the matters raised above.

Nevertheless, by this declaration I consider that I have done no more than pose a problem. The state of mind I have just described exists; today it is triumphant; even those who most firmly believe participate in it. These are facts that it is impossible not to take account of and that constitute, I repeat, the *formulation* of a question that has to be resolved. Let us see exactly what this question is.

I take it for granted from now on that there is no escape from the objections summarized above as long as the notion of dogma that they involve is retained. Is this to say that we must finally conclude that there is an absolute incompatibility between the idea of dogma and the conditions essential to rational thought? That, to think in a Christian way, it is necessary not to think any more at all? I certainly do not believe that this is so. But, in order to avoid the objections in question and to obtain the reconciliation we want, I ask myself, and I ask in general, whether it is not the very mode in which the idea of dogma is presented that is the true cause of the conflict and whether, in consequence, there is no way at all to change this mode?[8]

Now, when we examine the conception of dogma that is assumed and implied by the four objections set out above, we find surprisingly that it is common to the majority of Catholics and their adversaries. *It is a distinctively intellectualistic conception.* It assumes that the practical and moral meaning of dogma is secondary and derivative, and it puts its intellectual meaning first, considering that this latter *constitutes* dogma while the former is but a simple *consequence* of it. In short, it makes a dogma something like the formulation of a theorem, an intangible formulation of an indemonstrable theorem, but one having nevertheless a speculative and theoretical character and being related primarily to knowledge. This is the common assumption that analysis finds at the basis of the two opposed doctrines, I mean that which welcomes the idea of dogma and that which rejects it. And it is there, I believe, that the crux of the difficulty lies. It is from this presupposition and the conception that follows from it that, in my opinion, derive both the abuses to which the idea of dogma is subject and the objections of principle it raises. As long as we wish to define a dogma as playing the role

---

[8] I hope that the reader will take note of the limits within which this question is situated. It is not in any way a matter of modifying the content of the dogma nor even its traditional religious interpretation, but solely of determining the *modality* of the dogmatic judgment and the qualification proper to it.

of a theoretical formulation, and at the same time however, to attribute to it characteristics that are the inverse of those that make such formulations *true*, we must inevitably conclude that all dogmas are illegitimate.

It is a very curious thing that apologists have not more often recognized so serious a fact, namely that their conception of dogma destroys in advance the theses they wish to establish. On the other hand, this same intellectualistic notion of dogma leads to two very regrettable and unfortunately very frequent exaggerations: the one consisting in the confusion of dogmas properly so called with certain theological opinions and systems (that is, with accessory intellectual schemas); and the other consisting in not seeing that a dogma could never have any scientific meaning, and that there are not any dogmas about, for instance, biological evolution, any more than there are about the movement of the planets or the compressibility of gases.

By going more deeply into these various points we will come to see quite clearly that the problem of dogma is usually wrongly posed. If it is not so in the writings of the great theologians and in the best theological teaching (a matter about which my incompetence prevents me from deciding) it is certainly so in ordinary writings and teaching. At the same time I will show how, in my view, we must pose the question so that a satisfactory solution of it becomes possible.

* * *

From this point on I enter wholly into the sphere where I must limit myself to asking questions. This is quite explicitly my intention even though, for the sake of clarity, I retain a didactic tone. What follows must be taken as a simple exposition of what I usually reply to those who ask me how I think about the idea of dogma. Am I wrong to speak in this way? I am quite ready to recognize that I am wrong, if I am shown that in the eyes of the Church this is not the true way.

First of all, I want to say that a dogma cannot be likened to a theorem of which only the statement is known without demonstration and whose truth is guaranteed only by the master's say-so.

This is however, I well know, the most usual conception of dogma. God, in His act of revelation, is represented as a very wise teacher whose word must be believed when he communicates to his listeners certain conclusions whose proof his listeners are not capable of understanding. To me this seems quite unsatisfactory.[9]

Without going back over the general considerations I have already developed, let us take some examples that will make more precise what we have as yet only seen in general terms.

"God is personal." There we have a dogma. Let us try seeing it as a statement having primarily an intellectual meaning and a speculative import, a proposition belonging primarily to the sphere of theoretical knowledge. I pass over the difficulties raised by the word "God." But let us consider the word "personal." How must it be understood? If we say that the use of this word warns us to think of the divine personality in the image of what psychological experience shows us, on the basis of what common sense designates by the same word—as a human personality that has been idealised and raised to perfection—then we are being completely anthropomorphic. Catholics will certainly be in agreement with their adversaries in rejecting such a conception. We need not advert to the fact that taking things to the ideal limit is a rather tricky business, and one that lends itself to error or at least to pure verbiage; in any event it is incapable of providing us with anything more than very vague metaphors and finally perhaps, even contradictory conclusions.

Should we limit ourselves to saying that the divine personality is essentially incomparable and transcendent? Very well then, but it is now very badly named, in a way that seems bound to lead us into illusion. For if we say that the divine personality does not resemble anything that we know, by what right do we call it "personality"? Logically it must be designated by a word belonging to God alone and which cannot be used in any other instance. This word will therefore be radically indefinable. Imagine a set of syllables without any positive signification at all and let A be this

---

[9] God has spoken, so it is said. What does the word "spoken" mean here? Of course, it is a metaphor. But what reality does it conceal? The whole difficulty lies in this.

set. Then on our hypothesis, "God is personal" has no more meaning than "God is A." Is there any idea in this?

For anyone looking for an intellectualistic interpretation of the dogma "God is personal," the dilemma is inescapable. Either you define the word "personality" and then you fall inevitably into anthropomorphism; or you do not define it and then you fall no less inevitably into agnosticism. In other words, we are in a circle.[10]

Let us take yet another example: the resurrection of Jesus. If this dogma—whatever in the last resort may be its practical consequences—has as its main aim the increasing of our knowledge by guaranteeing the truth of a certain fact, if it is primarily a statement of an intellectual kind, then the first question it raises is this: what precise meaning does it suppose is to be given to the word "resurrection"? Jesus, after having gone through death, came to life again. What does that mean from a theoretical point of view? Not, doubtlessly, that after three days Jesus reappeared in a state identical with the state He was in before the crucifixion. The Gospel itself expressly tells us the contrary: the risen Jesus was no longer subject to ordinary physical or psychological laws; His "glorified" body was no longer perceivable under the same conditions as before, etc. What is being said here? The notion of "life" has not therefore the same content according to whether we apply it to the period that preceded the crucifixion or to the period following it. Well then, what does it represent with respect to this second period? Nothing that is expressible in concepts. It is a simple metaphor that cannot be converted into precise ideas. Here again it would be necessary, if we were to be logical, to invent another word, a word reserved for this single case, a word of which no standard definition would therefore be possible.

Let us borrow a final example from the dogma of the Real Presence. Here it is the term "presence" that needs interpretation. What does it usually mean? A being is said to be "present" when it is perceptible, or rather, although remaining in itself imperceptible to the senses, it manifests itself through perceptible effects. Now, according to the dogma itself, neither of these two conditions

---

[10] The same remarks could be made a propos the propositions, "God is self-aware," "God loves," "God wills," "God thinks," etc.

is realized in the present case. The presence in question is a mysterious presence, ineffable, extraordinary, without analogy with anything usually understood by this term. I ask then what idea there is in it for us? Something that can neither be analyzed nor even defined cannot be said to be an "idea" save by a misuse of words. You want the dogma to be a statement of an intellectual kind. But what does it state? It is impossible to indicate what it is with any precision. Does not this condemn the hypothesis then?

Ultimately, the attempt to conceive of dogmas as statements whose primary function is to communicate certain items of theoretical knowledge seemingly meets impossibilities at every turn. Inevitably it appears to have the effect of making dogmas into pure nonsense. Perhaps therefore we must give up the attempt altogether. Let us see then what other kind of meaning alone remains possible and licit.

* * *

If I am not mistaken, a dogma has first of all a *negative* sense. It excludes and condemns certain errors rather than positively determining their truth.[11]

Let us return to our examples. Take the dogma "God is personal." I do not see this at all as a definition of the divine personality. It teaches me nothing about this personality; it does not reveal its nature to me; it does not provide me with any explicit idea of it. But I do see that it tells me: "God is not impersonal," that is, God is not a simple law, a formal category, an ideal principle, an abstract entity, any more than He is a universal substance or some kind of cosmic force pervading everything. In short, the dogma "God is personal" does not contribute any new and positive idea, and it does not, moreover, guarantee the truth of one particular system among all those that the history of philosophy shows to have been put forward. Rather it warns me that such and such forms of pantheism are false and must be rejected.

I would say the same of the Real Presence. The dogma does

---

[11] We shall see in a moment how dogmas are more and better than this. But in order to begin I am taking up a strictly intellectual point of view.

not formulate for me a theory about this presence; it does not even teach me what it consists in. But it tells me very clearly that it should *not* be understood in such and such a way, nor again in other ways that have been proposed in the past—it tells me, for example, that the consecrated host should not be taken solely as a symbol or type of Jesus.

The resurrection of Christ lends itself to the same observations. The dogma does not teach me at all what the mechanics of this exceptional happening were, nor what the second life of Jesus is like. In a word, it does not communicate to me any idea. Rather, on the contrary, it excludes certain ideas that I could be tempted to assume. Death has not put an end to the action of Jesus on the things of this world; He still intervenes and lives among us, and not only as a dead thinker whose influence remains fruitful and perennial, and whose work has effects for a long time after. Jesus is literally our contemporary; in short, death has not been for Him, as it is for men in general, the definitive ending of His practical activity. That is what the dogma of the resurrection teaches us.[12]

Need we stress this point any more? To me that does not seem useful for the moment. The preceding examples are sufficient to make clear the principle of interpretation I have in view. No doubt, long discussions would be needed if we wanted to set out in detail all the consequences of this principle and all its possible applications, and a study of the different dogmas one by one would then become indispensable. But this is not my aim here. I wish to limit myself to merely indicating an idea. This is why I am not interested either in multiplying examples, or even in working any of them out completely.

Nevertheless, the idea in view is not a new one. It belongs to the most authentic tradition. Indeed, is it not in fact the classical teaching of the theologians and doctors that, in the supernatural order, the surest method of investigation is the *via negationis?* In this regard let me recall a well-known text of St Thomas: "The way of remotion is to be used above all in the investigation of the divine

---

[12] "Resumption of His body" can only mean "resumption of practical activity," since it is understood that it does not mean "recommencement of ordinary bodily phenomena."

nature. For the divine nature transcends every form that our intellect attains to; and thus we cannot apprehend it by knowing what it is, but we have some knowledge of it by knowing what it is not."[13]

I must, however, notice an objection that could be made. It may be allowed without difficulty that the dogmatic codification promulgated by the Church during the course of history has primarily a negative character, at least when it is envisaged from an intellectual point of view, as we are doing at present. The Church herself declares in fact that she has not any mission to produce new revelations, but solely to guard the deposit of faith. And the negative method that has been adopted is perfectly suited to this mission. All the same, what does the deposit itself consist in, if not in a certain set of basic affirmations? Take the first expression of the Christian faith, the *Credo*. What could be more positive? Now, this is precisely the basis of doctrine, that which characterizes it and constitutes it. Moreover, if we speak of *revelation* we are certainly speaking of *affirmations* and not of *negations*.

Most certainly, I do not contest anything of this. But we must distinguish. The Symbol of Nicaea and Constantinople already contains many traces of negative dogmatic elaboration—on the divinity of Jesus Christ against the Arian heresy, on the procession of the Holy Spirit against the Macedonians, etc.[14] To this extent, then, there is nothing contrary to our conclusions; it is the grammatical form alone that is affirmative here. Basically, it is a matter of errors being excluded rather than theories being formulated. But let us take the Symbol of the Apostles. In this case there is nothing negative at all; but there is also nothing that is strictly intellectual and theoretical, nothing that is strictly related to the sphere of speculative knowledge—in a word, nothing that resembles the statement of theorems. It is a profession of faith, a declaration of attitude. We will be looking at dogmas from this practical point of view in a moment—a view which, I hasten to say, is in my opinion the principal one. However, let us remain a moment more at the intellectual point of view. The Apostolic *Credo*, in its primary

[13] *Contra Gentiles*, I. 14.
[14] It would be easy to emphasize the example of the *consubstantialem* or that of the *Filoque*.

form, affirms the existence of realities about which it does not give any representative theory of even a rudimentary sort. Therefore its only role as regards abstract and reflective knowledge is as follows: To pose objects and, therefore, problems. Finally, it can be seen, the objection proposed above is not conclusive, and we can maintain our theses until further orders.

Thus, insofar as they are statements within the theoretical sphere, dogmas have a negative sense. History proves this, in that it makes us witnesses of their successive development corresponding to the development of heresies.[15] The birth of any dogma whatever has always followed the same path, always presented the same phases. At the beginning, there are purely human speculations, explanatory systems that are quite similar to other philosophical systems—in short, attempts at theories relative to the religious facts, to the mysterious realities that are lived by the Christian people in their practical religious belief. Only after this come the dogmas, in order to condemn certain of these attempts, to tax some of these conceptions with error, to exclude some of these intellectual schemas. From this derives the fact that dogmatic formulas often borrow expressions from various philosophies without troubling themselves to fuse together and unify these heterogeneous languages. There are no difficulties about this (save for those that attend the employment of concepts deriving from different sources) so long as the dogmas do not attempt to constitute by themselves a rational theory, an intelligible system of positive affirmations, but rather restrict themselves to ruling out of order certain hypotheses and conjectures of the human mind. On the contrary, it is natural that each dogma should adopt the point of view proper to the doctrine that it is proscribing, so as to get at it expressly without danger of ambiguity. From this also derives the fact that dogmatic formulas can legislate about the incomparable and the transcendent and yet not fall into the contradictions of anthropomorphism or agnosticism. It is man who, with his opinions, his theories, his systems, provides dogmas with their intelligible matter.[16] The dogmas sometimes restrict

---

[15] Cf. the usual formula of conciliar decrees: "Si quis dixerit . . . anathema sit."

[16] From the theoretical point of view, that is. Dogmas are thought out in terms of the human systems to which they are opposed.

themselves to declaring a *veto*, sometimes to declaring "This opinion, this theory, this system will not do," without ever indicating why they cannot be accepted nor with what we must replace them. Thus dogmatic definitions do not limit knowledge, do not stop progress; they simply close off false paths.

From a strictly intellectual point of view, dogmas have, it seems to me, only the negative or prohibitive meaning that I have just spoken about. If they were to formulate absolute truth adequately (assuming that this supposition is meaningful), they would be unintelligible to us. If they expressed merely an imperfect, relative, and changing truth, they could not legitimately command our assent. The only fundamental way to cut short all objections of principle against dogmas is to conceive these latter, as we have done, as definable as speculative propositions merely in relation to the already presupposed doctrines on which they pronounce judgement without giving any reasons. Is it not indeed the teaching of the theologians, even of the most intellectualistic of them, that in a dogmatic statement the reasons that can be incorporated in the text are not in themselves objects of faith requiring belief?

An important corollary follows at once from what has been said, namely that the true method for studying dogmas (that is, from the intellectual point of view) is the historical method. The discipline that is called Positive Theology attempts to carry out this task. It has, much more than so many purely dialectical discussions, a genuine apologetical value. In any case, it is impossible to understand dogmatic statements, let alone justify them, if we do not begin by resituating them within their historical context, outside of which their real meaning gradually evaporates into vagueness and sometimes ends by disappearing altogether.

Nevertheless, dogmas do not just have a negative meaning. And even the negative meaning that they exhibit when they are seen from a certain angle does not constitute their essential and fundamental meaning. This is because they are not merely propositions of a theoretical kind, and because they should not be examined solely from the intellectual point of view, from the point of view of knowledge. This is what we must now make clear.

* * *

Here more than ever I emphasize that the intention and drift of the following pages should not be misunderstood. My affirmative tone is, I repeat, simply a device of clarity. Basically, my intention is still the same as I defined it at the beginning.

This is, I would say, the form in which experience has shown me that the notion of dogma is most easily assimilable by the contemporary mind: Primarily a dogma has a *practical* meaning. Primarily, it states a *prescription of a practical kind*. Primarily it is the statement of a *rule of practical conduct*. There lies its principal value, and there lies its positive signification. This does not mean that it has no relation with thought, for (1) there are also duties concerning the activity of thinking; and (2) it is implicitly affirmed by the dogma itself that reality contains (in one form or another) what is needed to justify the prescribed conduct as reasonable and advantageous.

In this connection I would like to cite the following passage from Fr. Laberthonnière: "Dogmas are not simply puzzling and obscure formulas which God in His omnipotence promulgates so as to humble our intellect's pride. They have a moral and practical meaning; they have an essential meaning that is more or less accessible to us in proportion to the degree of spirituality that we possess."[17]

In a word, is not this how in daily life we answer those who have been converted and who find themselves in theoretical perplexity in which they flounder despite their good will: "Leave all that; it is not important. Don't think that God requires so many formalities. In Bossuet's words, go to Him honestly, openly, simply. Religion is less an intellectual adherence to a system of speculative proposition than a lived participation in mysterious realities." Why then do we not square our theory with our practice?

Let us keep to the same examples (especially in that they represent the different types of dogma). "God is personal" means, "Behave in your relations with God as you would in your relations with a human person." Likewise, "Jesus is risen" means, "Be in your relations with Him as you would have been before His death; as you are before a contemporary of yours." In the same way,

[17] *Essais de philosophie religieuse*, p. 272. Paris, Lethelleux.

again, the dogma of the Real Presence means that we must have before the consecrated host an attitude identical with that which we would have before Jesus if He became visible to us. And so on. It would be easy to multiply examples and, moreover, to develop each one in detail.[18]

It is not open to doubt, nor doubtless will anyone contest it, that dogmas can and must be interpreted in this way. It cannot be said too often that Christianity is not a system of speculative philosophy, but a source and rule of life, a discipline of moral and religious action, in short, a set of practical means for obtaining salvation. It is not surprising then, that its dogmas are concerned primarily with conduct rather than with pure reflective knowledge.[19]

I do not think it necessary to dwell on this point at length. However, I want to indicate in a few brief words the most important consequences of the principle that has just been put forward.

First of all, it is clear that the general objections rehearsed at the beginning of this article do not affect the above conception of dogma in the same way and to the same extent as the ordinary intellectualistic conception. This latter conception aggravates the quarrel and makes the difficulty insoluble. But now, on the other hand, the possibility of a solution may be glimpsed. As we no longer have to obtain a theoretical statement in conditions that are radically opposed to those laid down by logical method, we are no longer confronted with a logical scandal but solely with a problem regarding the relations between thought and action. No doubt, this is a difficult problem, but it is a tractable one and, in any event, it does not appear absurd in its very formulation.

There are, indeed, serious questions to be resolved. We must in some way provide a proof and justification of dogma. And that is not an easy thing to do at all. All the same, one of the largest obstacles has been removed. Practical truths are established in a

---

[18] I am not at all claiming that the above commentary gives the complete meaning of the dogmas cited; I simply want to indicate a direction for further study.

[19] This is why assent to dogmas is always an act of the will, not the inevitable result of a logically compelling train of reasoning.

different way from speculative truths. Recourse to authority, totally unacceptable in the sphere of pure thought, seems *a priori* less shocking in the sphere of action, for if authority has legitimate rights anywhere it is surely in the domain of practical action.

The First Vatican Council tells us, "If anyone should say that there are no true mysteries (in the strict sense) contained in divine revelation, but that all the dogmas of faith can be derived by reason from natural principles and so be understood and demonstrated, let him be anathema." But, if faith in dogmas were primarily a kind of knowledge, an adherence to statements of an intellectual kind, we would not be able to see how assent to irreducible mysteries could ever be legitimate or even possible, nor in what it could possibly consist, nor what kind of use or value it would have for us, nor how faith could be a virtue. On the other hand, all this becomes understandable if faith in dogmas is a practical submission to commandments regarding action. Nothing is more to be expected than that activity should present mysteries to the intellect.[20]

The Vatican Council tells us again: "If anyone says that assent to the Christian faith is not free . . . let him be anathema." This text is generally explained by recognizing that the reasons for belief, the motives of credibility, are not of invincible force, of mathematical evidence, and that consequently a decisive act of the will or heart is always necessary to bring our investigation to a definitive conclusion. Is not this to admit implicitly that we cannot see faith in dogma as an act that is primarily intellectual, without thereby making it inferior to ordinary acts of thought? How would such an act—an act performed in conditions that are contrary to the nature of thought—be legitimate or even possible? However, on the other hand, we can very well conceive how practical acceptance of commandments regarding action depends upon our free will and gains in merit from not being able to be brought about by logical necessity.

Let us emphasize this point a little, for it is of central importance in the problem of the relationship between reason and faith.

---

[20] For the believer submission to dogma is, then, from one point of view, what submission to facts is for the scholar.

At the outset, apologetic comes up against a very serious difficulty about which we are perhaps not always sufficiently concerned. On the one hand, it is taken for granted that the act of faith is a free act and that its object, as its supreme motive, is supernatural. But, on the other hand, an act of reason must precede and prepare for the act of faith, because the human mind must have a grip on the dogma to some extent if the dogma is to exist for it. As St Thomas well said: "With regard to those things that are of faith . . . no one would believe them unless he saw that they were to be believed."

Now, how can we reconcile these two contrary requirements in an intellectualistic system of interpretation? Either we maintain (as some have done in fact) that the apologetical proofs are absolutely certain and rigorous, and then what will become of the freedom of the act of faith? Or, in order to safeguard this freedom, we admit that the proofs are insufficient and only more or less probable, and then faith will lack a basis, since an insufficient proof is not an acceptable proof, above all in such a serious and difficult matter. An intellectualistic attitude leaves us at a loss before such a dilemma—freedom not belonging to the sphere of pure intelligence and not having any place nor any role in the proceedings of discursive reason.

But with the other attitude, the dilemma can be resolved since in this case the dialectic in question is one of action and life, not simply reasoning, and freedom bears on life and action.

In the same way, the objection about the intelligibility of the dogmatic formulas also fails. These latter, irremediably obscure, indeed inconceivable, if we expect them to provide positive determinations of the truth from a speculative and theoretical point of view, show, on the other hand, that they are capable of being understood if we agree to construe them merely as teachings concerning practical conduct. What difficulties, for instance, do we find in understanding dogmas about the divine personality, or the Real Presence, or the resurrection, within the practical system of interpretation outlined just now? Though they are mysteries for the mind that expects explanatory theories, these dogmas are nevertheless susceptible of being stated in a perfectly distinct way if they are seen as prescriptions about our activity. The language of common sense is then appropriate here, as is the usage of anthropomorphic symbols and of analogies and metaphors, and neither the one nor the other engenders insoluble complications, since in this case it is a matter solely of propositions relative to man and his attitudes.

We also see now what relationship dogmas have with real life. *A propos* this subject we foresee the possibility of an experimental study and of a gradual deepening of knowledge—something that has been lacking until now. We understand, finally, how dogmas can be common to everyone, accessible to everyone, despite the inequality of men's intellects, whereas when they were conceived in the intellectualistic mode we were inevitably led to make them the exclusive property of a select group. I do not have the time to develop here these various considerations as much as I would like; but I suppose that a simple indication will suffice for the moment and that the reader will fill in the detail for himself without difficulty.

However, to avoid all misunderstanding, I think it necessary to forestall a possible objection.

I have spoken of *practice*. This word must be properly understood. I take it in its widest sense. *Action* and *life* in this sense are synonyms. *Practice* does not in any way mean some kind of *blind procedure, at odds with thought, without relationship with knowledge*. In fact, there is an *activity of thought* that accompanies all our actions, a *life of thought* that permeates our whole life. In other words, knowing is a function of life, a practical act in its own proper way. This function, this act, is also called *experience*. This is a term that indicates that it is not a matter of actions being performed without any understanding at all, and also that the understanding in question is not at all that of simple discursive reason.

I have also spoken of activity presenting mysteries to the intelligence. By way of clarification I cited the example of scientific facts. To understand what I meant by this, it is important to remember that a scientific fact is not something that is just passively registered. If there is an appearance of a purely external datum, of a totally opaque mystery, of a brutal imposition coming from outside, this is with respect to the discursive understanding. But *thought-action*, of which I spoke just now, escapes this appearance. It infinitely transcends purely intellectual thought. I had no intention of saying anything else than this.[21]

There is therefore a necessary connection between dogmas and thought. It is at once a right and a duty not to be content with believing blindly in dogmas, but to work to the best of one's abilities at thinking about them. A general state of separation, of watertight compartments, of double-entry bookkeeping in one's consciousness, is not something desirable—not even, really, possible. It is contrary to the exigencies of philosophy which looks for spiritual unity. And, finally, it is contrary to the exigencies of morality, which cannot approve an action that is systematically thoughtless.

But thought, in its application to dogmas, should not misunderstand the primarily practical meaning of these latter. The test *of lived experience* and not *intellectualistic dialectic*—that is the procedure we need. The principle that inspires it is perfectly expressed in the sacred text: *Qui facit veritatem venit ad lucem.*

Translated thus into terms of action, the traditional methods of *analogy* and *eminence* take on a very exact meaning. They affirm, under the guise of metaphors and images, that supernatural reality contains what is necessary to make it obligatory that our attitude and conduct with respect to it should be of a particular kind. Images and metaphors—incurably vague and fallacious when one sees them as some kind of approximations to impossible concepts— become on the contrary wonderfully illuminating and suggestive as soon as one looks on them simply as a language of action expressing the truth in terms of its practical repercussions in us.

We have still to clarify finally the relations of dogmas, understood in the way we have just outlined, with theoretical and speculative thought, with pure knowledge. In what manner do they bear upon our intellectual life? How does their intangible and transcendent character leave complete freedom of inquiry untouched, as well as the unquestionable right of the mind to reject every conception that would claim to impose itself from the outside? It is easy enough to see this.

---

[21] The reader who wishes to go deeper into this point can look at the various articles that I have published since 1899 in the *Revue de Métaphysique et de Morale* and the *Bulletin de la Société française de philosophie*.

A Catholic is obliged to assent unreservedly to dogmas. But I cannot bring myself to think that this means that a theory, an intellectual schema, is thereby imposed on him. A constraint of this kind would in fact inevitably have quite unacceptable consequences: (1) Dogmas would then be nothing more than purely verbal formulas, mere passwords whose repetition would constitute a kind of unintelligible order; (2) these dogmas could not, moreover, be common either to all times or to all minds.[22]

No, dogmas are not at all like this. Their meaning, as we have seen, is above all practical and moral. The Catholic, obliged to admit them, is bound by them only to rules of conduct, not to particular ideas. So also he is not committed to receiving them as mere literal formulas. They present to him, on the contrary, a quite positive content, clearly intelligible and understandable. I add that this content, being related to practice alone, is not relative to the variable degrees of intelligence and knowledge; it remains exactly the same for the scholar and the unlettered man, for the clever and the lowly, for the ages of high civilization and for races that are still barbarous. In short, it is independent of the successive phases that human thought passes through in its urge towards knowledge, so that there is thus *one single faith for all men*.

This having been said, the Catholic, after having accepted dogma, retains complete freedom to postulate for himself this or that theory or intellectual schema as corresponding objects of, for example, the divine personality, the Real Presence, or the resurrection. It is up to him to give his preference to the theory that suits him best, to the intellectual schema that he may judge the better one. His position here is the same as before any scientific or philosophical speculation at all, and it is allowable for him to take up the same attitude in this case as in the latter. One thing only is demanded of him, one obligation only binds him: his theory must justify the practical rules stated by the dogma, his intellectual schema must account for the practical prescriptions laid down by the dogma. In a word, this latter appears almost as the statement of a *fact* about which it is possible to construct many different theories—a fact

---

[22] In two words, *esotericism* and *pharisaism:* this would be the inevitable dual danger.

which each theory must take account of, as the expression of a *datum* about which there are many legitimate intellectual schemas, but which no explanatory system could properly escape.[23]

The development that we have seen to be normal to religious thought as it is elaborated follows quite naturally from all this. Take any dogma at all: the divine personality, the Real Presence, the resurrection of Jesus. By itself and in itself it has only practical meaning. *But a mysterious reality corresponds to it and it therefore poses a theoretical problem to the intellect.* The human mind seizes upon this problem immediately and it thinks up explanations, solutions, systems, in all this simply following the laws of its own nature codified in the rules of method and in the principles of reason.[24] Insofar as the theory thus elaborated respects the practical meaning of the dogma, the latter allows it full scope. Judging the theory's value then remains a matter of pure human speculation and no authority external to thought itself has either the right or the power to intervene. But if a theory should perchance come up that affected the dogma in its own proper domain by altering its practical meaning, then immediately the dogma itself would rise up against it and condemn it, becoming thus a negative intellectual statement superimposed on the rule of conduct that it was purely and simply first of all.

We see then how the two meanings of dogma—the practical meaning and the negative meaning—come together, the latter being subordinated to the former. We can see, moreover, how dogmas are immutable and yet how there is an evolution of dogma. What is unchanging in a dogma is the orientation that it gives to our practical activity, the direction in which it influences our conduct. But the explanatory theories, the intellectual schemas, change constantly in the course of time in relation to individuals and epochs, exposed to every fluctuation and every relativity manifested by the history of the human mind. The Christians of the first centuries did not hold the same opinions as we do on the nature

---

[23] In this way we must distinguish within a dogma between its *intellectual formulation* and its *underlying reality*.

[24] In this respect, the Middle Ages had an independence and boldness that we have forgotten all about.

and person of Jesus, and neither did they pose the same problems. The unlearned person of today has not the same ideas on these lofty and difficult subjects nor the same intellectual preoccupations as the philosopher. However, unlearned or philosophers, men of the first or the twentieth century, all Catholics have always had and always will have the same practical attitude towards Jesus.

* * *

It is time to conclude. I will do so as briefly and as clearly as possible.

Two main conclusions appear to me to have come out of the preceding discussion:

1.   *The intellectualistic conception in vogue today makes most of the objections raised by the idea of dogma quite insoluble.*

2.   *A doctrine of the primacy of action allows us, on the contrary, to resolve the problem without abandoning any of the rights of pure thought, or any of the exigencies of dogma.*

If these conclusions were admitted, there would follow for present-day Apologetic an inescapable necessity to modify a number of its arguments and methods.

But now, can these conclusions be admitted without any harm resulting for faith? It is up to the theologians to tell us about this and, in the event of their reply being negative, to inform us how they think they can otherwise overcome the obstacles that stand in our way.

9

Religious language is
moral–emotive

Matthew Arnold

According to Arnold, religious language is not used in a scientific
way but in a *literary* way, that is, in the manner of "poetry and
eloquence." What distinguishes religious language from poetry
proper is that it is concerned with the guidance of human conduct.
Religious language is thus a species of moral language whose
general function it is to prescribe what we ought to do, the only
difference between religion and morality being one of degree.
Religion, says Arnold in a famous passage, is "ethics heightened,
enkindled, lit up by feeling"; it is "morality touched by emotion."
Insofar as we dwell upon the rules of morality and appreciate their
beneficence, we come to have favorable feelings or emotions
about them, and it is these feelings that we endeavor to express
(and so to evoke similar feelings in others) by religious
language.

In the sense that there is a scientific basis for human morality,
then there is a scientific basis for religion and religious language.
Thus, when we say that there is a God, what we mean in scientific
terms is that all things (including ourselves) have a law of their
being and tend to fulfill it, so that when it is said that we must
obey God's will, what we mean scientifically is that there is "a law
of things which is found in conscience, and which is an indication,
irrespective of our arbitrary wish and fancy, of what we ought to
do." However, the point of talking about God and God's will is

not to give us this scientific information, but rather to make us *feel* about it and so to act upon it.

Matthew Arnold (1822–1888) was a celebrated nineteenth-century English literary sage. These passages are taken from *Literature and Dogma*.

We have said elsewhere[1] how much it has contributed to the misunderstanding of St. Paul, that terms like *grace*, *new birth*, *justification*,—which he used in a fluid and passing way, as men use terms in common discourse or in eloquence and poetry, to describe approximately, but only approximately, what they have present before their mind, but do not profess that their mind does or can grasp exactly or adequately,—that such terms people have blunderingly taken in a fixed and rigid manner, as if they were symbols with as definite and fully grasped a meaning as the names *line* or *angle*, and proceeded to use them on this supposition; terms, in short, which with St. Paul are *literary* terms, theologians have employed as if they were *scientific* terms.

But if one desires to deal with this mistake thoroughly, one must observe it in that supreme term with which religion is filled,—the term *God*. The seemingly incurable ambiguity in the mode of employing this word is at the root of all our religious differences and difficulties. People use it as if it stood for a perfectly definite and ascertained idea, from which we might, without more ado, extract propositions and draw inferences, just as we should from any other definite and ascertained idea. For instance, I open a book which controverts what its author thinks dangerous views about religion, and I read: 'Our sense of morality tells us so-and-so; our sense of God, on the other hand, tells us so-and-so.' And again, 'the impulse in man to seek God' is distinguished, as if the distinction were self-evident and explained itself, from 'the impulse in man to seek his highest perfection.' Now, *morality* represents for everybody a thoroughly definite and ascertained idea:—the idea of human

From Matthew Arnold, *Literature and Dogma*, 4th ed. (London, Smith, Elder, 1874), pp. 10–24, 41–43.
[1] *Culture and Anarchy*, (London, Smith, Elder, 1869) p. 178.

conduct regulated in a certain manner. Everybody, again, understands distinctly enough what is meant by man's perfection:—his reaching the best which his powers and circumstances allow him to reach. And the word 'God' is used, in connection with both these words, morality and perfection, as if it stood for just as definite and ascertained an idea as they do; an idea drawn from experience, just as the ideas are which they stand for; an idea about which every one was agreed, and from which we might proceed to argue and to make inferences, with the certainty that, as in the case of morality and perfection, the basis on which we were going everyone knew and granted. But, in truth, the word 'God' is used in most cases,—not by the Bishops of Winchester and Gloucester, but by mankind in general,—as by no means a term of science or exact knowledge, but a term of poetry and eloquence, a term *thrown out*, so to speak, at a not fully grasped object of the speaker's consciousness, a *literary* term, in short; and mankind mean different things by it as their consciousness differs.

The first question, then, is, how people are using the word; whether in this literary way, or in the scientific way of the Bishops of Winchester and Gloucester. The second question is, what, supposing them to use the term as one of poetry and eloquence, and to import into it, therefore, a great deal of their own individual feelings and character, is yet the common substratum of idea on which, in using it, they all rest. For this will then be, so far as they are concerned, the scientific sense of the word, the sense in which we can use it for purposes of argument and inference without ambiguity. Is this *substratum*, at any rate, coincident with the scientific idea of the Bishops of Winchester and Gloucester?—will then be the question.

Strictly and formally the word 'God', we now learn from the philologists, means, like its kindred Aryan words *Theos*, *Deus*, and *Deva*, simply *brilliant*. In a certain narrow way, therefore, this is the one exact and scientific sense of the word. It was long thought to mean *good*, and so Luther took it to mean *the best that man knows or can know*; and in this sense, as a matter of fact and history, mankind constantly use the word. But then there is also the scientific sense held by theologians, deduced from the ideas of substance, identity, causation, design, and so on; but taught, they say, or at least implied in the Bible, and on which all the Bible rests. According to this scientific sense of theology, God is a person, the great first cause, the moral and intelligent governor of the universe; Jesus Christ consubstantial with him; and the Holy Ghost a person proceeding from the other two. This is the sense for which, or for portions of which, the Bishops of Winchester and Gloucester are so zealous to do something.

Other people, however, who fail to perceive the force of such a deduction from the abstract-ideas above mentioned, who indeed think it quite hollow, but who are told that this sense is in the Bible, and that they must receive it if they receive the Bible, conclude that in that case they had better receive neither the one nor the other. Something of this sort it was, no doubt, which made Professor Huxley tell the London School Board lately, that 'if these islands had no religion at all, it would not enter into his mind to introduce the religious idea by the agency of the Bible.' Of such people there are now a great many; and indeed there could hardly, for those who value the Bible, be a greater example of the sacrifices one is some-times called upon to make for the truth, than to find that, for the truth as held by the Bishops of Winchester and Gloucester, if it is the truth, one must sacrifice the allegiance of so many people to the Bible.

But surely, if there be anything with which metaphysics have nothing to do, and where a plain man, without skill to walk in the arduous paths of abstruse reasoning, may yet find himself at home, it is religion. For the object of religion is *conduct*; and conduct is really, however men may overlay it with philosophical disquisitions, the simplest thing in the world. That is to say, it is the simplest thing in the world as far as *understanding* is concerned; as regards *doing*, it is the hardest thing in the world. Here is the difficulty,—to *do* what we very well know ought to be done; and instead of facing this, men have searched out another with which they occupy them-selves by preference,—the origin of what is called the moral sense, the genesis and physiology of conscience, and so on. No one denies that here, too, is difficulty, or that the difficulty is a proper object for the human faculties to be exercised upon; but the difficulty here is speculative. It is not the difficulty of religion, which is a practical one; and it often tends to divert the attention from this. Yet surely the difficulty of religion is great enough by itself, if men would but consider it, to satisfy the most voracious appetite for difficulties. It extends to rightness in the whole range of what we call *conduct*; in three-fourths, therefore, at the very lowest computation, of human life. The only doubt is whether we ought not to make the range of conduct wider still, and to say it is four-fifths of human life, or five-sixths. But it is better to be under the mark than over it; so let us be content with reckoning conduct as three-fourths of human life.

And to recognise in what way conduct is this, let us eschew all school-terms, like *moral sense*, and *volitional*, and *altruistic*, which philosophers employ, and let us help ourselves by the most palpable and plain examples. When the rich man in the Bible-parable says: 'Soul, thou hast much goods laid up for many years; take thine ease, eat, drink, and be merry!'—those *goods* which he thus assigns as the stuff with which human life is mainly concerned (and so in practice it really is),—those goods and our dealings with them,—our taking our ease, eating, drinking, being merry,—are the matter of *conduct*, the range where it is exercised. Eating, drinking, ease, pleasure, money, the intercourse of the sexes, the giving free swing to one's temper and instincts,—these are the matters with which conduct is concerned, and with which all mankind know and feel it to be concerned.

Or when Protagoras points out of what things we are, from childhood till we die, being taught and admonished, and says (but it is lamentable that here we have not at hand Mr. Jowett, who so excellently introduces the enchanter Plato and his personages, but must use our own words): 'From the time he can understand what is said to him, nurse, and mother, and teacher, and father too, are bending their efforts to this end,—to make the child *good*; teaching and showing him, as to everything he has to do or say, how this is right and that not right, and this is honourable and that vile, and this is holy and that unholy, and this do and that do not;'—Protagoras, also, when he says this, bears his testimony to the scope and nature of *conduct*, tells us what conduct is. Or, once more, when Monsieur Littré (and we hope to make our peace with the Comtists by quoting an author of theirs in preference to those authors whom all the British public is now reading and quoting),—when Monsieur Littré, in a most ingenious essay on the origin of morals, traces up, better, perhaps, than any one else, all our impulses into two elementary instincts, the instinct of self-preservation and the reproductive instinct,—then we take his theory and we say, that all the impulses which can be conceived as derivable from the instinct of self-preservation in us and the reproductive instinct, these terms being applied in their ordinary sense, are the matter of *conduct*. It is evident this includes, to say no more, every impulse relating to temper, every impulse relating to sensuality; and we all know how much that is.

How we deal with these impulses is the matter of *conduct*,—how we obey, regulate, or restrain them;—that, and nothing else. Not whether M. Littré's theory is true or false; for whether it be true or false, there the impulses confessedly now are, and the business of conduct is to deal with them. But it is evident, if conduct deals with these, both how important a thing conduct is, and how simple a thing. Important, because it covers so large a portion of human life, and the portion common to all sorts of people; simple, because, though there needs perpetual admonition to form conduct, the admonition is needed not to determine what we ought to do, but to make us do it.

And as to this simplicity, all moralists are agreed. 'Let any plain honest man,' says Bishop Butler, 'before he engages in any course of action' (he means action of the very kind we call *conduct*), 'ask himself: Is this I am going about right or is it wrong? is it good or is it evil? I do not in the least doubt but that this question would be answered agreeably to truth and virtue by *almost any fair man in almost any circumstance*.' And Bishop Wilson says: 'Look up to God' (by which he means just this, consult your conscience,) 'at all times, and he will, *as in a glass*, discover what is fit to be done.' And the Preacher's well-known sentence is exactly to the same effect: 'God made man upright; but they have sought out many inventions,'—or, as it more correctly is, '*many abstruse reasonings*.' Let us hold fast to this, and we shall find we have a stay by the help of which even poor weak men, with no pretensions to be logical athletes, may stand firmly.

And so, when we are asked, what is the object of religion?— let us reply: *Conduct*. And when we are asked further, what is conduct?—let us answer: *Three-fourths of life*.

And certainly we need not go far about to prove that conduct, or 'righteousness,' which is the object of religion, is in a special manner the object of Bible-religion. The word 'righteousness' is the master-word of the Old Testament. *Keep judgment and do righteousness! Cease to do evil, learn to do well!* these words being taken in their plainest sense of conduct. *Offer the sacrifice*, not of victims and ceremonies, as the way of the world in religion then was, but: Offer the sacrifice *of righteousness!* The great concern of the New Testament is likewise righteousness, but righteousness reached through particular means, righteousness by the means of Jesus Christ. A sentence which sums up the New Testament, and assigns the ground whereon the Christian Church stands, is, as we have elsewhere said,[2] this: *Let every one that nameth the name of Christ depart from iniquity!* If we are to take a sentence which in like manner sums up the Old Testament, such a sentence is this: *O ye that love the Eternal, see that ye hate the thing which is evil! to him that ordereth his conversation right shall be shown the salvation of God.*

But instantly there will be raised the objection that this is morality, not religion; morality, ethics, conduct, being by many people, and above all by theologians, carefully contra-distinguished from religion, which is supposed in some special way to be connected with propositions about the Godhead of the Eternal Son, like those for which the Bishops of Winchester and Gloucester want to do something, or propositions about the personality of God, or about election or justification. Religion, however, means simply either a binding to righteousness, or else a serious attending to righteousness and dwelling upon it. Which of these two it most nearly means, depends upon the view we take of the word's derivation; but it means one of them, and they are really much the same. And the antithesis between *ethical* and *religious* is thus quite a false one. Ethical means *practical*, it relates to practice or conduct passing into habit or disposition. Religious also means *practical*, but practical in a still higher degree; and the right antithesis to both ethical and religious, is the same as the right antithesis to practical: namely, *theoretical*.

Now, the propositions of the Bishops of Winchester and

[2] *St. Paul and Protestantism*, (London, Smith, Elder, 1876) p. 159.

Gloucester are theoretical, and they therefore are very properly opposed to propositions which are moral or ethical; but they are with equal propriety opposed to propositions which are religious. They differ in kind from what is religious, while what is ethical agrees in kind with it. But is there, therefore, no difference between what is ethical, or morality, and religion? There *is* a difference; a difference of degree. Religion, if we follow the intention of human thought and human language in the use of the word, is ethics heightened, enkindled, lit up by feeling; the passage from morality to religion is made when to morality is applied emotion. And the true meaning of religion is thus not simply *morality*, but *morality touched by emotion*. And this new elevation and inspiration of morality is well marked by the word 'righteousness.' Conduct is the word of common life, morality is the word of philosophical disquisition, righteousness is the word of religion.

Some people, indeed, are for calling all high thought and feeling by the name of religion; according to that saying of Goethe: 'He who has art and science, has also religion.' But let us use words as mankind generally use them. We may call art and science touched by emotion *religion*, if we will; as we may make the instinct of self-preservation, into which M. Littré traces up all our private affections, include the perfecting ourselves by the study of what is beautiful in art; and the reproductive instinct, into which he traces up all our social affections, include the perfecting mankind by political science. But men have not yet got to that stage, when we think much of either their private or their social affections at all, except as exercising themselves in conduct; neither do we yet think of religion as otherwise exercising itself. When mankind speak of religion, they have before their mind an activity engaged, not with the whole of life, but with that three-fourths of life which is *conduct*. This is wide enough range for one word, surely; but at any rate, let us at present limit ourselves as mankind do.

And if some one now asks: But what *is* this application of emotion to morality, and by what marks may we know it?—we can quite easily satisfy him; not, indeed, by any disquisition of our own, but in a much better way, by examples. 'By the dispensation of Providence to mankind,' says Quintilian, 'goodness gives men most pleasure.' That is morality. 'The path of the just is as the shining light which shineth more and more into the perfect day.' That is morality touched with emotion, or religion. 'Hold off from sensuality,' says Cicero; 'for, if you have given yourself up to it, you will find yourself unable to think of anything else.' That is morality. 'Blessed are the pure in heart,' says Jesus Christ; 'for they shall see God.' That is religion. 'We all want to live honestly, but cannot,' says the Greek maxim-maker. That is morality. 'O wretched man that I am, who shall deliver me from the body of this death!' says St. Paul. That is religion. 'Would thou wert of as good conversation in deed as in word!' is morality. 'Not every one that saith unto me, Lord, Lord, shall enter into the kingdom of Heaven, but he that doeth the will of my Father which is in Heaven,' is religion. 'Live as you were meant to live!' is morality. 'Lay hold on eternal life!' is religion.

Or we may take the contrast within the bounds of the Bible itself. 'Love not sleep, lest thou come to poverty,' is morality; 'My meat is to do the will of him that sent me, and to finish his work,' is religion. Or we may even observe a third stage between these two stages, which shows to us the transition from one to the other. 'If thou givest thy soul the desires that please her, she will make thee a laughing-stock to thine enemies;'—that is morality. 'He that resisteth pleasure crowneth his life;'—that is morality with the tone heightened, passing, or trying to pass, into religion. 'Flesh and blood cannot inherit the kingdom of God;'—there the passage is made, and we have religion. Our religious examples are here all taken from the Bible, and from the Bible such examples can best be taken, but we might also find them elsewhere. 'Oh that my lot might lead me in the path of holy innocence of thought and deed, the path which august laws ordain, laws which in the highest heaven had their birth, neither did the race of mortal man beget them, nor shall oblivion ever put them to sleep; the power of God is mighty in them, and groweth not old!' That is from Sophocles, but it is as much religion as any of the things which we have quoted as religious. Like them, it is not the mere enjoining of conduct, but it is this enjoining touched, strengthened, and almost transformed by the addition of feeling.

So what is meant by the application of emotion to morality has now, it is to be hoped, been made clear. The next question will, I suppose, be: But how does one get the application made? Why, how does one get to feel much about any matter whatever? By dwelling upon it, by staying our thoughts upon it, by having it perpetually in our mind. The very words *mind, memory, remain*, come, probably, all from the same root, from the notion of staying, attending. Possibly even the word *man* comes from the same; so entirely does the idea of humanity, of intelligence, of looking before and after, of raising oneself out of the flux of things, rest upon the idea of steadying oneself, concentrating oneself, making order in the chaos of one's impressions, by attending to one impression rather than the other. The rules of conduct, of morality, were themselves, philosophers suppose, reached in this way;—the notion of a whole self as opposed to a partial self, a best self to an inferior, to a momentary self a permanent self requiring the restraint of impulses a man would naturally have indulged;—because, by *attending* to his life, man found it had a scope beyond the wants of the present moment. Suppose it was so; then the first man who, as 'a being,' comparatively, 'of a large discourse, looking before and after,' controlled the native, instantaneous, mechanical impulses of the instinct of self-preservation, controlled the native, instantaneous, mechanical impulses of the reproductive instinct, had morality revealed to him.

But there is a long way from this to that habitual dwelling on the rules thus reached, that constant turning them over in the mind, that near and lively experimental sense of their beneficence, which communicates emotion to our thought of them, and thus incalculably heightens their power. And the more mankind attended to the claims of that part of our nature which does *not* belong to conduct, properly so called, or to morality (and we have seen that, after all, about one-fourth of our nature is in this case), the more they would have distractions to take off their thoughts from those moral conclusions which all races of men, one may say, seem to have reached, and to prevent these moral conclusions from being quickened by emotion, and thus becoming religious.

The language of the Bible, then, is literary, not scientific language *thrown out* at an object of consciousness not fully grasped, which inspired emotion. Evidently, if the object be one not fully to be grasped, and one to inspire emotion, the language of figure and feeling will satisfy us better about it, will cover more of what we seek to express, than the language of literal fact and science; the language of science about it will be *below* what we feel to be the truth.

The question however has arisen and confronts us: what *was* the scientific basis of fact for this consciousness. When we have once satisfied ourselves both as to the tentative, poetic way in which the Bible-personages used language, and also as to their having no pretensions to metaphysics at all, let us, therefore, when there is this question raised as to the scientific account of what they had before their minds, be content with a very unpretending answer. And in this way such a phrase as that which we have formerly used concerning God, and have been much blamed for using,—the phrase, namely, that, 'for science, God is simply *the stream of tendency by which all things fulfil the law of their being*,'—may be allowed; and even prove useful. Certainly it is inadequate; certainly it is a less proper phrase than, for instance: 'Clouds and darkness are round about him, righteousness and judgment are the habitation of his seat.'[3] But then it is, in however humble a degree and with however narrow a reach, a *scientific* definition, which the other is not. The phrase, 'A Personal First Cause, the moral and intelligent Governor of the universe,' has also, when applied to God, the character, no doubt, of a scientific definition; but then it goes far beyond what is admittedly certain and verifiable, which is what we mean by scientific. It attempts far too much; if we want here, as we do want, to have what is admittedly certain and verifiable, we must content ourselves with very little. No one will say, that it is admittedly certain and verifiable, that there is a personal first cause, the moral and intelligent governor of the universe, whom we may call *God* if we will.

[3] It has been urged that if this personifying mode of expression is more proper and adequate, it must also be more scientifically exact. But surely it must on reflexion appear that this is by no means so. Wordsworth calls the earth 'the mighty mother of mankind', and the geographers call her 'an oblate spheroid'; Wordsworth's expression is more proper and adequate to convey what men feel about the earth, but it is not therefore the more scientifically exact.

But, that all things seem to us to have what we call a law of their being, and to tend to fulfil it, is certain and admitted; though whether we will call this *God* or not, is a matter of choice. Suppose, however, we call it *God*, we then give the name of *God* to a certain and admitted reality; this, at least, is an advantage.

And the notion of our definition does, in fact, enter into the term *God*, in men's common use of it. To please God, to serve God, to obey God's will, means to follow a law of things which is found in conscience, and which is an indication, irrespective of our arbitrary wish and fancy, of what we ought to do. There *is*, then, a real power which makes for righteousness; and it is the greatest of realities for us.[4] When Paul says, our business is 'to serve the spirit of God,' 'to serve the living and true God;' and when Epictetus says: 'What do I want?—to acquaint myself with the true order of things, and comply with it,' they both mean, so far, the same, in that they both mean we should obey a tendency, which is *not ourselves* but which appears in our consciousness, by which things fulfil the real law of their being.

[4] Prayer, about which so much has of late been said unadvisedly and ill, deals with this reality. All good and beneficial prayer is in truth, however men may describe it, at bottom nothing else than an energy of aspiration towards the Eternal *not ourselves* that makes for righteousness,—of aspiration towards it, and co-operation with it. Nothing, therefore, can be more efficacious, more right, and more real.

10

Religious language is poetic–ethic

George Santayana

The "Life of Reason" for Santayana consists in the pursuit of eternal or ideal aims proposed by reason, in which the individual "may lose what is mortal and accidental in himself and immortalise what is rational and human." Religion in its most general sense has the same aim, but what gives it its distinctive character is that it endeavors to realize this ideal life of reason through the imagination, that is to say by intuition, poetic vision, symbolism. The function of religious language is therefore a poetic one, but it differs from poetry in that it is concerned with "higher and more practical themes." Religious language may be more or less effective or adequate in promoting the life of reason by imaginative myth, but it is never true or false. Insofar as it mistakenly pretends to be descriptive in function, reporting the literal truth about "experience or reality elsewhere," then religious language is deceptive and harmful. Santayana's view of religious language, it will be seen, is a variation on the same theme exploited by Matthew Arnold.

George Santayana (1863–1952) was an American philosopher (of Spanish birth) of the early part of this century. The following extract is the first chapter of *Reason in Religion,* volume III of *The Life of Reason.*

Experience has repeatedly confirmed that well-known maxim of Bacon's, that "a little philosophy inclineth man's mind to atheism, but depth in philosophy bringeth men's mind about to religion." In every age the most comprehensive thinkers have found in the religion of their time and country something they could accept, interpreting and illustrating that religion so as to give it depth and universal application. Even the heretics and atheists, if they have had profundity, turn out after a while to be forerunners of some new orthodoxy. What they rebel against is a religion alien to their nature; they are atheists only by accident, and relatively to a convention which inwardly offends them, but they yearn mightily in their own souls after the religious acceptance of a world interpreted in their own fashion. So it appears in the end that their atheism and loud protestation were in fact the hastier part of their thought, since what emboldened them to deny the poor world's faith was that they were too impatient to understand it. Indeed, the enlightenment common to young wits and worm-eaten old satirists, who plume themselves on detecting the scientific ineptitude of religion—something which the blindest half see—is not nearly enlightened enough: it points to notorious facts incompatible with religious tenets literally taken, but it leaves unexplored the habits of thought from which those tenets sprang, their original meaning, and their true function. Such studies would bring the sceptic face to face with the mystery and pathos of mortal existence. They would make him understand why religion is so profoundly moving

From George Santayana, *Reason in Religion*, vol. III of *The Life of Reason* (1905–1906). Reprinted by permission of Constable Publishers. Reprinted with the permission of Charles Scribner's Sons from REASON IN RELIGION, pages 3–14, by George Santayana. Copyright 1905 Charles Scribner's Sons; renewal copyright 1933 George Santayana.

and in a sense so profoundly just. There must needs be something humane and necessary in an influence that has become the most general sanction of virtue, the chief occasion for art and philosophy, and the source, perhaps, of the best human happiness. If nothing, as Hooker said, is "so malapert as a splenetic religion," a sour irreligion is almost as perverse.

At the same time, when Bacon penned the sage epigram we have quoted he forgot to add that the God to whom depth in philosophy brings back men's minds is far from being the same from whom a little philosophy estranges them. It would be pitiful indeed if mature reflection bred no better conceptions than those which have drifted down the muddy stream of time, where tradition and passion have jumbled everything together. Traditional conceptions, when they are felicitous, may be adopted by the poet, but they must be purified by the moralist and disintegrated by the philosopher. Each religion, so dear to those whose life it sanctifies, and fulfilling so necessary a function in the society that has adopted it, necessarily contradicts every other religion, and probably contradicts itself. What religion a man shall have is a historical accident, quite as much as what language he shall speak. In the rare circumstances where a choice is possible, he may, with some difficulty, make an exchange; but even then he is only adopting a new convention which may be more agreeable to his personal temper but which is essentially as arbitrary as the old.

The attempt to speak without speaking any particular language is not more hopeless than the attempt to have a religion that shall be no religion in particular. A courier's or a dragoman's speech may indeed be often unusual and drawn from disparate sources, not without some mixture of personal originality; but that private jargon will have a meaning only because of its analogy to one or more conventional languages and its obvious derivation from them. So travellers from one religion to another, people who have lost their spiritual nationality, may often retain a neutral and confused residuum of belief, which they may egregiously regard as the essence of all religion, so little may they remember the graciousness and naturalness of that ancestral accent which a perfect religion should have. Yet a moment's probing of the conceptions surviving in such minds will show them to be nothing but vestiges of old beliefs, creases which thought, even if emptied of all dogmatic tenets, has not been able to smooth away at its first unfolding. Later generations, if they have any religion at all, will be found either to revert to ancient authority, or to attach themselves spontaneously to something wholly novel and immensely positive, to some faith promulgated by a fresh genius and passionately embraced by a converted people. Thus every living and healthy religion has a marked idiosyncrasy. Its power consists in its special and surprising message and in the bias which that revelation gives to life. The vistas it opens and the mysteries it propounds are another world to live in; and another world to live in—whether we expect ever to pass wholly into it or no—is what we mean by having a religion.

What relation, then, does this great business of the soul, which we call religion, bear to the Life of Reason? That the relation between the two is close seems clear from several circumstances. The Life of Reason is the seat of all ultimate values. Now the history of mankind will show us that whenever spirits at once lofty and intense have seemed to attain the highest joys, they have envisaged and attained them in religion. Religion would therefore seem to be a vehicle or a factor in rational life, since the ends of rational life are attained by it. Moreover, the Life of Reason is an ideal to which everything in the world should be subordinated; it establishes lines of moral cleavage everywhere and makes right eternally different from wrong. Religion does the same thing. It makes absolute moral decisions. It sanctions, unifies, and transforms ethics. Religion thus exercises a function of the Life of Reason. And a further function which is common to both is that of emancipating man from his personal limitations. In different ways religions promise to transfer the soul to better conditions. A supernaturally favoured kingdom is to be established for posterity upon earth, or for all the faithful in heaven, or the soul is to be free by repeated purgations from all taint and sorrow, or it is to be lost in the absolute, or it is to become an influence and an object of adoration in the places it once haunted or wherever the activities it once loved may be carried on by future generations of its kindred. Now reason in its way lays before us all these possibilities: it points to common objects, political and intellectual, in which an individual may lose what is mortal and accidental in himself and immortalise what is rational and human;

it teaches us how sweet and fortunate death may be to those whose spirit can still live in their country and in their ideas; it reveals the radiating effects of action and the eternal objects of thought.

Yet the difference in tone and language must strike us, so soon as it is philosophy that speaks. That change should remind us that even if the function of religion and that of reason coincide, this function is performed in the two cases by very different organs. Religions are many, reason one. Religion consists of conscious ideas, hopes, enthusiasms, and objects of worship; it operates by graces and flourishes by prayer. Reason, on the other hand, is a mere principle or potential order, on which, indeed, we may come to reflect, but which exists in us ideally only, without variation or stress of any kind. We conform or do not conform to it; it does not urge or chide us, nor call for any emotions on our part other than those naturally aroused by the various objects which it unfolds in their true nature and proportion. Religion brings some order into life by weighting it with new materials. Reason adds to the natural materials only the perfect order which it introduces into them. Rationality is nothing but a form, an ideal constitution which experience may more or less embody. Religion is a part of experience itself, a mass of sentiments and ideas. The one is an inviolate principle, the other a changing and struggling force. And yet this struggling and changing force of religion seems to direct man toward something eternal. It seems to make for an ultimate harmony within the soul and for an ultimate harmony between the soul and all the soul depends upon. So that religion, in its intent, is a more conscious and direct pursuit of the Life of Reason than is society, science, or art. For these approach and fill out the ideal life tentatively and piecemeal, hardly regarding the goal or caring for the ultimate justification of their instinctive aims. Religion also has an instinctive and blind side, and bubbles up in all manner of chance practices and intuitions; soon, however, it feels its way toward the heart of things, and, from whatever quarter it may come, veers in the direction of the ultimate.

Nevertheless, we must confess that this religious pursuit of the Life of Reason has been singularly abortive. Those within the pale of each religion may prevail upon themselves to express satisfaction with its results, thanks to a fond partiality in reading the past and generous draughts of hope for the future; but any one regarding the various religions at once and comparing their achievements with what reason requires, must feel how terrible is the disappointment which they have one and all prepared for mankind. Their chief anxiety has been to offer imaginary remedies for mortal ills, some of which are incurable essentially, while others might have been really cured by well-directed effort. The Greek oracles, for instance, pretended to heal our natural ignorance, which has its appropriate though difficult cure, while the Christian vision of heaven pretended to be an antidote to our natural death, the inevitable correlate of birth and of a changing and conditioned existence. By methods of this sort little can be done for the real betterment of life. To confuse intelligence and dislocate sentiment by gratuitous fictions is a short-sighted way of pursuing happiness. Nature is soon avenged. An unhealthy exaltation and a one-sided morality have to be followed by regrettable reactions. When these come, the real rewards of life may seem vain to a relaxed vitality, and the very name of virtue may irritate young spirits untrained in any natural excellence. Thus religion too often debauches the morality it comes to sanction, and impedes the science it ought to fulfil.

What is the secret of this ineptitude? Why does religion, so near to rationality in its purpose, fall so far short of it in its texture and in its results? The answer is easy: Religion pursues rationality through the imagination. When it explains events or assigns causes, it is an imaginative substitute for science. When it gives precepts, insinuates ideals, or remoulds aspiration, it is an imaginative substitute for wisdom—I mean for the deliberate and impartial pursuit of all good. The conditions and the aims of life are both represented in religion poetically, but this poetry tends to arrogate to itself literal truth and moral authority, neither of which it possesses. Hence the depth and importance of religion become intelligible no less than its contradictions and practical disasters. Its object is the same as that of reason, but its method is to proceed by intuition and by unchecked poetical conceits. These are repeated and vulgarised in proportion to their original fineness and significance, till they pass for reports of objective truth and come to constitute a world of faith, superposed upon the world of experience and regarded as materially enveloping it, if not in space at least in time and in existence. The only truth of religion comes from its interpretation of life, from its symbolic rendering of that moral experience which it springs out of and which it seeks to elucidate. Its falsehood comes from the insidious misunderstanding which clings to it, to the effect that these poetic conceptions are not merely representations of experience as it is or should be, but are rather information about experience or reality elsewhere—an experience and reality which, strangely enough, supply just the defects betrayed by reality and experience here.

Thus religion has the same original relation to life that poetry has; only poetry, which never pretends to literal validity, adds a pure value to existence, the value of a liberal imaginative exercise. The poetic value of religion would initially be greater than that of poetry itself, because religion deals with higher and more practical themes, with sides of life which are in greater need of some imaginative touch and ideal interpretation than are those pleasant or pompous things which ordinary poetry dwells upon. But this initial advantage is neutralised in part by the abuse to which religion is subject, whenever its symbolic rightness is taken for scientific truth. Like poetry, it improves the world only by imagining it improved, but not content with making this addition to the mind's furniture— an addition which might be useful and ennobling—it thinks to confer a more radical benefit by persuading mankind that, in spite of appearances, the world is really such as that rather arbitrary idealisation has painted it. This spurious satisfaction is naturally the prelude to many a disappointment, and the soul has infinite trouble to emerge again from the artificial problems and sentiments into which it is thus plunged. The value of religion becomes equivocal. Religion remains an imaginative achievement, a symbolic representation of moral reality which may have a most important function in vitalising the mind and in transmitting, by way of parables, the lessons of experience. But it becomes at the same time a continuous incidental deception; and this deception, in proportion as it is strenuously denied to be such, can work indefinite harm in the world and in the conscience.

On the whole, however, religion should not be conceived as having taken the place of anything better, but rather as having come to relieve situations which, but for its presence, would have been infinitely worse. In the thick of active life, or in the monotony of practical slavery, there is more need to stimulate fancy than to control it. Natural instinct is not much disturbed in the human brain by what may happen in that thin superstratum of ideas which commonly overlays it. We must not blame religion for preventing the development of a moral and natural science which at any rate would seldom have appeared; we must rather thank it for the sensibility, the reverence, the speculative insight which it has introduced into the world.

We may therefore proceed to analyse the significance and the function which religion has had at its different stages, and, without disguising or in the least condoning its confusion with literal truth, we may allow ourselves to enter as sympathetically as possible into its various conceptions and emotions. They have made up the inner life of many sages, and of all those who without great genius or learning have lived steadfastly in the spirit. The feeling of reverence should itself be treated with reverence, although not at a sacrifice of truth, with which alone, in the end, reverence is compatible. Nor have we any reason to be intolerant of the partialities and contradictions which religions display. Were we dealing with a science, such contradictions would have to be instantly solved and removed; but when we are concerned with the poetic interpretation of experience, contradiction means only variety, and variety means spontaneity, wealth of resource, and a nearer approach to total adequacy.

If we hope to gain any understanding of these matters we must begin by taking them out of that heated and fanatical atmosphere in which the Hebrew tradition has enveloped them. The Jews had no philosophy, and when their national traditions came to be theoretically explicated and justified, they were made to issue in a puerile scholasticism and a rabid intolerance. The question of monotheism, for instance, was a terrible question to the Jews. Idolatry did not consist in worshipping a god who, not being ideal, might be unworthy of worship, but rather in recognising other gods than the one worshipped in Jerusalem. To the Greeks, on the contrary, whose philosophy was enlightened and ingenuous, monotheism and polytheism seemed perfectly innocent and compatible. To say God or the gods was only to use different expressions for the same influence, now viewed in its abstract unity and correlation with all existence, now viewed in its various manifestations in moral life, in nature, or in history. So that what in Plato, Aristotle, and the Stoics meets us at every step—the combination of monotheism with polytheism—is no contradiction, but merely an intelligent variation of phrase to indicate various aspects or functions in physical and moral things. When religion appears to us in this light its contradictions and controversies lose all their bitterness. Each doctrine will simply represent the moral plane on which they live who have devised or adopted it. Religions will thus be better or worse, never true or false. We shall be able to lend ourselves to each in turn, and seek to draw from it the secret of its inspiration.

11

Religious language expresses quasi-metaphysical "attitudes"

R. M. Hare

Moral language and some kinds of religious language show various points of similarity; indeed, there is a close connection between the two, for acceptance of a religion involves acceptance of the moral precepts connected with it. In part, at least, then religious language has the same "logic" as moral discourse and therefore cannot be dismissed as senseless any more than moral language can. However, while moral judgments arise out of religious belief, they do not constitute it, and we still have to define the distinctive features of religious language. We can get a clue about how religious discourse functions, so Hare claims, by looking at the connection between a man's actions on the one hand, and his factual beliefs and his "springs of action" (desires, purposes, and moral principles) on the other. Action involves both factual beliefs and "springs of action," so that sometimes a particular action will mean that the agent has a particular factual belief, and sometimes it will mean that he has a particular purpose or evaluative principle. Similarly, religious language involves reference both to factual beliefs on the one hand, and to attitudes and evaluative principles on the other. Thus to say "Jesus is Lord" involves certain beliefs about Jesus and also the taking up of an attitude of worship to Jesus, evaluating him in a certain way. There are, Hare says, no specifically religious or supernatural "facts" as such, but we evaluate certain facts as having special importance or relevance. From this point of view, to believe religiously is to adopt certain attitudes. However, Hare argues, the distinction between belief in facts and attitudes to them, or between descriptions and evaluations, itself depends upon quasi-evaluative rules or principles (e.g. rules for discriminating between facts and illusions) and the taking up of certain basic attitudes to the world. If then we say that religious language is concerned not with describing special facts but with declaring and prescribing attitudes, perhaps some religious statements (for example, "God created the world *ex nihilo*") are concerned with these primordial or metaphysical "attitudes" without which the notion of "fact" (and presumably the distinction between facts and "first order" attitudes) would have no meaning, just as for Plato the Form of the Good was not itself a being but that whereby the world of beings was possible. From this point of view we might say that, for Hare, the function of some religious statements is to declare and prescribe certain quasi-metaphysical attitudes.

R. M. Hare is Professor of Philosophy at the University of Oxford. The following essay, "Religion and Morals," was published in its present form in *Faith and Logic.*

This paper is an attempt to indicate the bearing on the philosophy of religion of recent discussions in the field of moral philosophy.* I am still not at all certain what I want to say about this difficult subject; and I have been persuaded to publish the paper in the present volume by two considerations only. The first is that the type of view here tentatively put forward is attacked by some other contributors to the volume; and readers may therefore find it useful to have to hand a statement of the view which is being rebutted. The second is that, since I am at the moment not able to make much progress in this enquiry, others may be helped to do so by my setting out some considerations which seem to me important. They are to be warned, however, that much in this paper is un-digested, and the last section, at least, positively indigestible.

The recent history of moral philosophy has been the history of the impact upon it of that philosophical movement which is usually referred to loosely as Logical Empiricism or Logical Positivism. From the point of view of moral philosophy the most challenging thing the Logical Empiricists did was this: they directed their attention to a certain type of language, namely to those sentences which express 'scientific propositions' and other statements of fact, in the narrow sense; and they examined the conditions under which we are prepared to allow that such sentences are meaningful. They claimed that the criterion which we employ is this: to know the meaning of such a sentence is to know what would have to be the case for the statement which it expresses to be called true, or false. There are various ways of formulating this criterion; but I will not

R. M. Hare, "Religion and Morals," in *Faith and Logic*, ed. Basil Mitchell (London, Allen and Unwin, 1957), pp. 176–193. Reprinted by permission.
* It is adapted from a lecture given at the Royal Institute of Philosophy in February, 1954.

here discuss their relative merits, nor whether the criterion *can* be formulated in a satisfactory way. It is enough to say that this criterion, when it was first propounded, aroused much enthusiasm among empiricist philosophers. For here, they thought, was a way of eliminating from the pages of philosophy, once for all, those sentences (of which there are, it must be confessed, too many) that do not carry any weight of meaning. Philosophical books, it was said, are full of statements or so-called statements to which, when we examine them in the light of this criterion, we cannot assign any significance at all; we cannot think what would have to be the case for us to call them true, or false. Such books the empiricists, following Hume's prescription, were prepared to commit to the flames as containing nothing but sophistry and illusion.

The result of following this prescription was to sweep language too clean. At the time, the impact on both moral philosophy and the philosophy of religion was startling; for by this criterion it was thought that both moral statements and statements of religious belief could be shown to be only 'pseudo-propositions' and the sentences expressing them 'literally senseless'. But it later appeared that all that had been done was to isolate *one* kind of use we make of language, and to give a criterion of meaningfulness for statements made in this field. If we confine ourselves to what are ordinarily called statements of empirical fact, the criterion is enormously useful. Indeed, it might be said that the criterion provides us with a way of ascertaining, not whether what somebody says has meaning *of any sort*, but at least whether it has empirical meaning. For to call a statement an empirical one is perhaps to include it in the class of those statements of which we can say or show what would have to be the case in our own experience or somebody else's for us to call them true or false. What we have here, then, is not really a criterion of meaningfulness (a way of separating wheat from chaff) but a criterion of empiricality (a way, as we might say, of separating wheat from oats, or barley, or rice). Or, to use St Paul's metaphor, our language

is not one member, but many. If the foot shall say, Because I am not the hand, I am not of the body; is it therefore not of the body? And if the ear shall say, Because I am not the eye, I am not of the body; is it therefore not of the body? If the whole body were an eye, where were the hearing? If the whole were hearing, where were the smelling? But now God hath set the members every one of them in the body, as it hath pleased Him. And if they were all one member, where were the body? But now they are many members, yet but one body.[1]

Anatomy and its related disciplines (physiology, pathology, etc.) are the study of the several parts of the body to see what they are like, how related to one another, what the function of each is, and how it can go wrong. The more these sciences have progressed, the less inclined people have become to despise or depreciate parts of the body whose use they do not yet know. It has often been discovered that some insignificant-looking piece of the body, to which nobody had paid any attention, is in fact so important that we could not live without it—that some small organ, which seemed to be only a part of a larger one, has in fact its own peculiar function, without which the whole body would perish.

Logic, as it is being studied in many of the most important philosophical schools at the present time, is the anatomy of language. Since among the functions of language are thought and communication, the physiology of language, which goes along with its anatomy, is the study of the different ways in which we think and the different sorts of things that we communicate to each other. The most important result of the challenge made by the Logical Empiricists has been to stimulate an intensive study of these various uses of language. We have been forced to recognize that there is a very large number of different things that we do with words, and that they all have a vital part to play in our thought and discourse. The logician who thinks that he can confine his attention to one of them and ignore the rest is not doing the whole of his job.

About some kinds of words quite a lot has been discovered; this applies, I think, to various kinds of words used in scientific discourse, and also to moral words. How much has been discovered about any kind of discourse has depended, first of all on the amount of time and interest philosophers have given to it; but more on the

[1] I Cor. xii. 14.

relative complexity and difficulty of the kind of discourse in question. Religious discourse has come off badly on both these counts. For in the first place few philosophers nowadays are interested enough in religious questions to make them their main study; not many are even sufficiently conversant with the use of religious language to succeed in such an enquiry. And secondly, religious language is, as I hope to make clear, a very difficult subject; there are a great many different kinds of things that we say, which are all part of religious language; and some of these things can be said or listened to with comprehension only by people whose experience of the religious life has gone much further than that of most of us modern philosophers. But, on the other hand, many of the logical problems raised are not such as can be dealt with by logical amateurs. For this reason some who know very well how to use religious language have not been able to give a very convincing *account* of its use, just as some gardeners can grow very good vegetables without being able to tell us clearly or even correctly how they do it.

The present essay is intended only as a first attempt to explore part of this field. I wish first of all to draw attention to some points of similarity between moral language and some sorts of religious language. At the very least it will, I hope, be agreed that all or nearly all religions have what may be called a moral aspect. By this I mean, not merely that the adherents of a particular religion have in fact usually adhered to a particular set of moral principles, but that the moral principles are linked in some intimate way with the religious belief. Thus we find religious teachers, as part of their religious teaching, uttering moral precepts. The most tangible way (if I may so put it) of distinguishing between different religions is to see how their adherents behave. What was it that happened to St Paul when he stopped being an ordinary Jew and became a Christian? There may be a more recondite answer to this question; but at any rate there is this obvious answer, that he stopped doing one sort of thing (persecuting Christians) and started doing another (converting new Christians). Thus one obvious thing that happened to him was that his ideas about what he ought to do (his principles of action, or, in a wide sense, his moral principles) changed radically. And this is also true of lesser converts. Part of what it means to stop being a drunkard or a cannibal and become, say, a Methodist, is that one stops thinking it right to consume gin or human flesh. That religion is very intimately linked with morals, so that one cannot be said to adhere to or accept a religion, unless one accepts and at least tries to act on its moral precepts, is implied by St James:

> If any man thinketh himself to be religious, while he bridleth not his tongue but deceiveth his heart, this man's religion is vain. Pure religion and undefiled before our God and Father is this, to visit the fatherless and widows in their affliction, and to keep himself unspotted from the world.[2]

This may afford some comfort to the Christian empiricist; for the logical character and significance of moral judgments can by this time, I think, be stated in a way that would meet with fairly general acceptance among empiricists. To realize, therefore, that what religious people say in the course of their religious activities is in part moral is to realize that at any rate not all religious discourse is senseless. But this will be regarded, perhaps, as only a small contribution to the solution of the problem; for, it will be said, the *distinctive* character of religious discourse is not thereby illuminated. We may admit that part of this discourse consists of moral judgments; but not the central part. The moral judgments, as we may say, arise out of the religious belief; they do not constitute it. St Paul thought that he ought to stop persecuting Christians because he had changed his belief about a specifically religious matter which was not itself a matter of how one ought to behave, but more like a matter of fact; he had come to believe that Jesus was the Christ, the Son of God.

I do not think that it is possible to sort out this question without a more thorough investigation of the way in which factual beliefs and principles of action are related to each other, and the way in which both are related to our actual conduct. There is a famous doctrine of Aristotle's which, I am convinced, offers the key to a great range of problems in this field, namely the theory of the practical syllogism.[3] Aristotle said, roughly, that when a man does

---

[2] St James, i. sub. fin.; cf. ii, 14 ff.

[3] For references see D. J. Allan, "The Practical Syllogism," in *Autour d'Aristote: Recueil d'Etudes offert à Mgr. A. Mansion*, (Louvain, Publications Universitaires, 1955) p. 325.

anything, there are two things that lie behind what he does. He calls these two things the two premisses of the practical syllogism. The major premiss is some kind of precept or aim or prescription. The minor premiss is a statement of fact. The conclusion of the syllogism is an action. Thus, if I accept the principle that one ought always, if one has a streaming cold, to stay away from public places, and if I know that I have a streaming cold, I do stay away. Aristotle includes among major premisses of this sort of syllogism everything that can be called, in a phrase that Professor Braithwaite has used, 'springs of action'.[4] That is to say, he includes both desires, and purposes, and principles. Since what I wish to say can be said without discussing the important though troublesome distinctions between these different things, I shall adopt Professor Braithwaite's phrase. I shall also from time to time use the particular expression 'moral principles', although I should more correctly express what I have in mind if I used some more general and cumbrous expression such as 'principles governing conduct.' That is to say, I do not wish here to raise, any more than did Aristotle, the important and difficult question of what distinguishes moral principles from other principles of action.

I have said elsewhere that a man's moral principles are most reliably ascertained by seeing what he *does*.[5] This view has been strongly attacked; but I still hold it. For I think that if a man consistently breaks a moral principle which he professes, this inclines us to say that his professions are insincere. But it has also been commonly held that the way to find out about *any* of a man's beliefs, factual or otherwise, is to study what he does. And this must be true, provided that the word 'does' is given a sufficiently wide interpretation. For the only thing that we *can* study about a man is what he does. We cannot take his mind out and look at it (even if such an expression is meaningful); and, therefore, if we are to find out

---

[4] *Proceedings of the Aristotelian Society*, Supp. Vol. 20 (1946) p. 9. Professor Braithwaite's Eddington Memorial Lecture on 'An Empiricist's View of the Nature of Religious Belief" (Cambridge University Press, 1955) was delivered too late for consideration in this paper. I have, however, benefited greatly from the study of his other published and unpublished writings on this subject. Few writers indeed can match his sincerity, courage, and understanding of the question.

[5] *Language of Morals*, (Oxford, Clarendon Press, 1952) p. 1.

anything about his thoughts, we can do so only by studying his actions (including, of course, those actions which consist in his talking to us). I need not now raise the question whether the actions are merely *evidence* of the thoughts, or whether, as some have held, thinking *consists* in acting in a certain way. But at any rate it follows from what I have said that if believing something is a kind of thinking, we can only find out what a man believes by studying his actions; and likewise, if holding a moral principle, or desiring something, or having a certain-purpose, are in a wide sense kinds of thinking, we can only find out about a man's principles or purposes or desires by studying his actions.

An example will help to illustrate the view which I am presenting, and some of its difficulties. If we see a visitor from another town, who has no other means of conveyance than the train, looking at the clock, which says 10.25, and going on talking unconcernedly, we may conclude either that he *believes* that the last train leaves after about 10.30 or that he does not *want* to get home to-night. The possibility of drawing *either* of these two conclusions presents us with a problem. If we assume that he wants to get home to-night we can conclude from his behaviour that he believes that there is a train after 10.30. If, on the other hand, we assume that he believes that there is no train after 10.30, we can conclude from his behaviour that he does not want to get home to-night. What we cannot do is to draw both these conclusions at once without making any assumptions. In Aristotelian terms, from the premisses 'Let me do whatever is necessary to get home tonight' (major) and 'To get home to-night it is necessary to catch a train at or before 10.30' (minor) there follows the conclusion 'Let me catch a train at or before 10.30'; and this conclusion would be expressed in action by catching the train. So if the man does not catch the train we can conclude that he does not accept one of the premisses, if we assume that he does accept the other. In short, actions are evidence for springs of action, if we assume beliefs; or for beliefs, if we assume springs of action; but they cannot be evidence for both at the same time. This, it may be noticed in passing, presents a very real, though perhaps not insuperable, difficulty for those who wish to analyse statements about *all* mental states, including both desires and beliefs, in terms of statements about behaviour.

Let us now return to St Paul. He had always believed that he ought to follow the Christ when He appeared. Thus, it might be said, his conversion was not an alteration in his moral principles; they did not change at all. What was altered was the minor premiss —his factual belief. For whereas he had previously believed that Jesus was a pretender, he now came to believe that He was the Christ. This altered his actions, not through altering his moral principles, but through altering his opinion about a matter of fact.

Yet I find it very difficult to accept this view either. For when a man says 'Jesus is Christ' or 'Jesus is Lord' is he stating a fact (in the ordinary sense) at all? I think it would be agreed that of the people who were familiar with Jesus in His earthly life, some were ready to make this affirmation, and some were not. St Paul, perhaps, knew in one sense all the facts about Jesus *before* his conversion. He even knew, perhaps, that He cast out devils—but then non-Christian Jews had an explanation of this; He cast out devils, they said, by Beelzebub, the prince of the devils. Now what is the *factual* difference between casting out devils by Beelzebub, and casting them out by the finger of God? Or between either of these and curing mental disorders by suggestion (if that is the correct term)? The *fact* is that the symptoms of the disorder cease. It seems to me that one might, in one sense of the word 'fact', know all the facts about Jesus and still refuse to call Him 'Lord' or 'Christ'.

'But' it might be said, 'this leaves out what from St Paul's point of view was the most important fact of all, namely what actually happened to him upon the road to Damascus. Surely here was a new fact, and one which made him ready to acknowledge that Jesus was the Christ.' Yet someone else might say 'What happened to St Paul was that he had a very powerful emotional experience, accompanied by an illusion of someone talking to him, which shook him a great deal, so that he couldn't even see for a bit, and after which he changed his pattern of behaviour.' The same objector would, no doubt, say the same sort of thing about the other appearances of Jesus after His death. What, then, when we are dealing with 'supernatural' facts, is the difference between facts and illusions?

There is another possibility which might be suggested at this point. It might be said: 'If one person says "Jesus is Christ" and another denies this, they may not be differing about the facts; it may be that they have different attitudes to the facts. St Paul, when this thing happened to him, changed his whole way of life; another person, if the same thing happened to him, might have said "Sign of overstrain! I've been driving myself too hard, persecuting these Christians; I must take a holiday and then I'll feel better"'. According to this view St Peter, when he said 'Thou art the Christ', was not stating a fact; he was *doing* something, namely worshipping.

Now there is indeed such a thing as an attitude of worship; and it is plausible to say that to take up this attitude is part at any rate of what a person does when he is converted. It is therefore necessary to consider, in what can only be a superficial way, what is meant by 'worship'. The first thing to notice is that it is nearly always much easier to say of somebody *that* he is worshipping than to say *what* he is worshipping. 'The heathen in his blindness bows down to wood and stone'; but can we say that wood and stone, considered in themselves, are the real objects of his worship? We are not, for our present purposes, concerned with the answer to this old question, but with the logical character of the question itself. If we find a heathen bowing down to a piece of wood, and doing all the other things that would normally be called 'worshipping' it (suppose, for example, that he will not use the wood of that kind of tree for any profane purpose), then we can surely say that he is worshipping the piece of wood. If someone says 'He isn't really worshipping the piece of wood, but some invisible god whom he conceives of as resident in the piece of wood', then we may if we like agree with this; but I can think of cases in which this might well seem a distinction without a difference. We are reminded here of Professor Ryle's views about the mind.[6] Suppose that we ask 'What is the difference between, on the one hand, doing all the things that I habitually do to my wife, and on the other, doing all the same things and in addition thinking of her as a person?' It is not at all clear to me how one would answer such a question. It may be said 'If you can love something in the way that you love your wife, you must be thinking of it (her) as a person.' But this remark is two-edged. For it is intended to be an analytic statement; and therefore it would seem that on this view thinking of something as a person is an analytically necessary condition for being said to love it (him, her). But if so, then loving it (him, her) is an analytically sufficient

[6] G. Ryle, *The Concept of Mind*, (London, Hutchinson, 1949).

condition for being said to think of it (him, her) as a person. And if this is applicable to worship as well as to love, then we may say that worshipping something is an analytically sufficient condition for being said to think of it as a person. By this I mean, not that if we find someone worshipping something we are entitled to say that that thing *is* a person; but only that we are entitled in such a case to say that he *thinks* of it as a person. The further question remains, how we tell whether he is *right* to think of it as a person.

How then do I tell whether I am right to think of my wife as a person? I do not wish to answer this question at too great length. But if she does all the things which I expect persons to do, does not that show that I am right? And can we not say this of the piece of wood? Of course the piece of wood does not walk about or talk. But that is not what its worshipper expects. He expects only that worship of the piece of wood will be followed by a course of events favourable to him (rain at the right time, for example) whereas neglect of its worship will be followed by an opposite course of events.

Now if a person adopts an attitude of worship towards some object, and therefore thinks of it (or of something resident in it) as a person; and if everything which he expects to happen actually happens, shall we not say that he is right to worship it? Shall we not say that it is for him a proper object of worship? And if a proper object of worship, then a god; for only a god can be a proper object of worship (this statement is analytic). Moreover, on this interpretation the statement 'This piece of wood is a god' is falsifiable; for when the missionary comes and casts down the piece of wood, and the results which its worshippers expect do not follow, this is just the sort of thing that makes people say that it was false to call it a god, or, for short, that it was a false god. The more primitive a religion is, the more readily are its statements open to empirical falsification; religion has advanced from its more primitive to its less primitive forms partly by the empirical falsification of the claims of the more primitive forms, which then come to be known as superstitions. The less primitive a religion becomes, the less willing are its adherents to make predictions about what their god will do; in particular, they become less certain that he will act to what *they* conceive to be their advantage. Thus the prescriptive, attitudinal element in religious belief gains at the expense of the descriptive factual element.

> If it be so, our God whom we serve is able to deliver us from the burning fiery furnace; and he will deliver us out of thine hand, O king. But if not, be it known unto thee, O king, that we will not serve thy gods, nor worship the golden image which thou hast set up.[7]

This process, as is well known, has caused certain empiricist philosophers to maintain that religious 'advances' have been made at the cost of making statements of religious faith less open to empirical falsification, and, therefore, by the empiricist criterion, less meaningful. A possible answer to this attack is that, first, as it is the purpose of this paper to show, the empirical component in the meaning of religious language is not the only one, nor even, perhaps, the most important; and secondly, that even advanced religions require of their adherents *some* empirical expectations.

Likewise, even in the most primitive forms of religion, what is being stated is not just empirical fact. For if, as I have implied, the meaning of the word 'god' (with a small 'g') is 'a proper object of worship', the word 'proper' in the *definiens* is a value-word. Here we come back to something rather like morals (for 'proper' as used here, though not a moral word, is, like moral words, prescriptive). According to this view, in calling something a god, we are saying, not merely that worshipping it will have certain results, but that it is *proper* to worship it; that is to say, we are at least in part prescribing the taking up of a certain attitude towards it. And whether we are to say that a person really believes in a certain god will depend on what attitude he takes up to the object which is said to be a god; that is, it will depend on what he *does*. Those who have followed recent discussions of the various elements of meaning possessed by value-words will recognize here familiar features. The word 'god' has both evaluative and descriptive meaning. In virtue of its descriptive meaning statements containing it may be said to be verifiable and falsifiable by those who accept the same standards of evaluation as the speaker (and this does not necessarily involve

[7] Daniel iii. 17.

accepting the *whole* of his religious beliefs). In virtue of its evaluative meaning we say that a person who does not behave in a certain way towards a certain object is not treating it as a god.

I return now for the last time to St Paul. It seems fairly clear that it will not do to try to find some one thing about St Paul which changed when he became a Christian. If we ask 'Was it his beliefs about matters of fact which changed, or his moral principles, or some other kind of value-principles, or his attitude to something or other, or something else?' then we are asking for trouble. Surely we must say that almost everything about St Paul changed; he became 'a new creature'. If this is true, we shall not find a single simple analysis of religious statements which solves all philosophical problems concerning them; for not only are there many kinds of utterances which religious people make in the course of their religion (this would be difficult enough); but almost all these kinds of utterances are, so to speak, in circuit with all the rest. A religious person may make what is *prima facie* a statement of fact—perhaps even a statement of quite ordinary empirical fact like 'If I do but touch His garment I shall be made whole'—and yet perhaps he would not have made this statement at all unless it were bound up with all sorts of other beliefs, dispositions, attitudes, and so on. This is, to my mind, the chief reason why religious discourse has always baffled philosophers—and, I am inclined to add, long may it continue to baffle them if they think that to understand it is a merely *philosophical* problem.

I wish, therefore, to conclude this paper by giving what is little more than a bare classification of some of the chief sorts of things that religious people say and do in the course of their religion, and which, taken together, constitute religious belief. I do not wish to claim that the list is either comprehensive or sufficiently finely distinguished. It will be noticed that the items group themselves into a triad rather like the thesis, antithesis and synthesis of an earlier philosophy. I started, it will be remembered, by considering the suggestion that moral judgments are the distinctive constituents of religious discourse. This view I rejected, and then considered in turn the claim of statements of religious belief to be called statements of fact in the ordinary sense; and this, too, appeared unsatisfactory. If we take religious language as a whole, it is too factual to be called specifically moral, and yet too closely bound up with our conduct to be called in the ordinary sense factual.

I therefore came back to a position which has affinities with both the preceding ones. Taking up an attitude of worship to an object considered as a person is not quite like adopting a purely factual belief; nor is it simply subscribing to certain principles of conduct; but it involves both these things. The person who worships is bound to govern his conduct (or let it be governed) in a certain way; and he is also bound to believe in the truth of certain factual statements (empirical ones about what has actually happened in the world, and what is likely to happen). As a first sketch of a synthesis, it is plausible to say that in so far as religious discourse seems to refer to supernatural facts, this is the result of the superimposition of the attitude of worship upon factual beliefs which are themselves not other than empirical; that, in fact, we have here a case like that of 'non-natural qualities' in ethics. When we say that a strawberry is good because it is a sweet, and yet by calling it good mean to say something else of it than simply that it is sweet, we are tempted to think that by calling it good we are attributing to it some *quality*, somehow like sweetness yet of a different, 'non-natural' kind—a quality which cannot be tasted but only grasped by thought, and which is the consequence of the natural quality of sweetness. In truth, however, what we are doing is not attributing to the strawberry any other quality at all besides sweetness; but we are, as well as attributing to it that perfectly ordinary quality, *commending* it for having the quality. In the same way it might be that the *facts* that religious discourse deals with are perfectly ordinary empirical facts like what happens when you pray; but we are tempted to call them supernatural facts because our whole way of living is organized round them; they have for us value, relevance, importance, which they would not have if we were atheists. If this view were correct, then the belief that there are specifically religious, supernatural facts could be said to be the result of failing to distinguish in logic what cannot be distinguished in practice, namely, facts, and our attitudes to them.

Even this, however, will not do. For it implies that there *is* a clear distinction in logic between facts and our attitudes to them.

But though it is most important to start by making this distinction, it is important to end, not by blurring it, as is often done, but by articulating the relations between these two kinds of thing.

People sometimes talk as if facts were somehow given us entirely independently of any dispositions of our own with regard to them. Kant saw that this is not so; but I will not attempt to formulate what I wish to say in his language. I can put the point briefly (at the cost of obscurity) by saying that any statement of fact which claims *objectivity* will be found on analysis to contain an element which is ineradicably *modal* (a reference to causal necessity); and that such modal statements are not analysable in purely descriptive terms, but have a prescriptive element. This element is not the same as, but it presents certain analogies with, the prescriptive element in moral judgments. From this it follows that without principles of some sort we do not get any facts; there is no distinction between fact and illusion for a person who does not take up a certain attitude to the world.

This is obviously not the place to expand these somewhat pregnant remarks. But fortunately, in a subject the full logical discussion of which is too complicated to be attempted until logical studies have advanced further, a great deal of light has been shed by recent discoveries and probable conjectures of physiologists. That physiology should shed light on a logical problem may seem impossible to a philosophical purist; but if the thinking which is expressed in language is done by, or involves the use of, the brain, it is to be expected that there will be certain formal analogies between the features of language which logicians study and the processes which physiologists find going on in the brain. In the same way, if a calculating-machine does mathematics there will be formal analogies between the expression in mathematical language of the calculations which it does and the physical operations of the parts of the machine.

It is therefore extremely significant that, in his recent Reith Lectures, Professor Young, speaking of the brain, said some things which must have a familiar ring to any philosopher who has read Kant.[8] This is all the more paradoxical in that Kant himself would

---

[8] J. Z. Young, *Doubt and Certainty in Science*, (Oxford, University Press, 1951). See esp. pp. 61, 108.

have considered it outrageous that empirical discoveries about the brain should have any relevance to his doctrines. But to us it may appear that, since to talk we have to use our brains, the fact that a student of the brain echoes what has been said several centuries before by a student of metaphysics shows that the latter's studies were very firmly based, as they should be, in the facts of our use of words. At any rate it seems to me that Professor Young has paid to Kant the same sort of back-handed compliment as Kant paid to Swedenborg; the dreams of the metaphysician have been considerably elucidated by the dreams of the neuro-physiologist.

'We cannot speak', says Professor Young, 'as if there is a world around us of which our senses give us true information. In trying to speak about what the world is like we must remember all the time that what we see and what we say depends on what we have learned; we ourselves come into the process.' And elsewhere he says: 'The brain of each one of us does literally create his or her own world. To explain this we must answer the question: How does each brain set up its own characteristic rules? How do those regular patterns of activity in the cells of the brain . . . develop? This is the process that I call the establishment of certainty, and it is a process that we may consider as beginning in each human being at the moment when, as a newly born baby, his eyes open on to the world.' In his lectures Professor Young gives an account in some detail of how these rules, as he calls them, are formed in the brain (how, we might say, we learn to distinguish facts, or to understand the concept 'fact'). It is to be hoped that these new discoveries will finally and effectively remove from the repertory of philosophical theories that one which Professor Popper has called 'the bucket theory of the mind' [9]—the theory that facts drip into the mind like water into a bucket, where they accumulate and are called 'knowledge'. The lesson that is to be learnt from Professor Young, as from Kant, is that (as Kant might put it) nothing can become an object (or a fact) for us unless in our thinking we follow certain rules or principles— that the mind plays an active part in cognition, and that therefore

[9] K. R. Popper, *The Open Society and Its Enemies* (London, Routledge and Kegan Paul, 1945), Vol. II, pp. 201 ff.

the principles which govern its action are part-determinants of what we experience.[10]

Considerations like these make one very chary of working uncritically with a terminology which relies on an absolutely hard-and-fast distinction between principles or rules or dispositions on the one hand and facts on the other. For it would appear that until we have accepted rules for discriminating between facts and illusions, we cannot talk of facts at all, or for that matter of objects or entities in the sense of 'things really existing'. Now Christians believe that God created the world out of chaos, or out of nothing, in the sense of no *thing*. What I am now going to say I say very tentatively. Is it possible that this is our way of expressing the truth that without belief in a divine order—a belief expressed in other terms by means of worshipping assent to principles for discriminating between fact and illusion—there could be no belief in matters of fact or in real objects? Certainly it is salutary to recognize that *even* our belief in so-called hard facts rests in the end on a faith, a commitment, which is not in or to facts, but in that without which there would not be any facts. Plato, it will be remembered, said of the Idea of the Good, which was his name for God, that it was not itself a being, but the source or cause of being; the passage is worth quoting in full, and I will end with it:

> In the case of those things which we see by the light of the sun, the sun is the source, not merely of the possibility of our seeing them, but also of their very coming to be, their growth and their sustenance. But it is not itself a coming to be. And in the same way in the case of those things which we know by the light of the Idea of the Good, it is the source, not merely of the possibility of our knowing them, but also of their very being—for from it their being comes. Yet the Good itself is not a being, but rather lies even further off, on the yonder side of being, excelling it in majesty and power.[11]

[10] Cf. Kant, *Critique of Pure Reason*, 14, "Transition to the Transcendental Deduction of the Categories", (Trans. N. Kemp Smith, London, Macmillan, 1933) pp. 125ff.

[11] Plato, *Republic*, 509b.

12

Religious language has its own proper meaning

W. D. Hudson

Wittgenstein (1889–1951), the central figure in the British movement of Philosophical Analysis, adopted varying views about
religious language. In his earlier work, the *Tractatus Logico–
Philosophicus* (1922) he held that religion belonged to the realm
of "what cannot be said," so that religious realities could not be
expressed in language. But in his later thinking he seemed to admit
that religious language had its own distinctive "logic" and was
meaningful in its own way. It is this latter strain in Wittgenstein's
thinking that Hudson takes up here and develops. We can, he
argues, only see what meaning religious statements have by
looking at the whole context or "form of life" in which they are
appropriately used. When we do this, we discover that they have
their own characteristic kind of meaning which is not reducible
either to the descriptive meaning that is typical of scientific
language or to the prescriptive meaning that is typical of moral
language. To say, for example, "I believe in the Last Judgment,"
is in effect to say, "I adopt a certain picture (a way of looking at
the world and life) that regulates my whole life." The term "God"
plays a central part in the theist's conceptual scheme, and, in this
sense, to say that "God exists" means that one is prepared to
adopt this scheme or, as Wittgenstein puts it, to play "the religious
language game."

We cannot stand outside a conceptual scheme and justify it

"absolutely" from the outside, and from this point of view one's adoption of the religious conceptual scheme or "language game" cannot be justified, any more than our adoption of the language games of morals or science can be justified in any "absolute" sense. But insofar as religious language is expressive of experience that represents an essential dimension of human life, (so that one to whom religious language was really meaningless would be an impoverished personality), then we can say not only that the religious language game is played, but that it *must* be played.

W.D. Hudson is a philosopher at the University of Exeter, England. This extract is taken from his book *Ludwig Wittgenstein: The Bearing of His Philosophy upon Religious Belief.*

'Theology as grammar': this heading occurs only in a parenthesis in the *Investigations:* 'Grammar tells us what kind of object anything is. (Theology as grammar)' (373). To be a religious believer, whatever else it may mean, is to participate in a language-game or universe of discourse. If the belief in question is theistic, this will involve talking about, or to, God and sharing in the experiences and activities connected with such discourse, which characterize the theistic form of life. Theology stands to religious belief, so understood, as its grammar does to a language. The grammar of any language reveals its logical structure. A language and its grammar could not exist independently of one another but working out, or learning, the grammar is distinct from using the language— for instance, knowing which mood the sentence 'A book is a good present' is in, or what is its subject and what its object, etc., is not the same thing as knowing that a book is a good present. Somewhat similarly, if religious belief did not exist, there would be no point in theology, but the two are not identical. Grammar has to show what it would, or would not, make sense to say in a language; theology—and I include the most naive as well as the most sophisticated attempts to answer the whys and wherefores of those who reflect on religious belief—has to show what it does, or does not, make sense to say in a religion.

Following Wittgenstein, we spoke above of religious belief as using a picture. Theology has to do with what was called the 'technique' of using the picture. Just as a child learns to speak his

From W. D. Hudson, *Ludwig Wittgenstein: The Bearing of His Philosophy upon Religious Belief* (Richmond, John Knox Press, 1968), pp. 58–71. By permission of John Knox Press, Richmond, Virginia. © 1968. W. D. Hudson. By permission of Lutterworth Press, London.

native language before he is given lessons in its grammar, so, in religion, most people learn to use the picture before they concern themselves with questions which call for that clearer definition of technique which it is the theologian's job to provide. We will confine our discussion to theism, since that is a familiar form of religious belief. Suppose, for instance, that we have grown up using the picture of God as, without qualification, a good and powerful creator. We have been told stories which so describe him; and we have said prayers which assume that this is what he is. But now we begin to ask questions. For instance: then why are half the people in God's world hungry? Or, at a more sophisticated level: then why did there have to be an Atonement—if God is good why did he insist on a penalty being paid for sin, and if he is powerful, why did he not make men incapable of sin so that there would have been no occasion for a penalty? The theologian's task is to find answers to such questions. As we noted above, any man's *blik*, 'picture', or way of looking at the world, determines what, for him, does, and what does not, constitute an explanation. The Christian theologian has to work out explanations of world hunger, the Atonement, or whatever is in question, which are consistent with the Christian picture of God. In so doing, he has to take the picture as he finds it used by believers; but, at the same time, he has to define it, or the technique of using it, more clearly. If, for instance, he were to say that world hunger occurs because God does not care whether his creatures starve or not, this would be so inconsistent with the picture of God, which Christians use, that it would be quite unacceptable as an explanation. However, suppose our theologian were to say that world hunger is due to human selfishness; and go on to argue that God evinces his goodness in giving men freewill, but in so doing necessarily limits his power over them to that of persuasion. This explanation would define more precisely for some believers, what is meant by the goodness and power, attributed to God in the picture which they use.

Wittgenstein, I think, would have said that the philosopher of religion, like the theologian, is concerned with the technique of using the picture. The philosopher's task, however, is somewhat different from the theologian's. There are two aspects to it. (i) The philosopher must examine the guidance in using the picture, which the theologian gives, to see whether it is self-consistent or not. (ii) He must try to understand and reveal the 'depth grammar' of this technique.

The theologian's explanation of world hunger, suggested a moment ago, will serve to illustrate the first aspect of the philosopher's task. In saying that God evinces his goodness in giving men freewill, our theologian, presumably, purports to be taking 'goodness' and 'freewill' in their normal senses; but is he, in fact, doing so, when he goes on to argue that this necessarily involves creating men who are capable of the selfishness which causes world hunger?

At first blush, it seems that he is; but closer scrutiny raises doubts. Take 'goodness'. There is, to say the least, something in the contention of the those philosophers who point out that, if a man had to choose between producing a state of affairs, which would result in great suffering, and not producing anything at all, we should consider him good only if he chose the latter; and so, when our theologian claims that it is a mark of goodness in God to have created a world in which millions upon millions are starving, the word 'goodness' is being used in a very odd sense. Now take 'freewill'. Some philosophers recently have argued that it would not—as our theologian obviously supposes—be self-contradictory to say that God had given men freewill, in the normal sense of that word, and at the same time made them incapable of selfishness. 'Having freewill', as normally used, means: not being under certain kinds of compulsion, not doing what you do because, for instance, you are pushed, or intimidated, or ignorant of what you are doing, etc. In other words, 'freewill' means that the agent concerned does what *he* wills to do; he is *self-determined*. But there is nothing logically impossible in the idea of a man who is so made that, when he does what he wills to do, he always does what is unselfish. If God had made all men like that, they could (logically) have had freewill, in the sense of doing only what they willed to do, and at the same time been incapable of the selfishness which causes world hunger. Our theologian's assumption that this is self-contradictory is not in accordance with the normal sense of 'freewill', though that is the sense in which he purports to be using the term.

I am not saying that these arguments are conclusive against our theologian's explanation of evils like world hunger; and elsewhere I have tried to say why.[1] Here it is not necessary to take the discussion further. Enough has been said to show what was meant by describing the first aspect of the philosopher's task as that of examining for consistency the theologian's 'grammar', that is, his explication of the technique of religious belief.

The second aspect of the philosopher's task, we said, was to understand, and reveal, the 'depth grammar' of this technique. I think that Wittgenstein would have said that this involves two things at least: (i) discovering the tacit presuppositions of religious belief, and (ii) mapping its logical frontiers.

As for the former, depth grammar can show us 'what kind of object' God is. It will be remembered that Wittgenstein said this was its purpose: 'to show us what kind of object anything is'. The concept of God is constitutive of theistic belief and theology in the way that the concepts of number, obligation or a physical object are constitutive of arithmetic, morality and natural science respectively. As R. G. Collingwood insisted, everything that is said is said in answer to a question and every question is based on some presupposition(s).[2] Theism deals in questions and answers about God, and certain presuppositions about him are built into both the questions and the answers. When, for instance, Goethe asked, at the time of the Lisbon earthquake, 'Where is God and what is he doing?', he did not expect some such answer as 'Over there, standing next to the man in the red shirt, and wielding a shovel!' What he asked was to be shown some point in the earthquake which would make it consistent with the purpose of a God, whom both he and those who tried to answer him took to be good, but whom neither he nor they took to have a physical body. Presuppositions about the sense in which God can be conceived as an agent are built into the question and anything which would be intelligible as an answer to it. To reveal such presuppositions is to discover the internal logic of theism, or to 'show what kind of object' God is.

By mapping the logical frontiers of religious belief, I mean avoiding the confusions which arise from failure to mark off its

---

[1] "An Attempt to Defend Theism," *Philosophy*, Vol. 39 (January 1964), pp. 18–28.

[2] *Metaphysics*, (Oxford, Clarendon Press, 1958).

questions and answers from those of other kinds. One such confusion is that of which apologists for or against religion are guilty when they take belief in God to be the same kind of logical thing as a scientific hypothesis. Another example is Professor P. van Buren's attempt in *The Secular Meaning of the Gospel* (London, 1963) to reduce theology (God raised Christ from the dead) to human psychology (The disciples experienced a new freedom). This is a paradigm case of the kind of logical frontier-violation which depth grammar must condemn. It is just muddle-headed to suppose that, when you say something about God what you 'really mean' is something about men. Of course, it does not necessarily follow that acts of God and human feelings cannot, in certain ways, be related; but for there to be a relation between them, they must (logically) be two things, not one.

A great many dilemmas, connected with religious belief, as I tried to show above in discussing theology and falsification and the problem of transcendence, can be resolved, when the character of religious discourse as *sui generis* is clearly recognized. A remark of Professor G. Ryle comes to mind: 'If the seeming feuds between science and theology . . . are to be dissolved at all, their dissolution can come not from making polite compromises but only from drawing uncompromising contrasts between their businesses.'[3] But, when we have discovered the tacit presuppositions and mapped the logical frontiers of religious belief, have we disposed of all the philosophical problems to which it gives rise?

The question raised above, at the end of our discussion of Wittgenstein's lectures on religious belief, has not been faced as yet. It is all very well to show, if one can, that theistic belief is a distinctive language-game, constituted by the concept of God. But does God really exist? It tells us much, maybe, to say that the religious believer uses a picture in accordance with a certain technique, but is this a picture of anything objectively real? The question seems to be not only legitimate but inescapable.

We must consider it now. Some modern philosophers, I think under the influence of the later Wittgenstein, would say that it rests on a misconception. Professor T. R. Miles in *Religion and the Scientific*

---

[3] *Dilemmas*, (Cambridge, University Press, 1954) p. 81.

Outlook (London, 1959) spoke of 'the absolute existence mistake'. He pointed out that we know well enough how to differentiate what exists from what does not, or what is real from what is unreal, in certain spheres. Take as examples the questions: 'Does the Loch Ness monster really exist?' 'Is six times thirty shillings really nine pounds?' 'Have children a real duty to support their parents in old age?', 'Is it really God's will that a penurious mother of six should not take "the pill"?' There are techniques in natural science, arithmetic, ethics, and theology respectively for answering such questions. But how are we to deal with a question which concerns the reality or otherwise of the constitutive concept of a universe of discourse, e.g. 'Does the physical world really exist?' or 'Does God really exist?' Such questions—and any answers to them—presuppose that we can give an ontologically ultimate definition to 'really exists' and justify it, but can we? The matter is complex and I must content myself with making two points only here.

(i) 'Really exists' seems to be indefinable in somewhat the way that G. E. Moore said 'good' was.[4] Take *any* proposed definition of 'really exists', e.g. 'being part of the physical world'. If this definition is correct—i.e. if in normal use this is what 'really exists' means—notice what follows. The statement, 'What is part of the physical world really exists' must then appear to most people to be an insignificant tautology, equivalent to 'What is part of the physical world is part of the physical world'. And the question 'Does what is part of the physical world really exist' must appear self-answering, equivalent to 'Is what is part of the physical world part of the physical world?' However, is this how the statement and the question do appear? Would the reader say that 'What is part of the physical world really exists' seems to him a mere tautology, similar to 'Apples are apples'? Or would he say that the question, 'Does the physical world really exist?' can be answered simply by consulting an accurate dictionary, as the question, 'Is a bachelor an unmarried male?' can? I think not.

Materialists, most of all, have to agree with what I have just been saying. Their belief may be stated thus: if anything really exists, then it is part of the physical world. This belief is held in

[4] *Principia Ethica*, (Cambridge, University Press, 1903) chapter 1.

conscious opposition to various alternatives, e.g. that God, Platonic ideas, the Unconscious, or whatever, really exist. Materialists undoubtedly want the statement of their belief to be understood as ontologically significant and informative. But if 'really exists' meant 'being part of the physical world', the statement, 'If anything really exists, then it is part of the physical world' would be neither significant nor informative ontologically. All it would amount to is: if anything is part of the physical world, then it is part of the physical world. Materialists are misguided if they try to make their beliefs true by definition. Statements which are true by definition have to do only with the meanings of words. But materialists, as such, do not hold beliefs about the meanings of words, but about the nature of ultimate reality.

The point which I am making here does not, of course, apply only to materialistic definitions of 'really exists'. Suppose I believe that what really exists is God. Do I mean by this only what I would mean by 'God is God'? Surely not! And if some inquirer asked, 'But does God really exist?' should I reply 'My dear chap, you have only to look at your dictionary!'? *Whatever* X is taken to be, if 'X really exists' purports to be an ontologically significant and informative remark, then X cannot logically be the *definition* of 'really exists'. This is the sense in which I claim that 'really exists' is indefinable.

(ii) The second point which I want to make about 'really exists' arises from the fact that people sometimes talk as though it made sense to speak of getting outside all conceptual schemes whatsoever and discovering what really exists. But what would be involved in such an ontologically ultimate discovery and would it make sense to say that anyone had made it? Every conceptual scheme, I have claimed earlier, has its constitutive concept or concepts: science, that of a physical object; morality, that of obligation, etc. Suppose we say that it is not enough to know that these are the ultimate presuppositions of certain ways of thinking; we must find out which of them really exist and which do not. We might conceivably invent a conceptual scheme, distinct from science and morality, within which the questions, 'Do physical objects really exist?' and 'Does obligation really exist?', could both be asked and possibly answered. Let us call this metaphysical and metamoral scheme M. There will necessarily be some concept or concepts—perhaps one called the

Absolute—which constitute, i.e. give its logical features to—M. But what if somebody wants to know whether the Absolute, in its turn, is not just the presupposition of a way of thinking, but really exists? We shall have to invent another scheme within which that question —together with those about physical objects and obligation—can intelligibly be asked and answered. But now; does the constitutive concept of this new scheme really exist? And so on. We are in an infinite regress.

To *know* anything we must be aware of it as something; and this is simply to say that we must think or speak of it in terms of some conceptual scheme—as a physical object, or a duty, or a mode of the Absolute, or whatever. This follows from the meaning of 'know'. We cannot therefore meaningfully say that we know anything outside any conceptual scheme whatsoever. Since it is nonsense to say that we have discovered something which we could not know, neither does it make sense to say that we had got outside all conceptual schemes and discovered what, in that sense, really exists.

I must emphasize that there are two things which *do not follow* from these two points which I have made about 'really exists'.

(i) Professor E. L. Mascall seems to think that, if we cannot do what I have said that we cannot—namely, define 'really exists' in an ontologically ultimate sense, or discover outside all conceptual schemes which of their constitutive concepts really exist and which do not—it must then be 'impossible to distinguish significantly between the existence or non-existence of anything: you can say significantly that the cat is on the mat, but you cannot say significantly whether it is a real or an imaginary cat to which you are referring'.[5] But of course you can! We know well enough what is normally meant by a real cat, as opposed to an imaginary one. Real cats meow, drink milk, squeal when trodden on, chase other cats on the tiles, etc. An imaginary cat is simply one which does not pass such tests. But if someone said that he knew a cat which was, in all these respects, just like a real cat, but was imaginary what should we make of that remark? He would have, in effect, stepped outside the universe of discourse in which we normally differentiate

[5] *The Secularization of Christianity*, (London, Darton, Longman & Todd, 1965) p. 19n.

real from imaginary cats. Within that universe his cat is a real one—it passes all the tests. What would he mean by calling it imaginary? And how could he know that that was what it was? If you say that he could not know, it does not follow for a moment, as Mascall evidently supposes, that the normal distinction between real and imaginary cats loses its significance.

(ii) Neither does it follow that, if we cannot know, apart from the presuppositions of the theistic conceptual scheme, that God really exists, the bottom is knocked out of theism. A thing which cannot be said is simply a thing which cannot be said. To say that the statement, 'I know outside any conceptual scheme that God really exists' would make no sense, is to say something about language but not necessarily about anything else. Compare that statement with this: God cannot do the logically impossible. People sometimes think that the latter denies the omnipotence of God, but it does nothing of the kind. It does not say anything about what God, in fact, can or cannot do. All it says is that, if anyone uttered the remark, 'God can do the logically impossible', he would be contradicting himself and so what he said would be meaningless. Similarly, if anyone said 'I have got outside all conceptual schemes whatsoever and away from their presuppositions, and discovered that what really exists is God', it would, in my opinion, be impos- to make any sense of what he said. But it does not follow from this that questions such as 'Is this really God's will?' or 'Does there exist in God an everlasting mercy?', and the answers which Christianity, for example, offers to them, do not make sense. These questions belong *within* the conceptual scheme of theism, and that is where answers to them will be found, if found at all. To say that they become insignificant, if a remark, which belongs outside that scheme altogether, is meaningless—namely, the one I quoted a moment ago about '. . . what really exists is God'—would be like saying that because God cannot do the logically impossible, he cannot do anything at all.

In the end, I think, we must say of religion in general, and theism in particular, what Wittgenstein said with wider reference. 'Our mistake is to look for an explanation where we ought to look at what happens as a "proto-phenomenon". That is, where we ought to have said: *this language-game is played*' (654). And again:

'What has to be accepted, the given, is—so one could say—*forms of life*' (p. 226). Like any other conceptual scheme, a religion is based logically upon presupposition, and is bounded logically by frontiers; the former must be accepted, and the latter respected, if the game is to be played or the form of life taken up. In the case of theism, we must decide whether or not to deal in questions and answers which have to do with God. This decision is logically like deciding whether or not to do science, think morally, or take up some branch of mathematics. It is the decision to give, or not give, a certain frame to experience.

I think Wittgenstein would have agreed with this account of the matter, at any rate to some degree. He once said of his later philosophy: 'Its advantage is that if you believe, say, Spinoza or Kant, this inferferes with what you believe in religion; but if you believe me, nothing of the sort.' We have neither justified nor discredited theism in any ultimate sense. The difficulty is to conceive of what would be involved in doing so. There are, of course, all kinds of things to be said about theism: how it compares with other religions, what experiences are characteristic of it, what its theology of science, morality, history, is, etc. etc. But it would seem that it is an illusion to think that philosophy can do more than reveal its presupposition and draw its logical frontiers. That presupposition is God and those frontiers mark off talk about God from other kinds of talk.

It would, however, be dishonest to conceal the fact that, given this philosophical account of theism, there are still lingering philosophical questions which trouble one, as a theist. I can do little more than mention them here.

(i) How is talk about God to be differentiated logically from, say, talk about Santa Claus? Despite all that has been said above about 'really exists', this question persists. Surely God is believed by theists to be there—to be objective—in some sense in which Santa Claus is not But in precisely what sense, and how does one show that he is, in a philosophically convincing way? Scientists test their theories by deducing from them empirically observable predictions. However conditioned their view of objective reality may be by the presuppositions of their science, they do commit their theories to 'what is there' and let them stand or fall by whether or not the predictions which they have deduced are fulfilled. When they are fulfilled, one can speak of the theory from which they have been deduced as 'knowledge', or as 'objectively true', in an intelligible sense. Objectivity here means being established in this way. But I have argued that religious beliefs are not to be treated as though they were scientific hypotheses. In what sense, then, do we speak of them as objectively grounded, i.e. as more than shared fantasies like that of Santa Claus? This seems to me to be the most urgent question confronting Christian philosophers today, but I must confess that I have not come upon any way of dealing with it which appears to me entirely satisfactory from a philosophical point of view.

(ii) How does one dispose of the contention that talk about God is unintelligible to modern man because it is obsolete? Wittgenstein, it will be remembered, said that language-games may become 'obsolete and get forgotten'. Professor A. C. MacIntyre has recently argued that this is just what has happened to Christianity.[6] His point, if I rightly interpret it, is this. It will not do to say that understanding Christianity is simply a matter of accepting the presupposition(s) of a certain language-game or form of life and thinking or acting accordingly. One must consider what it involves for modern man to do so. When mediaeval man had to explain an occurrence or decide upon an action, the questions which he most naturally asked were, respectively, 'Why has God sent this upon us?' or 'What does God will us to do?' But these are not the questions which modern man naturally asks. He normally explains things, or decides upon action, in accordance with the presuppositions of natural science or utilitarian ethics. He can, of course, see that, *given* the presupposition of God, the above (mediaeval) questions make sense. But the point is that this is just a way of saying that he has to see how his normal criteria of intelligibility need to be changed in order to see how these questions make sense. To understand, for example, 'Why did God allow the Lisbon earthquake?', a modern man has to see how the answer to this differs from the way in which he normally explains earthquakes. So the normal way of explaining them in terms of natural cause and effect is still the determinative factor in understanding. For modern man, the criteria of

[6] "Is Understanding Religion Compatible with Believing?," *Faith and the Philosophers*, ed. J. Hick (London, Macmillan, 1964), pp. 103–110.

intelligibility—even in the case of religious belief—are, in the last analysis, those of unbelief! In reply, two lines may be taken here. On the one hand, there is what might be called the 'fundamentalist' line: 'If modern man finds Christianity unintelligible, so much the worse for modern man!' On the other, the 'radical Christian' line: 'If the traditional presuppositions of Christianity are unintelligible to modern man, then we must replace them by those of natural science or utilitarian ethics and call these Christian!' But I find neither the move of the fundamentalist nor that of the radical Christian altogether satisfactory here.

(iii) The theistic language-game is played, but is it rational to take this game seriously? What constitutes rationality is, of course, a vexed question. But, to say the least, it is arguable that the rational man, as such, is the man who believes nothing unless he has good reasons for doing so, *and* who recognises that what appears to him a good reason today may, in the light of fuller knowledge, not do so tomorrow. In a word, he is a sceptic, though not an absolute one. He holds his beliefs, as it were, subject to modification. It is true enough, as preachers are fond of saying, that unbelievers must have faith of some kind just as much as believers: that, in order to think or act at all, they must presuppose the uniformity of nature, or the value of human happiness, or whatever. Nevertheless, the religious believer, as such, is committed to his presuppositions as the unbeliever is not, and as it is arguable that no rational man ought to be. Dr. W. W. Bartley has recently pointed out that the rationalist can remain a rationalist, whatever presupposition he finds himself compelled to abandon, but the Christian cannot remain a Christian and cease to believe that God has revealed himself in Jesus Christ.[7] There is, therefore, a limit to scepticism in the Christian position, which is not paralleled in that of the rational man, as such. Of course, one may simply reply to Bartley that, if that is how it is with Christianity, that is how it is; why should we be disturbed to find a Christian less sceptical than an unbeliever? But the worry is: does such a reply forfeit any claim to be taken seriously by the philosophically-minded unbeliever? Does it imply that Christianity is irrational?

[7] *The Retreat to Commitment*, (London, Chatto, 1964).

These three questions take us, so to speak, to the front line of apologetics. Any adequate defence of Christian theism must take account of them. As I have indicated it is not easy to find convincing answers and work needs to be done by Christian thinkers on each of them.

They focus doubts about the view which has been put forward here that a body of religious belief, such as Christianity, must be regarded as a 'proto-phenomenon', that is, a form of life, or language-game, which neither requires nor admits of any justification beyond itself. But even if it should turn out that this view is the most that analytical philosophy can say about Christianity, I suggest that there is something important which might be added.

Some language-games, or forms of life, seem to be definitive of humanity in the sense that it is essential to our concept of man, as man, that he should engage in them. Morality would be a case in point. It is, I suppose, conceivable that men should cease to use moral language: that words such as 'right', 'good', 'ought', as they are now used in a moral sense, should drop out of our language. With them would go such activities as moral persuasion or argument; and, no doubt, also such experiences as those which we call remorse or a sense of duty. I say that this is conceivable; but when we imagine it, do we not have to add that, if it happened to *homo sapiens*, he would be deprived of something essential to what we have always meant by his humanity—in a real sense, he would cease to be man?

What I suggest, very tentatively, is that somewhat the same might be said of religious belief. It is true, of course that there are individuals who have no religious beliefs and, I am not for a moment disputing that many of them are admirable human beings. But could it be argued that there is a dimension, at once mysterious and magnificent, which religious language, and the kind of experience which goes with it, add to human life; and that if this dimension were lost something essential to what we mean by calling our life 'human' would be lost also? Could it even be said that the unbeliever, who finds it necessary to argue about, or propagate, his unbelief, is witnessing to the impossibility of man, as man, ceasing to talk about God? 'This game is played'. But more: to play it is the nature of man.